Companion to the Bible ..

COMPANION

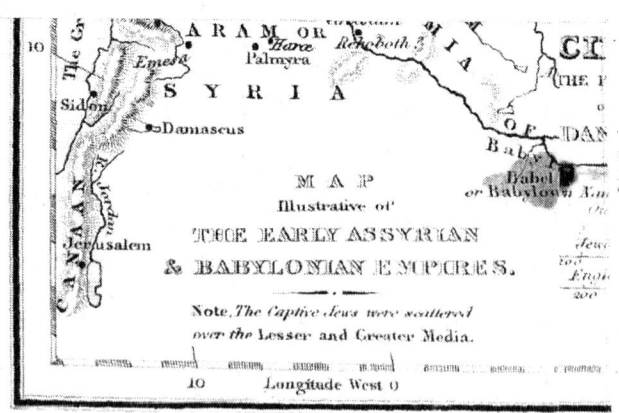

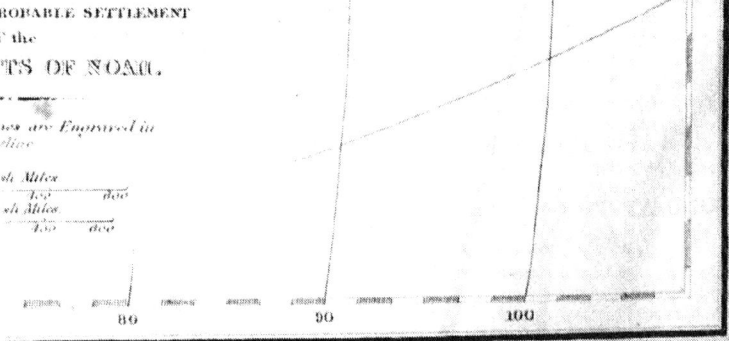

COMPANION

TO

THE BIBLE.

INTENDED FOR BIBLE CLASSES, FAMILIES, AND
YOUNG PERSONS IN GENERAL.

WITH MAPS OF THE ANCIENT WORLD, CANAAN, AND THE
TRAVELS OF THE APOSTLE PAUL.

A NEW EDITION,

REVISED AND CORRECTED.

LONDON:
THE RELIGIOUS TRACT SOCIETY;
Instituted 1799.
SOLD AT THE DEPOSITORY, 56, PATERNOSTER ROW,
AND 65, ST. PAUL'S CHURCHYARD;
AND BY THE BOOKSELLERS.

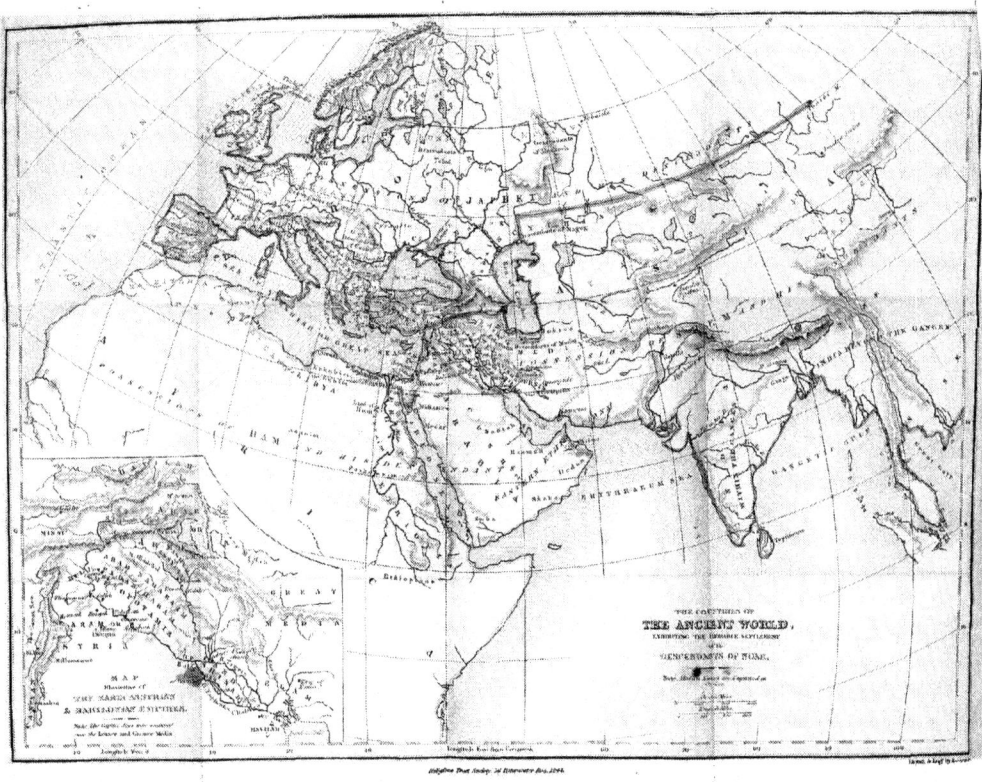

BS475
.C5
1844

CONTENTS.

Chap.		Page
I.	Title of the Bible	1
II.	Antiquity of the Bible	1
III.	Excellency of the Bible	3
IV.	Inspiration of the Bible	5
V.	Design of the Bible	7
VI.	Authenticity of the Bible	8
VII.	Translation of the Bible	13
VIII.	State of Mind necessary to read the Bible	17
IX.	Rules for the profitable reading of the Bible	21
X.	Geography of the Bible, particularly of the Old Testament	29
XI.	Hebrew Offices	31
XII.	Hebrew Festivals	34
XIII.	Divisions of the Bible	42
XIV.	Analysis of the Books of the Old Testament	44
XV.	Chronological Order of the Books of the Old Testament	99
	Chronological Arrangement of the Psalms	101
XVI.	Jewish History between the Times of the Old and New Testament	103
XVII.	Title of the New Testament	111
XVIII.	Biography of the Writers of the New Testament	112
XIX.	Analysis of the Books of the New Testament	117
XX.	Harmony of the Gospels	178
XXI.	Chronological Table of the New Testament Scriptures	182
XXII.	The Miracles of Christ	183
XXIII.	Recorded Parables of Jesus Christ	184
XXIV.	Remarkable Discourses of Christ	185
XXV.	Jewish Sects	186
XXVI.	Heresies among the Apostolical Churches	189
XXVII.	Fulfilled Prophecies of Scripture	191
XXVIII.	Unfulfilled Prophecies of Scripture	237
XXIX.	Figurative Language of the Bible	242
XXX.	Index to the Symbolical Language of the Bible	245
XXXI.	Character and Influence of Christianity, and its Claims upon all Mankind	256
XXXII.	Plan for the annual Reading through of the Bible	260
XXXIII.	Geographical Gazetteer of the New Testament	265
XXXIV.	Scripture Money, Weights, and Measures	270
XXXV.	Chronological Index to the whole Bible	272
XXXVI.	Scripture Names	280

OUTLINES FOR BIBLE-CLASS INSTRUCTION.

The following plan was originally drawn up by the Rev. Dr. Romeyn, of New York, and recommended by the General Assembly of the Presbyterian Church in America: it has been revised for this work.

I. Observe the historical part of the scripture lessons, relating to the two great divisions of mankind—the church and the world.

II. The biographical part, embracing the two distinct classes, believers and unbelievers; with the different effects which their good and bad examples have had upon the church and the world.

III. The doctrinal part, teaching the nature and perfections of God; the character, person, offices, and work of Christ; the influences of the Holy Spirit; the actual state of man by the fall, and his renovated character by grace, marking distinctly the gradual increase of knowledge on these points from age to age, through the patriarchal and Levitical dispensations, till the Christian revelation furnished mankind with the clear and full developement of God's merciful purposes towards our world.

IV. The preceptive part, including the whole range of our duties agreeably to the moral law.

V. The positive ordinances, comprising the sacrifices, types, the priesthood, the temple-service, of the Old Testament, with Baptism and the Lord's supper of the New Testament; distinguishing between these positive institutions and moral duties,— the first dependent on the will of God, and therefore mutable; the last on his nature, and therefore immutable: marking the changes of the first from time to time, with the reasons for the change, and unfolding the influence which they were obviously intended to have upon the spiritual exercises of our hearts, and our obedience to the moral law.

VI. The practical lessons which the historical and biographical parts furnish for the regulation of human conduct, in all the relations of life.

In these outlines it will be understood, that general questions, under each division, should be proposed to the pupils, and full instruction given by the teacher.

COMPANION TO THE BIBLE.

PART I.

Chapter I.—Title of the Bible.

The word Bible is taken from the Greek word *Biblos*, which signifies *book;* and the volume to which Christians give that title, by way of eminence, is called The Bible, because of its supreme excellency, being the book of books, the best book, the book of the knowledge of God.

The Bible is called The Scriptures, from the Latin word *Scriptura,* which signifies a writing; and it is called The Holy Scriptures, because it contains the collection of the writings of holy men, who, at different times, were raised up and inspired of God, for the purpose of publishing his commandments and promises, and the records of his mercies and judgments, for the instruction and salvation of mankind, by faith in the Divine Redeemer.

The two parts of the Bible are called the Old and New Testaments, (2 Cor. iii. 6, and 14,) or covenants. They are so named because they contain the revelations or testaments of God's covenant of mercy, for the redemption, salvation, and glorification of sinful man, by the interposition of the Messiah, the Son of God, the Lord Jesus Christ, as the only Mediator between God and man.

Ch. II.—The Antiquity of the Bible.

That the Bible has existed from very remote ages, will not be disputed, except by those who are grossly ignorant. The proofs of its antiquity are, beyond all comparison, more numerous and convincing, than can be advanced in

favour of any other book in existence. It has never been without its intelligent witnesses, and zealous guardians; though some of them have been the greatest perverters of its peculiar principles, or the bitterest enemies of the Christian name.

The Old Testament has been preserved by the Jews, in every age, with a scrupulous jealousy, and with a veneration for its words and letters, bordering on superstition; demonstrating their regard for it as divinely inspired. The Hebrews never were guilty of negligence in relation even to the words of their sacred books; for they used to transcribe and compare them so carefully, that they could tell how often every letter came over again in writing any book of the Old Testament.

The Old Testament contains, besides the account of the former ages of the world, the code of the Jewish laws, both civil and religious; and the records of their national history, for more than one thousand nine hundred years, from the call of Abraham; as well as prophecies, which regarded the Israelites and many other nations in a distant futurity, and which have respect to times yet to come. The celebrated Roman historian Tacitus, who lived in the apostolic age, speaks of the Jewish books as very ancient in his time. They were translated from the Hebrew into the Greek language more than two thousand and one hundred years ago; and they were possessed in both those languages by the Jews. By those Jews who lived among the Greeks, they were read in their synagogues every sabbath day, in the Greek translation, the same as the Hebrew Scriptures were read by the native Jews: commentaries were written upon them by their learned doctors; copies of them were circulated in every nation where the Jews were scattered, and thus the sacred books were multiplied without number.

The books of Moses, including Genesis, Exodus, Leviticus, Numbers, and Deuteronomy, were written more than three thousand and three hundred years ago, and nearly fifteen hundred years before the Christian era: many of the other books were published above a thousand

years, and those of the elder prophets about eight hundred years before the advent of Christ!

As to the writings of uninspired men, they are modern compared with the Holy Scriptures. The earliest profane history which is known is that of Herodotus, in Greek; which was written no earlier than the time of Malachi, the last of the Old Testament writers. Somewhat more ancient than Herodotus, are the poems of Homer and Hesiod: the period in which they were written cannot be correctly ascertained; but those who allow them the remotest antiquity, place Homer only in the days of Isaiah the prophet, and Hesiod in the age of Elijah. It is not, indeed, agreed among the learned, whether there ever was such a person as Hesiod. The books of these ancient, uninspired writers are of a quite different character from the Holy Scriptures; they are filled with silly and absurd fables, and contain many impurities. They make no discovery of the just character of the only living and true God, though they contain much concerning religion. As to the history by Herodotus, though very valuable in many respects, it contains much that is merely fabulous and untrue; but as far as it records the transactions of his own age, or describes the things within the compass of his own observation, or details matters of fact of which he was correctly informed, his statements confirm the faithfulness and accuracy of the records contained in the holy and inspired word of the Lord.

Ch. III.—The Excellency of the Bible.

That the Bible is the best book, might be proved sufficiently from its sanctifying and transforming influence upon the minds of all its devout readers. But this is manifest more especially from the fact of its having God for its author: and that God is its author is evident, from its being the only book which teaches every thing that our Creator requires of us, either to know, or believe, or do, that we may escape his deserved displeasure, obtain

his sovereign favour, and dwell for ever in the bliss of his immediate presence. 1. It opens to us the mystery of the creation; 2. The nature of God, of angels, and of men; 3. The immortality of the soul; 4. The end for which man was created; 5. The origin of evil, and the inseparable connexion between sin and misery; 6. The vanity of the present world, and the glory reserved in a future state for the pious servants of God. In the Bible we are taught the purest morality, perfectly accordant with the dictates of sound reason, and confirmed by the witness of our conscience, which God has placed for himself in our breasts. In this volume we see described all the secret workings of the human mind, in a manner which demonstrates the inspiration of Him, who is the Searcher of hearts. It gives us a particular account of all the spiritual maladies of man, with their various symptoms, and the methods of their cure. From this source flow all the pure streams of spiritual and healing knowledge, to bless mankind with recovery from his fallen state, with salvation and immortality.

Although many hundreds of thousands of books have been written in different ages by wise and learned men, even the best of them will bear no comparison with the Bible, in respect either of religion, morality, history, or purity and sublimity of composition. Perhaps no man was ever better qualified to pronounce his judgment in this matter than the late Sir William Jones, who was one of the most learned men that ever lived. He says, "I have regularly and attentively read the Holy Scriptures, and am of opinion that this volume, independent of its divine origin, contains more true sublimity, more exquisite beauty, purer morality, more important history, and finer strains both of poetry and eloquence, than could be collected within the same compass, from all other books that were ever composed in any age or nation. The antiquity of those compositions no man doubts, and the unstrained application of them to events long subsequent to their publication, is a solid ground of belief that they were genuine predictions, and consequently inspired."

The commendation which bishop Horne gives to the

book of Psalms, is found to be true of the whole Bible, by the devout Christian, who, alone, is capable of perceiving its excellency. That pious prelate says, "Indited under the influence of Him, to whom all hearts are known, and all secrets foreknown, they suit mankind in all situations, grateful as the manna which descended from above, and conformed itself to every palate. The fairest productions of human art, after a few perusals, like gathered flowers, wither in our hands, and lose their fragrancy; but these unfading plants of paradise become, as we are accustomed to them, still more and more beautiful; their bloom appears to be daily heightened, fresh odours are emitted, and new sweets are extracted from them. He who hath once tasted their excellences, will desire to taste them yet again; and he who tastes them oftenest, will relish them best."

CH. IV.—THE INSPIRATION OF THE BIBLE.

THE books of the Old Testament, in the number and order in which we now possess them, were held sacred by the Jewish church. Concerning them especially the apostle Paul declares, "All Scripture is given by inspiration of God," 2 Tim. iii. 16; and the apostle Peter, in reference to the same, testifies, "No prophecy of the Scripture is of any private interpretation. For the prophecy came not in old time by the will of man; but holy men of God spake as they were moved by the Holy Ghost," 2 Pet. i. 20, 21.

Being inspired of God, signifies being supernaturally influenced by his Holy Spirit: thus the ancient prophets are said to have spoken by divine inspiration. The inspiration of the sacred writers consisted, 1. In their being infallibly excited and effectually moved to undertake their work; 2. Being furnished by special revelation from God with the knowledge of things which they had not previously possessed; 3. Being directed in the choice of proper words to express their conceptions; and, 4.

Being fully guided in all things to write according to the will of God.

That the Holy Scriptures were inspired, is evident from their divine sentiments in religion: 1. The glorious character under which they represent Almighty God; 2. The purity and reasonableness of their morality; 3. The majestic simplicity of their style; 4. Their wonderful efficacy on the minds of believers; 5. The faithfulness and disinterestedness of the writers; 6. The miracles by which they confirmed their doctrines; 7. The astonishing preservation of the several books to our times; and, 8. The fulfilment of their numerous and various prophecies.

"The inspiration pleaded for extends to all the books of the sacred Scriptures, and to all the writers of them, and principal speakers introduced in them; and though all that is contained in them is not of God, or inspired by him, as the quotations from heathen writers, the words of Satan, the speeches of bad men, and even of good men, in which some things not right are said of God, as by Job and his three friends; yet the writers of the books in which these sayings are, were under a divine impulse, inspiration, and direction to commit these several things to writing; partly for the truth of historical facts, and partly to show the malice of devils and wicked men, as well as the weaknesses and frailties of good men, and all are for our caution and instruction."—*Dr. Gill.*

"Inspiration belongs to the original writings. No one contends for any degree of inspiration to the transcribers in different ages. Accuracy in the copies they have made, is, under God, secured by the fidelity of the keepers of Scripture, by the opposition of parties watching each other, as of Jews and Christians, and various sects, and by the great multiplication of copies and translations into different languages, which took place so early. The agreement among the ancient manuscripts, both of the Old and New Testaments, has been ascertained, by the strictest examination, to be astonishingly exact."—*Huldane.* It certainly is so as to all points of importance, and the differences do not affect any article of faith, or any moral precept.

Ch. V.—The Design of the Bible.

The Bible having God for its author, and having been given by the special inspiration of the Holy Spirit, we may be assured that it has been written for the most important purposes. The Bible is evidently designed to give us correct information concerning our relation to God as his creatures, and all things that it was necessary for us to know, that we might glorify him on earth and enjoy him for ever: it was given to declare to us the creation of all things by the omnipotent word of God; to make known to us the state of holiness and happiness of our first parents in Paradise, and their dreadful fall from that condition by transgression against God, which is the original cause of all our sin and misery. Also to show us the duty we owe to him, who is our almighty Creator, our bountiful Benefactor, and our righteous Judge; the method by which we can secure his eternal friendship, and be prepared for the possession of everlasting mansions in his glorious kingdom. The Scriptures are specially designed to make us wise unto salvation through faith in Christ Jesus; 1. To reveal to us the mercy of the Lord in him; 2. To form our minds after the likeness of God our Saviour; 3. To build up our souls in wisdom and faith, in love and holiness; 4. To make us thoroughly furnished unto good works, enabling us to glorify God on earth; and, 5. To lead us to an imperishable inheritance among the spirits of just men made perfect, and finally to be glorified with Christ in heaven.

If such be the design of the Bible, how necessary must it be for every one to understand its declarations, and to pay a serious and proper attention to what it reveals. The word of God invites our attentive and prayerful regards in terms the most engaging and persuasive. It closes its gracious appeals by proclaiming, " Whosoever will, let him take the water of life freely," Rev. xxii. 17. The infinite tenderness of the Divine compassion to sinners, flows in the language of the inspired writers with which they address the children of

men, and the most gracious promises of the Lord of glory accompany the Divine invitations.

But those who oppose the merciful designs of the Bible with all its wondrous grace, will not be held guiltless in the great day of the Lord. "How shall we escape," says an apostle, "if we neglect so great salvation?" Heb. ii. 3. Neglect of the Bible, under the Christian dispensation, is despising the pity and tender mercy of God, and the blessings of his gracious covenant. The apostle, by the Holy Spirit, appeals to the careless in those awfully awakening words; "He that despised Moses's law died without mercy under two or three witnesses; of how much sorer punishment, suppose ye, shall he be thought worthy who hath trodden under foot the Son of God, and hath counted the blood of the covenant wherewith he was sanctified an unholy thing, and hath done despite unto the Spirit of grace," Heb. x. 28, 29. Our merciful Lord and Saviour himself has declared, "He that believeth not shall be damned!" Mark xvi. 16.

CH. VI.—The Authenticity of the Bible.

WE have the most ample and satisfactory proofs that the books of the Bible are authentic and genuine. The Scriptures of the Old Testament were collected and completed under the scrupulous care of inspired prophets. The singular providence of God is evident in the translation of the Old Testament into Greek, nearly three hundred years before the birth of Christ, for the benefit of the Jews who were living in countries where that language was used. The testimony which our Saviour bore to the Old Testament used by the Jews in Judea, and the quotations which the New Testament writers have made from its several books, generally from the Greek translation, confirm what has already been said on the antiquity of the Bible, and prove its authenticity. This will appear in a much stronger point of view when we consider the Jews as the keepers of this Old Testament— their own sacred volume, which contains the most ex-

traordinary predictions concerning the infidelity of their nation, and the rise, progress, and extensive prevalence of Christianity;—their still existing and remaining the irreconcilable enemies of its claims;—and that their enmity should also be foretold.

That all the books which convey to us the history of the events of the New Testament were written, and immediately published, by persons living at the time of the things mentioned, and whose names they bear, is most fully proved by the clearest and most forcible arguments. 1. By an unbroken series of Christian authors, reaching from the days of the apostles down to the present time. 2. By the concurrent and well-informed belief of all denominations of Christians. 3. By the unreserved acknowledgment of the most learned and intelligent enemies of Christianity.

That the books we possess under the titles of Matthew, Mark, Luke, and John, were written by the persons whose names they bear, cannot be doubted by any well-informed and candid mind; because, from the time of their first publication, they have been uniformly attributed to them by all Christian writers. That all the facts related in these writings, and all the accounts given of our Saviour's actions and sayings are strictly true, we have the most substantial grounds for believing. Matthew and John were two of our Lord's apostles; his constant attendants throughout the whole of his ministry; eye-witnesses of the facts, and ear-witnesses of the discourses which they relate. Mark and Luke were not of the twelve apostles; but they were contemporaries and associates with the apostles, and living in habits of friendship and intercourse with those who had been present at the transactions which they record. Many suppose that Luke was one of the seventy disciples who were ordained by our Lord to preach his gospel; and if so, his personal knowledge of Christ must have been almost equal to that of the twelve apostles. However, if not one of the seventy, he was the constant companion of Paul for many years, and well knew the things concerning which he wrote. In the beginning of his Gospel,

therefore, Luke declares his intimate acquaintance with his subject. "Forasmuch as many have taken in hand to set forth in order a declaration of those things which are most surely believed among us, even as they delivered them unto us, who from the beginning were eye-witnesses and ministers of the word: it seemed good to me also, having had perfect understanding of all things from the very first, to write unto thee in order, most excellent Theophilus, that thou mightest know the certainty of those things wherein thou hast been instructed," Luke i. 1—4.

Luke being also the author of the Acts of the Apostles, we have for the writers of these five books, men who had the most accurate knowledge of the things which they relate, either from their own personal observation, or by means of immediate communication with those who saw and heard every thing recorded. They could not, therefore, have been themselves deceived; nor had they any inducement or inclination to deceive others. They were men of honesty, simplicity, eminent integrity, and amiable candour, which are qualities singularly manifest in all their writings; and their greatest enemies have never attempted to cast the least stain upon the purity of their characters. It was not possible for them to gain any thing by false statements; and the doctrines which they published, they themselves at length ratified with their own blood.

But, besides all these qualifications, to compose those writings which contain the gospel of our salvation, they were moved, not only by a benevolent regard for the souls of men, but by the sovereign influences of the Holy Spirit; and his gracious and infallible directions secured them from every possible error and mistake, in writing books adapted for the edification and sanctification of all nations, and for all succeeding generations..

The same effectual inspiration of the Holy Spirit influenced the apostles, in writing the epistles to the newly-founded churches, agreeably to the promises of their Master, Christ. About the commencement of the second century, copies of most of the New Testament books

CH. VI.—THE AUTHENTICITY OF THE BIBLE.

were collected into one volume. At first, indeed, for want of full information, the Epistles and Gospels being in the care of different and distant churches, and as several books, falsely attributed to the apostles, were published, and widely circulated, some of the churches hesitated about receiving the Epistle to the Hebrews, the Second Epistle of Peter, the Second and Third Epistles of John, the Epistle of Jude, and the Book of the Revelation. A scrupulous investigation of their claims was therefore instituted; and after a rigorous examination, it appeared evidently clear that they were the inspired productions of the apostles of Christ; and, therefore, they were admitted by consent of all the churches, as of equal authority with the other parts of the New Testament.

As to the preservation of the sacred books down to our times, it is certain, that although the original copies may have been lost, the books of the New Testament have been preserved without any material alteration, much less corruption; and that they are, in all essential matters, the same as they came from the hands of their authors. In taking copies of these books by writing, from time to time, as the art of printing was then unknown, some letters, syllables, or even words, may have been omitted, altered, or even changed in some manuscripts; but no important doctrine, precept, or passage of history, has been designedly or fraudulently corrupted. This would have been impossible: because, as soon as the original writings were published, great numbers of copies were immediately taken, carried by the evangelical missionaries wherever they went, and sent to the different churches; they were soon translated into foreign languages, and conveyed into the most distant countries; they were constantly read in the Christian assemblies, diligently perused by many private Christians, some of whom had whole books by heart; they were quoted by numerous writers, and appealed to, as the inspired standard of doctrine, by various sects, who differed from each other, some on important points; and, consequently, they were jealously watchful against the least

attempt, either to falsify or to alter the word of Divine revelation.

"Who can imagine that God, who sent his Son to declare this doctrine, and his apostles, by the assistance of the Holy Spirit, to indite and speak it, and by so many miracles confirmed it to the world, should suffer any wicked persons to corrupt and alter any of those terms on which the happiness of mankind depends? It is absurd to say that God repented of his good will and kindness to mankind, in vouchsafing the gospel to them; or that he so far maligned the good of future generations, that he suffered wicked men to rob them of all the good intended to them by this declaration of his holy will."—*Dr. Whitby.*

That there should be differences found to exist in the manuscripts of the Holy Scriptures, cannot be surprising to any one, who recollects that before the invention of printing, in the fifteenth century, copies of all books were made by transcribers; some of whom were ignorant, rash, or careless, though skilful in the art of writing. These persons were not supernaturally guarded against the possibility of error; and a mistake in one copy would necessarily be propagated through all that were taken from it; each of which copies might likewise have peculiar faults of its own: so that various, or different readings, would be thus increased in proportion to the number of transcripts that were made. Besides actual oversights, transcribers might have occasioned various readings, by substituting, through ignorance, one letter, or even word, in place of another; or being inattentive, they might have omitted a line or period. In these different ways, it is very natural to expect, reckoning all the little diversities of single words, syllables, and letters, that many thousands of various readings should be discovered, in collating several hundred manuscripts of the whole Scriptures.

The manuscripts of the whole or parts of the sacred books are found in every ancient library in all parts of the Christian world; and amount in number to several thousands. Almost all these have been actually ex-

amined and compared by learned men with extraordinary care. Many of them were evidently transcribed as early as the eighth, seventh, sixth, and even the fourth centuries. Thus we are carried up to very near the times of the apostles, and the promulgation of the inspired writings. The prodigious number of these manuscripts, the remote countries whence they have been collected, and the identity of their contents with the quotations which the fathers of different ages have made, demonstrate the authenticity of the New Testament. It has been, indeed, asserted by learned men, that if the New Testament were lost, its contents might be wholly supplied by the quotations from it, which are found in the writings of the fathers of the first four centuries of the Christian church!

CH. VII.—THE TRANSLATION OF THE BIBLE.

THE authenticity of the Bible will be more fully established, by a consideration of some of its translations; and young believers cannot fail to be interested, in being informed some particulars concerning the history and character of that in the English language.

The Old Testament, as has been noticed in the preceding chapter, was translated into Greek nearly three hundred years before the birth of Christ. This version is commonly called The Septuagint, from the reported number of seventy-two, or, in round numbers, seventy Jewish elders, who were employed in the work. Soon after the publication of the apostolic writings, the Bible was translated into Latin, for the use of the Christians using that language. This version was called the Italic, which being in the vulgar tongue of the Romans, was called the Vulgate, of which, A. D. 384, Jerome, who died A. D. 420, published an improved translation, containing both the Old and New Testament, with prefaces to the several books: this is the only authorized Bible of the Romish church at the present time.

In French, the Waldenses had a translation of the

CH. VII.—THE TRANSLATION OF THE BIBLE.

Bible, made by their celebrated leader, Peter Waldo, about A. D. 1160, and another, more generally published, about A. D. 1383.

In Spain, Alphonsus, king of Castile, had a translation of the Sacred Books made into his native dialect, about A. D. 1280.

In Germany, a translation of the Bible was made about A. D. 1460. Luther published a new translation of the New Testament, A. D. 1522, and of the whole Bible, A. D. 1532.

In England, several attempts were made at different times to translate the Bible into the vulgar language, especially by Bede, a learned and pious monk, who died A. D. 735; and by king Alfred, who died A. D. 900: but the first complete English translation of the Bible, it is generally admitted, was made by Wickliff, about A. D. 1380. The New Testament by that great man has been printed; and there are, in several libraries, manuscript copies of his translation of the whole Bible. The first printed English Bible was a translation made by William Tindal, who retired to the continent, to prosecute that work in security. He was assisted by Miles Coverdale, another English exile. The New Testament was printed at Antwerp, A. D. 1526, but most of the copies were bought up and burnt, by order of Tonstal, bishop of London. An improved edition was published in 1530. In 1535 the whole Bible was published by Coverdale, and rapidly sold; but while this edition was being prepared, Tindal was seized by the papists, through the treachery of Henry Philips, an Englishman, and, being strangled, he was burnt as a heretic at Filford castle, between Antwerp and Brussels. This Christian martyr expired, praying, "Lord! open the eyes of the king of England!" Two of Tindal's assistants shared a similar fate; John Frith at Smithfield, and William Roye in Portugal. On the death of Tindal, the good work was carried on by Miles Coverdale, assisted by John Rogers, who was afterwards the first martyr in the reign of queen Mary. They revised the whole Bible, comparing it with the Hebrew, Greek, Latin, and German; adding notes

and prefaces from the German translation by Luther. It was dedicated to Henry VIII., and issued in 1537, under the borrowed name of Thomas Matthews. It was printed on the continent; but a licence was obtained for publishing it in England, by the influence of archbishop Cranmer, lord Cromwell, and bishops Latimer and Shaxton. This translation of the Bible, revised by Coverdale, with prefaces added by Cranmer, was printed in England in 1539, and called Cranmer's Bible. Another edition of this Bible was printed in the following year, 1540, and, by royal proclamation, every parish was obliged to place a copy of it in the church, for public use, under the penalty of forty shillings a month. Two years afterwards the popish bishops procured its suppression by the king: it was restored under Edward VI., suppressed under Mary, and again restored under Elizabeth. In the reign of Mary, some English exiles at Geneva, among whom were Coverdale and John Knox, the celebrated Scotch reformer, made a new translation, which was printed in 1560. This is called the Geneva Bible: it contains marginal readings and annotations, the chapters divided into verses, and other important helps; on which account it was greatly prized. Archbishop Parker engaged some learned men to make a new revision or edition, which was published in 1568, and was called the Bishop's Bible. This translation was used in the churches, though the Geneva Bible was generally read in private families; more than thirty editions of which were printed in as many years. King James disliked the Geneva Bible, on account of the notes: and when many objections against the Bishop's Bible were made at the Hampton Court conference in 1603, in consequence of the request of Dr. Reynolds, the king gave orders for a new translation. Forty-seven learned divines were engaged in the work, which was commenced in 1607, and completed and published in 1611, with a learned preface, and a dedication to king James. After this publication, all the other versions fell into disuse, and king James's version has continued to this day to be the

only Bible allowed to be printed, without a commentary or notes, in Great Britain.

The translators did not pretend that it was a perfect and faultless version; and as it was made so long ago, it may reasonably be supposed that it is capable of some improvements: but of its general excellence, the following testimonies, given by learned divines of different communions, may be regarded as sufficient to satisfy any unlearned reader.

About a hundred years ago, Dr. John Taylor wrote,—" You may rest fully satisfied, that as our English translation is in itself by far the most excellent book in our language, so it is a pure and plentiful fountain of divine knowledge; giving a true, clear, and full account of the Divine dispensations, and the gospel of our salvation: so that whoever studies the Bible, the English Bible, is sure of gaining that knowledge, which, if duly applied to the heart and conversation, will infallibly guide him to eternal life."

Dr. Geddes says,—" If accuracy, fidelity, and the strictest attention to the letter of the text, be supposed to constitute the qualities of an excellent version, this, of all versions, must in general be accounted the most excellent."

Dr. Doddridge observes,—" On some occasions, we do not scruple to animadvert upon it; but these remarks affect not the fundamentals of religion, and seldom reach any further than the beauty of a figure, or at best the connexion of an argument."

Dr. Adam Clarke declares,—" It is the most accurate and faithful of all translations. Nor is this its only praise: the translators have seized the very soul and spirit of the original, and expressed this, almost every where, with pathos and energy."

Dr. Moses Stuart, Professor of Sacred Literature in one of the most distinguished Theological Institutions in America, says of the English Bible,—" Ours is, on the whole, a most noble production for the time in which it was made. The divines of that day were very differ-

ent Hebrew scholars from what most of their successors have been, in England or Scotland."

The Rev. Thomas Scott writes,—" It may be asked, How can unlearned persons know, how our translation may be depended on, as in general faithful and correct? Let the inquirer remember, that Episcopalians, Presbyterians, and Independents, Baptists and Pædobaptists, Calvinists and Arminians, persons who maintain eager controversies with each other in various ways, all appeal to the same version, and in no matter of consequence object to it. This demonstrates that the translation, on the whole, is just. The same consideration proves the impossibility of the primitive Christians corrupting the Sacred Records."

Thus we see a merciful Providence has marvellously appeared in raising up learned men to translate the Holy Scriptures: and there are at this time more than one hundred and fifty languages in which the oracles of God are circulated, making known to many nations the salvation of our Lord Jesus Christ!

CH. VIII.—STATE OF MIND NECESSARY TO THE READING OF THE BIBLE.

THE sovereign goodness of God has been singularly manifested in the wisdom and skill with which he has endowed his servants in relation to his inspired word. Through his gracious providence, the Holy Scriptures have not only been preserved down to our times, but they have been translated into our language by pious and learned men; and by the same providence, skilful mechanics have been led to discover and to improve the wonderful art of printing; by which means, the Bible is now become the commonest book among us, so as to have been our lesson-book from childhood; while four hundred years ago a copy cost many pounds, even if it could be obtained at all, as it required almost the whole labour of a life in writing it. But to derive saving and eternal benefit from the Scriptures, it is necessary to

read them, not merely as at school, but as deeply and personally interested in their precious contents; as heirs of an eternal existence, and candidates for a glorious immortality.

Some persons read the Bible only as a book of amusement; others peruse it as the most ancient record of authentic and faithful history; and others again—as scholars, as critics in its refined classic language, and on account of the beauties of its style and composition. But there are not a few, who, according to its principal design, read it with devout veneration, and with earnest prayer for the Divine illumination, and the sanctifying influences of the Holy Spirit.

To read the word of God with saving benefit, the heart must be prepared with suitable dispositions.

1. The Bible must be read with reverence. It is to be remembered, that it is the inspired revelation of the Lord God Almighty. This appears to be lamentably forgotten, even by many pious persons. We are so much accustomed to the sight of a Bible, that we are in danger of looking upon it merely as a common book: but every time we cast our eyes upon the sacred volume, our minds should be impressed with its character, as a standing miracle of sovereign and divine mercy. " My heart standeth in awe of thy word," said the royal psalmist, Psa. cxix. 161. This wonderful book bears upon its communications, the evident impress of God: it carries with it divine authority: it is the only rule of our duty in this life, and the law by which we shall all be judged at the last day! " Thus saith the LORD,—To this man will I look, even to him that is poor, and of a contrite spirit, and that trembleth at my word," Isa. lxvi. 2. Nothing, surely, can be more unbecoming, than to read the word of Almighty God with an irreverent, careless, trifling state of mind: and can there be any thing more dangerous?

2. Docility or teachableness is indispensable to a profitable reading of the Scriptures. They are the " Oracles of God;" and he who would read them to edification and salvation, must humbly receive their infallible instruc-

tions as the dictates of infinite wisdom. "The meek will he guide in judgment; and the meek will he teach his way. The secret of the LORD is with them that fear him; and he will show them his covenant—(so the marginal reading,) to make them to know it," Psa. xxv. 9 and 14. Prejudices, preconceived notions, and favourite opinions must be laid aside; and the mind must yield to the truth of God as wax to the seal. Every beloved lust must be denied, and every darling sin must be sacrificed. The apostle James gives this inspired direction—"Lay apart all filthiness and superfluity of naughtiness, and receive with meekness the engrafted word, which is able to save your souls," James i. 21. The manner in which the early Christians regarded the Scriptures, at once evinces both reverence and humility. "When ye received the word of God which ye heard of us, ye received it not as the word of man, but, as it is in truth, the word of God, which effectually worketh also in you that believe," 1 Thess. ii. 13.

3. Devout reliance on the influences of the Holy Spirit, is necessary to a beneficial reading of the Bible. "The natural man," however he may be polished in his manners, and possess a mind furnished with various stores of knowledge, being prayerless, "receiveth not the things of the Spirit of God; for they are foolishness unto him: neither can he know them, because they are spiritually discerned," 1 Cor. ii. 14. To prepare our sensual minds savingly to regard the inspired Scriptures, God, our heavenly Father, has graciously promised his Holy Spirit to those who pray for his illuminating and sanctifying influences: "If any of you lack wisdom, let him ask of God, that giveth to all men liberally, and upbraideth not; and it shall be given him," James i. 5. "If ye then, being evil, know how to give good gifts unto your children, how much more shall your heavenly Father give the Holy Spirit to them that ask him!" Luke xi. 13.

"Many of the things of God in the Scriptures are very deep, so that they cannot be discovered but by the help of the Spirit of God. This is the great and principal

rule, which is to be given to those who would find out the mind of God in the Scripture. Let them be earnest, diligent, constant, fervent in their supplications and prayers, that God, according to his promise, would graciously send his Holy Spirit, to guide, lead, instruct, and teach them; to open their understandings, that they may understand the Scriptures, as our Lord did for his disciples. Unless we have his guidance, we shall labour to little purpose in this matter. Yea, woe be to him who leans to his own understanding herein."—*Dr. Owen.*

4. The Bible must be read with ardent desire to enjoy its consolations, and to obey its precepts. If the Bible has been given to us by Divine inspiration, and if it is designed to make sinners wise unto salvation, through faith in Christ Jesus; if it is able to build us up in faith and holiness, to qualify us for communion with God on earth, and to give us an inheritance among all them that are sanctified through faith in Christ Jesus, it must be read and studied, with a humble, believing, prayerful mind; so that its soul-renewing doctrines may be understood and loved, and its holy precepts cordially and universally obeyed. In this manner, as a recorded example to us, did the devout psalmist study the word of God, and realize its divine blessings. Psalms xix. and cxix. are most beautifully edifying specimens of a profitable manner of studying the Bible. May every reader of these pages, possessing the spirit, be led to adopt the language of the psalmist—" Open thou mine eyes, that I may behold wondrous things out of thy law. The law of thy mouth is better unto me than thousands of gold and silver. Let my heart be sound in thy statutes, that I be not ashamed. Thy testimonies have I taken as an heritage for ever: for they are the rejoicing of my heart," Psa. cxix. 18, 72, 80, 111. "If any man will do his will, he shall know of the doctrine, whether it be of God," John vii. 17. "The whole Scripture is divinely inspired and profitable; being written by the Holy Ghost for this purpose, that in it, as a common healing office for souls, all men may choose the medicine suited to cure their own distempers. It searches

their hearts, discovers their thoughts, fixes principles in their consciences, judges their acts, supports their spirits, comforts their souls, enlightens their minds, guides them in their hope, confidence, and love to God, directs them in all their communion with him and obedience unto him, and leads them to an enjoyment of him. And this work of the Holy Ghost in it, and by it, seals its divine authority unto them, so that they find rest, spiritual satisfaction, and great assurance therein. When once they have obtained this experience of its divine power, it is vain for men or devils to oppose canonical authority with their frivolous cavils and objections."—*Dr. Owen.*

Ch. IX.—Rules for the profitable Reading of the Bible.

Besides the proper state of mind in which the word of God may be read profitably, there are many rules, of more or less importance, yet essentially requisite to be observed in order to derive the full amount of benefit in this employment. The following have been found by many pious persons eminently useful.

1. Read the Bible daily. An equal portion cannot be read every day by all persons. Thomas Gouge, an eminent minister, read fifteen chapters daily. Chrysostom, a bishop of the fourth century, besides other portions, read through the Epistle to the Romans twice every week: but such a measure is not practicable by every one; nor is it to be recommended as indispensable. Probably, however, there are few or none who could not read a chapter in the morning, and another in the evening. But even if it were only a verse at each time, with larger portions on the Lord's day, very great profit would arise to the meditative, devout believer. "His delight is in the law of the Lord; and in his law doth he meditate day and night," Psa. i. 2. "Blessed is the man that heareth me, watching daily at my gates, waiting at the posts of my doors," Prov. viii. 34.

2. Read through each book of the Bible. It indicates a trifling mind, to read any important book only in parts, and those irregularly: but this is a common evil. How much more unwise and criminal must such a proceeding be in relation to the word of God! Merely "to dip into a book," especially the volume of inspiration, is not the way to understand the full meaning of its author. Many of the books of Scripture are, in a great measure, independent of the others. Thus Genesis, the four Gospels, the Acts, Romans, and Hebrews, cannot be clearly understood by parts only being read. Each book should be read throughout in course before another is begun, that the full sense and scope of the writer may be perceived.

Though all are necessary, and designed for our instruction, yet all the books of the Bible are not of equal interest, especially to the plain Christian; and, therefore, they do not claim so much of his attention. The Psalms, each of which is an independent writing, the Gospels, and the Epistles, generally engage the minds of believers in the greatest degree; as they seem peculiarly adapted to edify, sanctify, and console them in their pilgrimage: but the scope, and force, and design, and benefit of them can be fully realized, only in perusing each as a whole.

3. Regard the design of each book. Detached passages of Scripture are often misunderstood and misapplied, even by good men, through inattention to the design of the inspiring Spirit. Ungodly men often pervert the word of God, as Satan did when he tempted our Saviour, Matt. iv. 6. Peter, admonishing his brethren against such an evil, especially in relation to difficult passages in Paul's Epistles, observes, "Which they that are unlearned and unstable wrest, as they do also the other Scriptures, unto their own destruction," 2 Pet. iii. 16. To illustrate this rule we may refer to the Epistles of Paul to the Romans and to the Hebrews. They both contain the same divine doctrines of salvation, but his manner of setting them forth is strikingly different. The Epistle to the Romans was written for the instruc-

tion of believers generally, while that to the Hebrews was addressed to the Jewish people specially, and designed to show that the ceremonial institutions established by Moses were intended only for a time; while the various services of the priesthood, the sacrifices, and the purifications, prefigured the all-glorious priesthood and atonement of Christ as our surety, and the sanctification of the church by the blessings of his grace.

4. Consider the Bible as an harmonious whole. "The writers plainly make it appear, that they wrote, not of themselves, but as they were moved by the Holy Ghost. For though they were men that lived in different ages of the world, and in different parts of it, and were of different interests and capacities, and in different conditions and circumstances, yet they are all of the same sentiment; they speak and write of the same things, deliver out the same doctrines and truths, enjoin the same moral duties of religion, and the same positive precepts, according to the different dispensations under which they wrote, and relate the same historical facts. There are no contradictions to one another, no jar nor discord between them, but all uniform and of a piece. What seeming contradictions may be observed, are easily reconciled with a little care and study."—*Dr. Gill.*

5. Remark the testimony of the ancient prophets to Christ. The spirit of the whole Bible is to direct its readers to Jesus Christ. One of the glorified elders declared to John, that "the testimony of Jesus is the spirit of prophecy," Rev. xix. 10. So said our Lord himself, "Search the Scriptures, for they are they which testify of me," John v. 39. He conversed on this subject, after his resurrection, with two of his disciples. "And beginning at Moses, and all the prophets, he expounded unto them in all the Scriptures the things concerning himself.—And he said unto them, These are the words which I spake unto you, while I was yet with you, that all things must be fulfilled which were written in the law of Moses, and in the prophets, and in the Psalms, concerning me," Luke xxiv. 27, 44. "To him," said Peter,

"give all the prophets witness, that through his name, whosoever believeth in him shall receive remission of sins," Acts x. 43. By this, it is not intended that every part or passage refers to Jesus Christ; but that the doctrinal spirit of the whole volume testifies the necessity, sufficiency, and blessings of a Mediator between God and man; while very many passages point out the glory, the offices, and the grace of Jesus Christ, as the only Saviour of sinners. "Let this also commend the Scriptures much to our diligence and affection, that their great theme is our Redeemer, and salvation wrought by him."—*Archbishop Leighton.*

6. Make the Bible its own expositor. In consulting parallel passages of Scripture, by the help of a Bible with marginal references, or by means of a concordance, incalculable advantage may be gained. While we are required to "search the Scriptures," we are directed to be diligent in "comparing spiritual things with spiritual," 1 Cor. ii. 13. "I will not scruple to assert, that the most illiterate Christian, if he can but read his English Bible, and will take the pains to read it in this manner, will not only attain all that practical knowledge which is necessary to his salvation, but, by God's blessing, he will become learned in every thing relating to his religion, in such a degree that he will not be liable to be misled, either by the refined arguments or false assertions of those who endeavour to engraft their own opinions upon the oracles of God. He may safely be ignorant of all philosophy, except what is learned from the sacred books; which, indeed, contain the highest philosophy, adapted to the lowest apprehensions. He may safely remain ignorant of all history, except so much of the history of the first ages of the Jewish and Christian church as is to be gathered from the canonical books of the Old and New Testaments. Let him study these in the manner I recommend; and let him never cease to pray for the illumination of that Spirit by which these books were dictated; and the whole history of abstruse philosophy and recondite his-

tory shall furnish no argument with which the perverse will of man shall be able to shake this learned Christian's faith."—*Bishop Horsley.*

7. Possess correct ideas of the method in which alone a sinner can attain to a state of justification before God, and be qualified to dwell in his presence in heaven. " We are accounted righteous before God, only for the merit of our Lord and Saviour Jesus Christ, by faith, and not for our works and deservings."—*Church of England*, Art. XI. " Justification is an act of God's free grace, wherein he pardoneth all our sins, and accepteth us as righteous in his sight, only for the righteousness of Christ imputed to us, and received by faith alone."—*Assembly's Catechism.* See Isa. liii. 10—12; Rom. v. 17—19; 2 Cor. v. 21.

The scripture doctrine of sanctification should be well understood. A sinful creature can be prepared for the kingdom of God only by being regenerated, " born again," John iii. 3, 5, " born of the Spirit," " with the word of truth," James i. 18; " not of corruptible seed, but of incorruptible, by the word of God," 1 Pet. i. 23: the alienated and unholy mind being renewed and sanctified by the Holy Spirit. " Not by works of righteousness which we have done, but according to his mercy he saved us, by the washing of regeneration and renewing of the Holy Ghost; which he shed on us abundantly, through Jesus Christ our Saviour," Titus iii. 5, 6. Allowing these leading principles to rule in the mind, it will be prepared to understand many passages of Scripture, which would otherwise appear obscure or inexplicable to an inconsiderate reader.

8. Remember, that many things in the Old Testament were designed by God as types or emblematical representations of Jesus Christ and his relation to his church. That which was prefigured is called the antitype. The apostle declares, " The law had a shadow of good things to come;" by which were prefigured many things concerning the mediation of Christ and his redemption of the church, Heb. viii. 5; ix. 8, 12, 24; x. 1.

Great caution is indeed necessary in the interpretation

of the types; for many, by their indiscretion and unrestrained fancies, have exposed the doctrine of types to ridicule. There is one certain and infallible rule which we have for the interpretation of types. " Whatever persons or things recorded in the Old Testament, were expressly declared by Christ or his apostles to have been designed as prefigurations of persons or things relating to the New Testament, such persons or things, so recorded in the former, are types of persons or things with which they are compared in the latter."—*Bishop Marsh.*

Many persons were typical, as Adam, Melchisedec, Moses, and David were of our Lord and Saviour. Things were typical, as Noah's ark, the manna, and the tabernacle. Places were typical, as Canaan, Jerusalem, and the cities of refuge. Institutions were typical, as the passover, the repeated atonements for sin, and the purifications; of which the Epistle to the Hebrews is an inspired exposition.

9. Preserve in mind an accurate idea of the term *covenant*, as used in the Bible. It generally signifies a league, contract, or mutual agreement made between two parties; but in the Scriptures it most frequently denotes a solemn promise made by God, to a certain person or persons, for important purposes. There are several covenants mentioned in the Bible, of which the following ought to be attentively considered.

(1.) The Covenant of Obedience, commonly called the Covenant of Works, between God the Creator and our first parents, and with all mankind in them: of this covenant the tree of life was the sacramental sign, Gen. ii. 9; iii. 22—24.

(2.) The Covenant of Safety with Noah, for all mankind, of which the rainbow was the appointed token, Gen. ix. 9—17.

(3.) The Covenant of Property with Abraham and his seed, renewed with the children of Israel at Sinai: the seal of his covenant was circumcision, Gen. xvii. 1—13; Exod. xix. 1—8; Deut. ix. 5—11.

(4.) The Covenant of Royalty with David, 2 Sam. vii.; Psa. lxxxix. 19—37.

(5.) The Covenant of Redemption and Grace, with Christ as its surety. Hence the apostle declares of believers, " God hath saved us, and called us, with a holy calling, not according to our works, but according to his own purpose and grace, which was given us in Christ Jesus before the world began," 2 Tim. i. 9.

The covenant of grace is a merciful constitution of things, in which God takes sinners into a new relation to himself as his peculiar people; stipulates blessings and privileges for them, gives them laws and ordinances as the rule of their obedience, and the means of their correspondence with him, the whole transaction being ratified with the blood of sacrifice. This covenant of mercy was made known to mankind in former ages of the world by means of the animal sacrifices; its awful conditions were sealed by the blood of Christ, and it is now commemorated by the people of God, in the communion of the Lord's supper. The covenant of grace is contrasted by the apostle with that of Moses; and its merciful provisions are declared as infinitely better than those of the Levitical dispensation. " He," Christ, "is the Mediator of a better covenant, which was established upon better promises. For this is the covenant that I will make with the house of Israel after those days, saith the Lord; I will put my laws into their minds, and write them in their hearts: and I will be to them a God, and they shall be to me a people: and they shall not teach every man his neighbour and every man his brother, saying, Know the Lord: for all shall know me, from the least to the greatest. For I will be merciful to their unrighteousness, and their sins and their iniquities will I remember no more," Heb. viii. 6, 10—12.

10. Right apprehensions concerning the law of God are of much consequence to the Scripture reader. The word *law* is variously used in the Bible, in reference to believers on Jesus Christ. It is employed to denote the Levitical institutions, which were partly of a political, partly of a moral, and partly of a religious character. From these the Hebrew Christians were delivered by virtue of their faith in Christ. Law is used in the New

Testament to signify that rule of our duty both to God and man, which was delivered to Moses in ten commandments, and which was summed up by our Lord in those two comprehensive precepts, "Thou shalt love the Lord thy God with all thy heart, and with all thy soul, and with all thy mind;" and, "Thou shalt love thy neighbour as thyself." This must necessarily be a rule of duty to all intelligent creatures; and though believers in Christ are not under it, as a condition of justification and life, it will be for ever obligatory upon all men.

11. Obtain a general acquaintance with the geography of the Bible, so as to be familiar with the relative situation of the principal countries mentioned in the Scriptures: this will, in numerous instances, serve as a key to the clear understanding of many significant passages, not only in the writings of the prophets, but in the books of the New Testament.

12. Get a correct acquaintance with the Hebrew offices; as those of the priests and Levites: and with the sacred festivals; as the feasts of the Passover and Tabernacles.

13. Times, seasons, and intervals of great events in the chronology of the Bible should be well considered by the reader of Scripture; by which much light will appear thrown upon various parts of the word of God. The principal epochs, or remarkable periods of time from which dates are made, ought to be familiar to the Christian reader: the creation of the world 4000 years before the advent of Christ: the deluge, B. C. 2348 years: the calling of Abraham, B. C. 1921 years: the exodus of Israel, B. C. 1491 years: the dedication of Solomon's temple, B. C. 1012 years: the captivity of Judah, B. C. 588 years: the close of the Old Testament, B. C. 400: the termination of the New Testament history, A. D. 100.

The dates of various events mentioned in the Bible, include a large system of chronology: they were added to the present English version, and are very useful: but many of the dates to the time of Abraham, are believed to be incorrect, as is shown in the notes to the CHRONOLOGICAL INDEX.

14. Ancient customs of the eastern nations should be considered. Besides the peculiar religious ceremonies of the Hebrews, there were many national customs, which, though not indecorous or improper, may yet appear singular to us, and which, therefore, are necessary to be known. The houses were generally built with flat roofs; upon which the inhabitants were accustomed to walk, and sometimes to sleep, and where pious persons were used to retire for prayer, Matt. xxiv. 17; Acts x. 9. The bottles mentioned in Scripture were made of the skins of animals; and their books were few and small, written upon pieces of parchment, which were wound upon rollers, etc. etc. See the books called "The Manners and Customs of the Jews:" and "The Rites and Worship of the Jews."

15. Notice several peculiarities in our version of the Bible. The words printed in Italic letters have not corresponding words in the original: they were added by the translators to complete the sense; but though in some instances they are very important, in others they make it obscure. The word LORD, when printed in capital letters, is, in the Hebrew, Jehovah, signifying that Being who is eternal and self-existent, and who gives being to others. Lord, in small letters in the original, signifies ruler or sustainer; see both, Psa. cx. 1. The larger Bibles have many words placed in the margin, which are the more literal renderings of the original words to which they refer: those in the Old Testament are distinguished by the letters Heb., signifying that such is the correct meaning in Hebrew; and those in the New Testament by Gr., denoting that such is the literal signification in the original Greek.

CH. X.—GEOGRAPHY OF THE BIBLE, PARTICULARLY OF THE OLD TESTAMENT.

THE principal countries mentioned in the Old Testament, except Egypt, are situated on the western border of the Asiatic continent. In that division of the world, the first man was created—there dwelt the first long-

lived patriarchs, and the descendants of Noah, till several ages after the deluge—there the great monarchies of Assyria, Babylon, and Persia were founded and flourished. The ruins of stately palaces, and of other magnificent buildings, which are still to be seen throughout the countries that formed the Assyrian, Babylonian, and Persian, and the Grecian and Roman empires in Asia, sufficiently attest the multitude and riches of its ancient inhabitants, and corroborate the astonishing accounts transmitted to us by different ancient historians, and the inspired writers of the Scriptures.

Paradise, or the garden of Eden, is supposed to have been situated in Armenia, near the celebrated river Euphrates. The country called Palestine, or the land of Judea; Syria, including Phœnicia; Asia Minor, now called Natolia; Mesopotamia, now termed Diarbeck; Chaldea, Assyria, and Arabia, constitute the principal countries noticed in the Old Testament Scriptures, and are all in Asia. Egypt, which is on the north-east coast of Africa, is separated from Asia only by a narrow neck of land, called the Isthmus of Suez, and the Red Sea, now called the Arabian Gulf.

Asia is celebrated as being far superior to Africa, or even Europe, both in the salubrious serenity of its air, and the rich fertility of its soil; producing abundance of corn, the most delicious fruits, and valuable timber, with the most fragrant and balsamic plants, gums, and spices, and the most precious stones.

The Scriptures, however, relate chiefly to the events connected with the family of Abraham, especially those regarding religion, and which took place in Palestine or Canaan—where the kingdoms of Israel and Judah flourished—where the temple of God was erected by king Solomon—where most of the inspired Scriptures were written—where our Lord Jesus Christ accomplished the all-important work of human redemption—and where the apostles of the Saviour were supernaturally qualified to go forth among all nations, to preach the gospel of eternal salvation, bringing sinners of every tribe and nation by faith and holiness into the kingdom of Messiah.

Canaan was so named from Canaan, the son of Ham, the son of Noah. It lay between the Mediterranean Sea and the mountains of Arabia, extending from Egypt on the south to Phœnicia on the north. It was bounded on the east by Arabia Deserta; on the south by Arabia Petræa, Idumea, and Egypt; on the west by the Mediterranean, called in Scripture The Great Sea; and on the north by the mountains of Lebanon in Syria. Its length from the city of Dan, which stood at the foot of those mountains, to Beersheba, which was situated at the southern extremity of the land, is about two hundred miles; and its breadth, from the shores of the Mediterranean to the eastern border, is about ninety miles. This country is known to us by several significant names besides that of Canaan: it is called The Land of Promise, from the fact of its having been promised to Abraham and his family: Palestine, from the Philistines: Judea, from the tribe of Judah possessing its most fertile division. It is frequently called The Holy Land, from the circumstances recorded in the Holy Scriptures, especially as the ministry of Christ was exercised in that country; and as there the obedience, and death, and resurrection of Christ took place for our eternal salvation.

On the completion of the work of redemption, the apostles were commissioned to "go into all the world, and preach the gospel to every creature;" and the fulfilment of their ministry opens to us a new field of geography. Asia Minor, Greece, and several other parts of the Roman empire, especially the countries around the shores of the Mediterranean Sea, might claim a particular notice in this place, did the nature of this work allow of an extension of the subject: but the reader is referred to Chapter XVII. in the second part, called, The Geographical Gazetteer to the New Testament.

Ch. XI.—Hebrew Offices.

Correct sentiments concerning the several Hebrew offices, will be valuable to the reader of the Bible.

1. The Patriarchs were the fathers who lived in the early ages of the world, and who became famous on account of their long lives, and their descendants. Adam, Seth, Enoch, etc. were eminent before the deluge: Noah, Shem, Ham, and Japhet, and their sons after that event. Job, Abraham, Ishmael, Isaac, Esau, Jacob, and their sons, are the other most celebrated patriarchs of the Old Testament: they were the founders of mighty families. The patriarchs exercised a kind of sovereign authority in their respective households, being both priests and princes. In Job and Abraham we see excellent examples of the patriarchal government.

2. The Prophets were illustrious persons who were divinely raised up, especially among the Israelites, to be the extraordinary ministers of religion under the several dispensations of God among men. To them the knowledge of secret things was revealed, particularly concerning what was future; that they might declare them to mankind, or write them for our instruction, as the infallible oracles of God. Colleges and schools were founded in different places, by many of those servants of God; for the propagation of divine doctrine: and hence their disciples were called Prophets; as we find one instituted by Samuel, and read of "a company of prophets coming down from the high place, with a psaltery, and a tabret, and a pipe, and a harp, before them; and they did prophesy," 1 Sam. x. 5. Those especially called Prophets are the writers of the several books which bear their names; and they flourished in a continued succession during a period of more than a thousand years, reckoning from Moses to Malachi; all co-operating in the same designs, uniting in one spirit to deliver the same doctrines, and to predict the same blessings to mankind, especially through the Redeemer.

3. The Priests were those persons whose office was to offer sacrifices to God for sin, and make intercession with him for themselves and for the people. Before the institution of the Levitical priesthood, by the call and consecration of Aaron, and among other worshippers of God, patriarchs, elder brothers, and princes, or

every man for himself, offered sacrifice; as appears evident from the history of Cain, Abel, Noah, Job, and Abraham. Moses performed this office, at the foot of Mount Sinai, for the Israelites, as their mediator with God, young men being chosen from among the people of Israel, to assist him in the duty of sacrificing, Exod. xxiv. 4, 8. But after the LORD had chosen the tribe of Levi to serve him in his tabernacle, and the priesthood was annexed to the family of Aaron, then the right to offer sacrifices to God, among the Israelites, was reserved alone to this family; and it was ordained "that no stranger, not of the seed of Aaron, should come near to offer incense before the LORD," Numb. xvi. 40.

The high priest was the first character among the Israelites, as he was the medium of communion with God. The priesthood was hereditary in the family of Aaron, and the first-born of the oldest branch of it, if he had no legal blemish, was always the high priest. He was consecrated with solemn pomp, and officiated at the daily sacrifice in splendid robes; especially on the day of atonement, on which occasion he wore the precious breastplate, with the names of the twelve tribes of Israel engraven on gems, set in it, that he might be admonished to bear on his heart the whole community, for whom the sacred ornament was a memorial before the Lord. In his appointment to his office, and in his consecration, sacrifice, and intercession for the people, the high priest was an eminent type of Jesus Christ, Exod. xxviii. xxix.; Lev. xvi.; Heb. iii. v. vii. viii. ix. x.

The Jewish priests were also of the family of Aaron: they were the ordinary ministers of religion, and their duty was to offer the daily and other sacrifices, under the direction of the high priest; to conduct all the various services of the tabernacle; to manage all the religious ceremonies of the people, and to instruct them in the law of God. They were divided into twenty-four ranks, each rank serving weekly in the temple.

The Jewish high priest, in his public character, as sacrificer and intercessor for the people of Israel, prefigured our Lord Jesus Christ, in his mediation with God

by atonement and intercession for mankind. The ministers of the gospel were represented by the ordinary priests, not in their office as sacrificers, but as intercessors for, and instructors of, the people in the worship and service of God.

4. The Levites were the descendants of Levi, but not of the family of Aaron: they were a lower order of ecclesiastical persons, inferior in office to the priests, and their assistants in the several parts of the sacred service. In this subordinate capacity were all the posterity of Moses; affording a proof that he was not influenced by ambition, but acted by the Divine direction. The Levites applied themselves to the study of the law, and they were dispersed through the country as the ordinary teachers, magistrates, and judges of the people. They had no landed property allotted to them except forty-eight cities; for God was their inheritance, and he appointed the tithes of the produce of the land of Israel, as a reward for their services among the people, Numb. xviii. 20—32; xxxv. 1—8.

5. The Nethinims, from the Hebrew word Nathan, "to give," were servants, who had been given up to the service of the tabernacle and temple, at which they officiated, in the more laborious duties of carrying wood and water. They were the Canaanites whose lives were spared, Josh. ix.; Ezra viii. 20.

6. Nazarites were persons devoted to the peculiar service of God, for a week, a month, a year, or for life. Samson and John the Baptist were Nazarites by birth; others were so by their own voluntary act, Numb. vi. 1—21; Acts xviii. 18; xxi. 21—26. The Rechabites were of this class of persons, Jer. xxxv.: their descendants are still found in the East.

7. The Scribes among the Israelites were writers of the law; persons who addicted themselves to literary pursuits. They were a class of lawyers by profession: at first they were only the copiers of the law, or secretaries to the government; but from transcribers of the sacred writings, they assumed the office of its expounders, till in the time of our Saviour, their popular

commentaries had, in many things, superseded the word of God, Matt. xv. 1—9; xxiii. 2—33.

Ch. XII.—Hebrew Festivals, Times, and Seasons.

To a serious reader of the Bible, a general acquaintance with the Hebrew times and seasons is important. The Israelites had two different periods, from which they began the computation of their year;—one for civil purposes, the other for the regulation of their religious festivals. The sacred year commenced in the month Abib, which corresponds with our March; because in that month the Israelites were emancipated from their slavery in Egypt: the civil year began in the month Tisri, answering to our September. The Hebrew mode of reckoning months was not as ours, but strictly lunar: they, therefore, cannot be reduced to correspond exactly with ours, as they consisted of 29 and 30 days alternately. To make their year equal to the solar, the Jews took care every three years to add a month to Adar, and called it Ve-Adar, or second Adar.

The natural day the Israelites distinguished from the civil: the civil day was from the rising to the setting of the sun; and the natural day was of 24 hours, reckoning from one sun setting to another. The night was divided into four watches, each watch containing the space of about three hours.

The following Table of Hebrew Time may serve to explain more clearly the periods of the several sacred festivals appointed to be observed by the Israelites.

CH. XII.—HEBREW FESTIVALS AND SEASONS.

TABLE OF HEBREW TIMES AND FESTIVALS.

Hebrew Months.	Nearly corresponding with Months of our	Months of the Sacred Year.	Months of the Civil Year.	Seasons.	Festivals.
Abib, or Nisan, Exod. xii. 2, 18. xiii. 4. Esth. iii. 7.	March.	1st	7th	Harvest.	14. Paschal Lamb killed. 15. PASSOVER. 16. First fruits of barley harvest presented to the Lord. 21. Passover ended.
Tyar, or Zif, 1 Kings vi. 1.	April.	2d	8th		
Sivan, Esth. viii. 9.	May.	3d	9th	Summer.	6. PENTECOST. First fruits of wheat presented to the Lord.
Tammuz, Ezek. viii. 14.	June.	4th	10th		
Ab.	July.	5th	11th	Hot Season.	
Elul, Neh. vi. 15.	August.	6th	12th		9. Temple taken on this day by the Chaldeans, and afterwards by the Romans.
Ethanim, or Tisri, 1 Kings viii. 2.	September.	7th	1st	Seed Time.	1. Feast of Trumpets. 10. Day of Atonement. 15. FEAST OF TABERNACLES. 22. Last day of it.
Marchesvan, or Bul, 1 Kings vi. 38.	October.	8th	2d		
Chisleu, Zech. vii. 1.	November.	9th	3d	Winter.	25. Feast of the Dedication of the Temple.
Tebeth, Esth. ii. 16.	December.	10th	4th		
Sebat, Zech. i. 7.	January.	11th	5th	Cold Season.	
Adar, Esth. iii. 7. Ve-Adar is added here when necessary.	February.	12th	6th		14 and 15. Feast of Purim. Esth. ix. 18—21.

CH. XII.—HEBREW FESTIVALS AND SEASONS.

1. The Sabbath was first and most important of the sacred festivals. The seventh day was so denominated from a Hebrew word signifying rest, because in it God had rested from his works of creation. From the beginning of the world it had been set apart for religious services; and by a special injunction it was afterwards observed by the Hebrews as a holy day. They were commanded to sanctify it for sacred purposes, in honour of God as their Creator, and likewise as a memorial of their redemption from slavery in the land of Egypt, Gen. ii. 2; Exod. xx. 8—11.

2. The Daily Sacrifice. The sacrifices of the Hebrews were exceedingly numerous: bullocks, sheep, goats, pigeons, and turtle-doves, were the animals used by appointment of God for this purpose. " There were four sorts of sacrifices, as one alone was not sufficient to represent the adorable sacrifice of Jesus Christ."—*Abbé Fleury*. The sacrifices were of two general kinds: 1. Such as were offered in the way of atonement for sin; 2. Such as were designed to express gratitude to God, as thank-offerings for his mercies and blessings, either on common or special occasions, Lev. i. vii.

The daily sacrifice was very remarkable: it was a lamb without blemish, offered to God by fire, as an atonement for sin; one in the morning daily throughout the year, for the sins of the nation during the night, and another in the evening for their sins during the day. Before the act of sacrificing, the devoted victim had the sins of the whole nation confessed over it, by the officiating priest, and the guilt ceremonially transferred to the animal, by the representatives of the people, chosen and delegated from time to time for that purpose, laying their hands upon its head. It was then slain, and offered as a burnt-offering for them: meanwhile the congregation worshipped in the court, and the priests burnt incense on the golden altar, making supplication for the people. On the sabbath the sacrifice was double, two lambs being offered at each service, Exod. xxix. 38—42; xxx. 6—8; Lev. vi. 9; Numb. xxviii. 3—9.

3. The Day of Atonement was distinguished with the

most solemn annual sacrifice; at which, after the high priest had offered a bullock, as an atonement for the sins of himself and his family, two goats were offered as an atonement for the nation. The manner of the sacrifice was affecting and instructive. After the sins of the nation had been confessed over their heads by the high priest, one was slain and offered by fire, after the manner of the daily sacrifice: the other was taken, bearing the sins of the people, into the wilderness, to be seen no more, Lev. xvi. An ancient form of confession, according to the Hebrew doctors, was, on the Day of Atonement, as follows: "O Lord, thy people, the house of Israel, have done wickedly; they have transgressed before thee; I beseech thee now, O Lord, pardon the sins, iniquities, and transgressions with which the people, the house of Israel, have sinned, done wickedly, and transgressed before thee, as it is written in the law of thy servant Moses: that in that day he shall make atonement for you, that he might becleanse you, and that you might be clean from all your iniquities before the Lord."—*Godwyn.*

Another form of confession at private sacrifices, is said to have been as follows: "Now, O Lord, I have sinned, I have committed iniquity, I have rebelled; but I return in repentance to thy presence, and be this my expiation."—*Dr. Outram.*

4. The New Moons were observed with much solemn festivity; for which special sacrifices were appointed, and the rejoicings of the nation were attended with the sounding of the silver trumpets by the priests, Numb. x. 10; xxviii. 11—15.

The annual festivals of the Israelites were three; at which all the males of the nation, above twelve years of age, were required to present themselves before the LORD at his sanctuary, Deut. xvi. 16.

5. The Passover was the first of the annual Jewish festivals: it was instituted to commemorate the wonderful preservation of the Hebrews, on the night of their deliverance from slavery, when the destroying angel slew the first-born of every Egyptian family, passing over the houses of the Israelites, their door-posts having been

CH. XII.—HEBREW FESTIVALS AND SEASONS. 39

sprinkled with the blood of the paschal lamb, which was sacrificed in the evening. That night was the termination of the four hundred and thirty years of the sojourning of the Hebrews, from the time of Abraham, Gen. xv. 13, 14; Exod. xii. 41, 42. It was the fourteenth day of the month Abib, answering to the beginning of our April; and which, from that most memorable event, became the chief of their months, and, as the period of Israel's redemption from slavery, the commencement of their ecclesiastical year, which had not been before that time distinguished from the civil, Exod. xii. 2—18; xxiii. 15.

The passover was typical of our Saviour, and hence the apostle says, "Christ our Passover is sacrificed for us," 1 Cor. v. 7. The spotless purity of his heart and life was prefigured by the paschal lamb, being without blemish. Christians are, therefore, redeemed not with "silver and gold, but with the precious blood of Christ, as of a lamb without blemish and without spot," 1 Pet. i. 18, 19. As the Israelites were passed over and delivered by the shedding of the blood, and feeding upon the flesh of the paschal lamb,—so the salvation of Christians is enjoyed by feeding, in faith, upon the flesh and blood of Christ, John vi. 51—63.

6. Pentecost is a Greek word signifying the fiftieth; this festival was so called because it was celebrated the fiftieth day after the second day of the passover. The feast of Pentecost was instituted to commemorate the giving of the law at Sinai, that being received fifty days after the deliverance from Egypt. It was called, also, the Feast of Weeks, Deut. xvi. 16, and the Feast of Harvest, as it was held at the close of the wheat harvest, the first-fruits of which, in two loaves of fine flour, were presented to the Lord, with sacrifices, thanksgiving, and rejoicing. The public sacrifice was seven lambs of that year, one calf, and two rams for a burnt-offering; two lambs for a peace-offering, and a goat for a sin-offering, Lev. xxiii. 10—20.

It is worthy of observation, that this feast happened on the Lord's day in that year in which our Saviour

was crucified, when the apostles were miraculously endowed by the Holy Spirit, to qualify them for preaching the gospel in all languages, so establishing the kingdom of Christ among all nations, and when three thousand converts were at one time brought into the church of the Redeemer.

7. The Feast of Tabernacles was held at the close of the whole harvest and vintage, Deut. xvi. 13, to acknowledge the bounty of God, in crowning the year with his blessings. It was designed to commemorate the goodness of God in protecting the Israelites in the wilderness: for which purpose, during this feast they dwelt in booths formed of the boughs of trees, and in these they continued seven days, to remind them of their forefathers sojourning in the desert. The Feast of Tabernacles commenced on the fifteenth day of Tisri, which was the first month of the civil year, on the first of which a festival was held called the Feast of Trumpets, a memorial of blowing of trumpets, or of triumph and shouting for joy. It began the year; the tenth was the Day of Atonement, Lev. xxiii. 24, 34—43; Deut. xvi. 13—15.

8. The Sabbatical Year, the Jubilee or Year of Release, was every seventh year among the Israelites. As the sabbath day signified that the people were the Lord's, for which reason they abstained from their own work to do the work of the Lord; so the sabbatical year was intended to remind them that both they and their land belonged to the Lord. The observation of this festival consisted principally in two things. 1. In not tilling the ground or pruning the vine; whence the land was said to keep a sabbath, Lev. xxv. 6. 2. In discharging all debtors and releasing all debts; from which it was called the Lord's Release, Deut. xv. 2—9. To remove all the fears of the timid concerning the want of a harvest, as they were not allowed to sow or cultivate the land, God mercifully promised to command his blessing upon the sixth year, that the land should bring forth the fruit of three years, Lev. xxv. 20—22. Religious instruction was to be particularly communicated

to the servants and to the poor in this year of release, that the knowledge and fear of God might be preserved among the people, Deut. xxxi. 10—13.

9. The Great Jubilee, or Grand Sabbatical Year, was appointed to be held every fiftieth year, at the end of seven of the smaller jubilees, Lev. xxv. 8—55. This was a year of general release to the Israelites, not only of all debts, but of all slaves and prisoners, and of all lands and possessions, whether they had been sold or mortgaged. This joyful period was announced in the evening after the solemn services of the day of atonement, ver. 9. This time was most wisely appointed; as the rich and the injured would be better prepared to remit the debts of their brethren, when they themselves had been imploring forgiveness of God; and when peace was made with God, by the sacrifices of atonement, it was peculiarly suitable to proclaim liberty and rejoicing throughout the country. The design of this institution was both political and typical. The jubilee was political, intended to prevent the oppression of the poor, as well as their being liable to perpetual slavery. By this means, the rich were prevented from getting the whole of the landed property into their own possession, and a kind of equality was maintained in all their families. By this means also, the distinction of tribes was preserved in Israel in respect both of their estates and families, and it was thus correctly ascertained from what tribe and family the Messiah descended.

The jubilee had a typical design, to which the prophet Isaiah refers in predicting the character and office of Messiah, ch. lxi. 1, 2; Luke iv. 17—21. The various terms which the prophet employs alluded to the blessings of the jubilee, but its full sense refers to the richer blessings of the gospel, which proclaims spiritual release from the bondage of sin and Satan, liberty of returning to our heavenly inheritance by Jesus Christ, and the privilege of being enriched with the treasures of his grace on earth, preparatory to the enjoyment of the celestial glory.

Ch. XIII.—Divisions of the Bible.

The Bible contains two collections of writings, distinguished by the titles, The Old Testament, and The New Testament. The former comprises the successive revelations of the Divine will to the Hebrews, both the Israelites and Jews, before the advent of Christ; and the latter contains the inspired writings of the apostles and evangelists of our Lord and Saviour, designed especially for all the nations converted to the faith of Jesus. The two parts include sixty-six books. The thirty-nine books of the Old Testament were classed in three divisions by the ancient Jews: these portions were called, 1. The Law: 2. The Prophets: and, 3. The Holy Writings. The law containing the five books of Moses, was called the Pentateuch, from a Greek word signifying five instruments. The Prophets included Joshua, Judges, the two books of Samuel, and the two books of Kings, which were called the Former Prophets: and the Latter Prophets comprised Isaiah, Jeremiah, Ezekiel, and the twelve lesser prophetical books from Hosea to Malachi, which were reckoned as one book. The Hagiographa, or Holy Writings, comprehended the Psalms, Proverbs, Job, Solomon's Song, Ruth, Lamentations, Ecclesiastes, Esther, Daniel, Ezra, with Nehemiah and the two books of Chronicles.

That arrangement of the sacred books, which has been adopted in our Bibles, is not regulated by the exact order of time in which they were severally written: the book of Genesis is, however, universally allowed to have been the first, (the book of Job being perfected by Moses about the same time,) and the prophecy of Malachi was the last of the Old Testament.

The Psalms were, from the first, distinct compositions; but the other sacred books were divided into fifty-three larger and smaller sections: so that one of each being read in the synagogue every sabbath day, the whole of the Old Testament was read publicly once a year, in the stated worship of the Jews, after the time of Ezra.

The sacred writings had, originally, no marks of punc-

tuation, and letter followed letter, as if every line were but a single word. Necessity, therefore, led to the adoption of some marks of distinction, both for public and private reading. The Jews began early to point their sections: some say in the time of Ezra; others attribute this improvement to the second century of the Christian era. The New Testament was first pointed by Jerome, in the fourth century; and divided into church lessons and sections by Ammonius and Euthalius in the century following.

The division of the Bible into chapters and verses (not however such small portions as the present verses) was made by cardinal Hugo, about A. D. 1240. The plan of Hugo having become known to Rabbi Nathan in the fifteenth century, he made a Hebrew concordance to the Old Testament, retaining the chapters, but improving the order of the verses. The New Testament was divided into verses, and numbered, A. D. 1545, by Robert Stephens, a very learned Frenchman, who was printer to the king of France. These divisions were made for the convenience of more readily finding the different passages of the Scriptures; and they are of incalculable advantage to us: but, notwithstanding this benefit, in some cases, they rather interrupt the connexion between one part and another: it is, therefore, especially necessary, in seeking correctly to understand any chapter or passage, to consider the whole design of the writer, as it may be perceived by means of the preceding and following parts of the book.

The following table has been published, as containing several particulars of the English version of the Bible; and they may interest some readers.

In the Old Testament	In the New Testament.	Total.
Books........ 39	Books.........27	Books.........66
Chapters..... 929	Chapters......260	Chapters.... 1,189
Verses.....23,214	Verses.......7,959	Verses.....31,173
Words....592,493	Words....181,253	Words....773,746
Letters..2,728,100	Letters....838,380	Letters..3,566,480

The middle chapter and the shortest in the Bible is the hundred and seventeenth Psalm; the middle verse is the

eighth of the hundred and eighteenth Psalm. The twenty-first verse of the seventh chapter of Ezra, in the English version, has all the letters of the alphabet in it. The nineteenth chapter of the second book of Kings and the thirty-seventh chapter of Isaiah are alike.

Ch. XIV.—Analysis of the Books of the Old Testament.

GENESIS,

Comprising a period of 2369 years.

GENESIS is a Greek word, which signifies creation or production, and the first book in the Bible is so called because it relates the history of the creation and production of all things by the word of Almighty God, and of the peopling of the earth by his blessing and providence. The book of Genesis is the oldest volume in the world, and contains the most really important information: it was written by Moses, the deliverer of the Israelites from Egypt, and it embraces a period of about two thousand three hundred and sixty-nine years, from the creation of the world to the death of Joseph in Egypt.

Genesis contains fifty chapters: but every chapter does not relate to a distinct and complete subject. A chapter is sometimes only part of a section, which includes several of these divisions. In Genesis there are eleven principal sections.

Section I. Includes the first and second chapters, which relate the wonderful history of the creation of all things in the heavens and on the earth.

Sec. II. The fall of our first parents, Adam and Eve, from their state of holiness and happiness, by transgression; their expulsion from Paradise, to labour for support in sorrow till death; and the gracious promise of Messiah as a Saviour, ch. iii.

Sec. III. The history of Adam and his descendants to the time of Noah, ch. iv. v.

Sec. IV. The increase of wickedness upon the earth,

and the destruction of the whole race of mankind, except Noah and his family, by the universal deluge, chap. vi. vii.

Sec. V. The repeopling of the earth, after the flood, by the family of Noah, ch. viii.—x.

Sec. VI. The impious attempt to build the tower of Babel,—the confusion of languages, and the dispersion of mankind over the earth, ch. xi.

Sec. VII. The history of Abraham and his family, ch. xii.—xxv.

Sec. VIII. The history of Isaac and his family, ch. xxvi. xxvii.

Sec. IX. The history of Jacob and his family, ch. xxviii.—xxxvi.

Sec. X. The story of Joseph and his brethren, ch. xxxvii.—xl.

Sec. XI. The history of Joseph's prosperity in Egypt and his kindness to his father and his brethren, till his death, ch. xli.—l.

In the book of Genesis there are contained several things which deserve to be most seriously considered and remembered, particularly by every young person. There are seven things especially of which no other book can give us true information.

1. The creation of all things by the omnipotent word of God.

2. The fall of our first parents from innocence and happiness by transgressing the commands of their Creator; whereby all mankind are sinners, and liable to sickness, pain, and death.

3. God's gracious promise of the Redeemer.

4. The great age to which men lived in the early period of the world.

5. The destruction of the world by a deluge, on account of the great and universal wickedness of mankind.

6. The confusion of speech at Babel, as the origin of different languages and nations.

7. The calling of Abraham from the Chaldean idolatry, for the purpose of preserving true religion in the world; and the separation of his family from all people, as the Messiah was promised to descend from him.

Besides these and some other memorable things, there were, in the first ages of the world, several persons of remarkable eminence: among whom were Adam and Eve our first parents—the first of human beings; Abel, the first who died, being murdered by his wicked brother Cain; Enoch, who, after pleasing God in a holy, active, and useful life, was taken to heaven without dying; Methuselah, the oldest man, who lived 969 years; Noah, who was saved when the world was drowned; Abraham, who, in faith, sacrificed his son at the command of God; and Joseph, who was sold to slavery by his own brethren, and who, afterwards, became lord and ruler of all Egypt.

From this divine record of those two most stupendous subjects, Creation and Providence, almost all the ancient philosophers, astronomers, chronologists, and historians, have taken their respective data; and all the modern improvements and accurate discoveries in different arts and sciences, have only served to confirm the facts detailed by Moses. The great fact of the Deluge, omitting the mention of every other, is not only fully confirmed by the remains of marine animals in every quarter of the globe, but is attested with more or less correctness by the traditions of many ancient pagan writers. In fine, without this history, the world would be in comparative darkness, not knowing whence it came, nor whither it is going. Even in the first page, a child may learn more in an hour, than all the philosophers in the world were able to discover without it in four thousand years.

"Reader, thou hast now before thee the most ancient and the most authentic history in the world; a history that contains the first written discovery that God has made of himself to mankind: a discovery of his own being in his wisdom, power, and goodness, in which thou and the whole human race are so intimately concerned. How much thou art indebted to him for this discovery he alone can teach thee, and cause thy heart to feel its obligations to his wisdom and mercy. God made thee and the universe, and governs all things ac-

cording to the counsel of his own will. While under the direction of this counsel thou canst not err; while under the influence of this will thou canst not be wretched. Give thyself up to his teaching, and submit to his authority; and after guiding thee here by his counsel, he will at last bring thee to glory."--*Dr. A. Clarke.*

References in Genesis.

Ch. i. 1.	Heb. xi. 3.	Ch. xv. 6.	Rom. iv. 3; Jas. ii. 23.
— iii. 4.	2 Cor. xi. 3.		
— — 6.	1 Tim. ii. 14.	— xvi. 15.	Gal. iv. 22.
— — 15.	John viii. 44; Matt. i. 23; 1 John iii. 8.	— xviii. 12.	1 Pet. iii. 6.
		— xix. 25.	2 Pet. ii. 6.
— iv. 4.	Heb. xi. 4.	— — 26.	Luke xvii. 32.
— — 8.	1 John iii. 12.	— xxii. 1-10.	Heb xi. 17; Jas. ii. 21.
— v 24.	Heb. xi. 5.		
— vi. 12.	1 Pet. iii. 20.	— xxv. 33.	Heb. xii. 16.
— — 14.	Heb. xi. 7.	— xlviii. 15.	Heb. xi. 21.
— vii. 7.	Matt. xxiv. 37, 38.	— xlix. 10.	Matt. ii 6, Luke i. 32, 33.
— xii. 1.	Heb. xi. 8.		
— xiv. 18.	— vii. 1.	l. 24, 25.	Heb. xi. 22.

EXODUS,

A period of 145 *years, from* A. M. 2369 *to* 2514.

Exodus is a Greek word, which signifies going out, or departure; and this book is so named, because it relates the departure of the children of Israel from Egypt. The book of Exodus was written by Moses. It was designed to serve as a memorial, 1. Of the wonderful deliverance of the Israelites from the horrors of Egyptian slavery; 2. Of their being formed, in the wilderness, into a religious community for the support of the public and constant worship of God; 3. Of the divine origin and obligation of their religious and political institutions, God graciously condescending to acknowledge himself as their King and their Father. The book of Exodus was further designed to show the exact fulfilment of the prophecies and promises delivered to Abraham, Gen. xv. 5—16; Exod. xii. 35, 36, 40, 41, that his descendants would be afflicted in a strange land, whence they should depart in the fourth generation with great substance.

CH. XIV.—ANALYSIS OF EXODUS.

Exodus is divided into forty chapters, and it contains eight principal sections.

Section I. Relates the surprising increase of the descendants of Jacob, while in Egypt, and their grievously oppressed condition, ch. i.

Sec. II. The birth and life of Moses till he was called and ordained by the LORD to be the deliverer of Israel from their bondage, ch. ii.—vi.

Sec. III. The wickedness of Pharaoh, and the ten plagues inflicted upon the land and people of Egypt, ch. vii.—xi.

Sec. IV. The institution of the passover, and the deliverance of the Israelites, ch. xii. xiii.

Sec. V. The miraculous passage of the Red Sea by the Israelites, and the overthrow of Pharaoh with his army, ch. xiv. xv.

Sec. VI. The account of several miracles wrought for the relief of the Israelites in the Arabian desert, ch. xvi.—xviii.

Sec. VII. The giving of the laws to Moses, by God, on the mountain of Sinai, ch. xix.—xxii.

Sec. VIII. The costly establishment for the public worship of God, with the manner of the ceremonies and sacrifices, ch. xxiii.—xl.

The things most deserving to be remembered, as recorded in the book of Exodus, are seven:

1. The ten plagues, brought as a punishment from God upon the wicked Egyptians.

2. The institution of the passover to commemorate the deliverance of Israel.

3. The Red Sea opening a passage to save the Israelites, and its closing upon the Egyptians for their destruction.

4. The various miracles which God wrought to feed and supply the Israelites during forty years in the deserts of Arabia.

5. God, in awful majesty, giving the law from Mount Sinai in Arabia.

6. The foolish and wicked idolatry of the Israelites in making a golden calf as an object of worship.

CH. XIV.—ANALYSIS OF EXODUS.

7. The costly and particular system of ceremonies for the public worship of God, designed to shadow forth the priesthood of our Lord Jesus Christ, and the way of salvation by him as our Mediator and Redeemer.

References in Exodus.

Ch ii. 2.	Heb. xi. 23.	Ch. xvi. 15.	1 Cor. x. 3.
—— 11.	—— — 24;	— xvii. 6.	—— — 4.
	Acts vii. 23.	— xix. 6.	1 Pet. ii 9.
— iii. 2.	Acts vii. 30.	—— — 12.	Heb. xii. 18—20.
— xii. 7.	Heb. xii. 24	— xxiv. 6, 8.	—— ix. 19—22.
— xiv. 22.	1 Cor. x. 2;	— xxvi. 35.	—— — 2.
	Heb. xi. 29.	xxxii. 6.	1 Cor. x. 7.
— xvi. 15.	John vi. 31—49.		

Observations on the Ten Plagues of Egypt.

These ten plagues were inflicted upon Egypt in a manner remarkably adapted to punish the stupid idolatries of that people, their monstrous wickedness, and their wanton cruelties. This will evidently appear from a few observations.

1. The waters turned to blood. The priests of Egypt held blood in abhorrence, yet they cruelly sported with the blood of the captive Israelites, whose children they had caused to be cast into the river. The Egyptians worshipped the river Nile as a god; partly on account of its delicious waters; but chiefly as the great means of the extraordinary fertility of their lands by its annual overflow: they called it The Ocean: but its waters being turned into blood, must have excited their loathing and detestation, while the calamity would cover them with confusion and shame, their fish having died, and their deity being degraded.

2. The plague of frogs. Frogs were consecrated to the Egyptian deity Osiris; and their swelling was regarded by the priests, as an emblem of divine inspiration. Their gross superstition, therefore, was suitably punished, when their sacred river was polluted with miraculous swarms of these creatures, so as to fill the land, and to enter even their houses, their beds, and the vessels of their food, making the whole country offensive.

3. The plague of lice. The idolatries of Egypt were accompanied with rites, the most unclean, foul, and abominable; but these were performed under the appearance of scrupulous external cleanliness, especially in respect to the priests. They were excessively cautious lest any lice should be found upon their garments, particularly when they officiated in the religious services of their idol temples: so that by this plague, their superstitious prejudices must have been distressingly shocked, and the people with the priests overwhelmed with a common disgrace: the magicians acknowledged, therefore, that this was "the finger of God."

4. The plague of flies. The Egyptians worshipped several deities, whose province it was to drive away flies, which swarmed in their country during the summer season. In many places they even offered an ox in sacrifice to these despicable insects. Beelzebub, or Baalzebul, the god of Ekron, 2 Kings i. 2, was a fly-deity of this people. The plague of flies, therefore, was the more grievous to them, as it so utterly degraded this revered divinity of Egypt.

5. The murrain of the cattle. The Egyptians held many beasts in idolatrous veneration. The lion, wolf, dog, cat, ape, and goat, among the wild animals, were held sacred by them; but especially the ox, heifer, and ram. The soul of their god Osiris was believed to reside in the body of the bull Apis: yet neither Osiris nor all the rest could save the beasts of Egypt from the fatal disease which fell upon them at the command of Moses the messenger of Jehovah. This must have been the more grievous to the Egyptians, as they found no injury befall the cattle of Israel.

6. The plague of boils. The Egyptians had several medical divinities, to whom, on particular occasions, they sacrificed living men. These were taken, it is supposed, in those times, from among the Israelites. They were burnt alive upon a high altar, and their ashes were cast into the air; that, with every scattered atom, a blessing might descend. Moses, therefore, took ashes from the furnace, perhaps where human bodies had been

offered as sacrifices, and cast them into the air; atoms of which were scattered by the wind, and overspread the land, and these descended upon both priests and people in curses, with tormenting boils, which shamed their honoured deities.

7. The plague of hail, rain, and fire. In Egypt it neither hails nor rains; and the Egyptians worshipped their fabulous deities, Isis and Osiris, as their protectors from fire: consequently this plague must have been very terrible. By the destruction of the barley, their supply of food must have been grievously diminished; and by the loss of the flax the trade in fine linen, which in Egypt was very great and important, must have been extensively spoiled, to the dishonour of their false divinities.

8. The plague of locusts. In Africa these destructive creatures so dreadfully abound, that their swarms sometimes cover an extent of land a hundred miles square; and, devouring in a single night every green herb, they produce a fearful famine, as described by the prophet Joel. Such havoc followed them in Egypt; nor could Isis, Serapis, and all the divinities of the land, avail to deliver them from under the rod of Moses, the appointed badge of his divine mission.

9. The plague of darkness. The Egyptians worshipped darkness as the origin of their gods. Orpheus, the most ancient pagan writer, who borrowed his notions from Egypt, in one of his hymns says, " I will sing of night, the parent of the gods and men: night, the origin of all things." They were therefore plagued with a horrible darkness — the blackness of darkness, with darkness which might be felt, and this seems to have been accompanied with fearful sights, which is referred to by the prophet, by *evil angels*, Psa. lxxviii. 49: these evils their gods had no power either to prevent or alleviate, while the Israelites enjoyed light in all their dwellings.

10. The death of the first-born in every family. The howlings of the Egyptians at their funerals, and at the decease of their friends, were dreadful beyond those of

every other people; but now they had cause for their lamentation. The principal reason of this last and heaviest calamity, was to avenge their unlamented cruelties upon the people of Israel. They had been preserved as a nation by one of that family, and yet they had enslaved the people, and murdered numbers of their male children; but now the awful vengeance of God overtook them, in righteous retribution visiting every house with the death of the eldest child in every family, "from the first-born of Pharaoh that sat on the throne, even unto the first-born of the maid-servant that was behind the mill, and all the first-born of beasts." This last judgment humbled the proud spirit of Pharaoh, and he in haste released the people of God.

LEVITICUS.

The third book in the Bible is called Leviticus, because it contains the laws relating to the ceremonies and offices of divine worship, instituted to be observed by the Israelites, among whom the Levites were divinely appointed to be the ministers of religion. Leviticus was written by Moses: it is divided into twenty-seven chapters, and includes four principal sections.

Section I. Contains the laws concerning the several kinds of sacrifices, ch. i.—vii.

Sect. II. The laws and ceremonies of consecrating the high priests, ch. viii.—x.

Sec. III. The laws relating to the various purifications, ch. xi.—xxii.

Sec. IV. The laws concerning the sacred festivals, ch. xxiii.—xxvii.

The book of Leviticus contains a code of laws, sacrificial, ceremonial, civil, and judicial, which, for the purity of their morality, the wisdom, justice, and beneficence of their enactments, and the simplicity, dignity, and impressive nature of their rites, are perfectly unrivalled, especially among the ancient nations, and altogether worthy of their Divine Author. All the ceremonies of the Mosaic ritual are at once dignified and

expressive: they evidently point out the holiness of their Author, the sinfulness of man, the necessity of an atonement for sin, and the state of moral excellence to which the mercy and grace of the Creator have destined to raise the human soul. They include, as well as point out, the gospel of the Son of God; from which they receive their consummation and perfection. The sacrifices and oblations were significant of the atonement of Christ; the requisite qualities of those sacrifices were emblematical of his immaculate character; and the prescribed mode in the form of those offerings, and the mystical rites ordained, were allusive institutions, calculated to enlighten the apprehensions of the Jews, and to prepare them for the reception of the gospel. The institution of the high priesthood typified Jesus the great High Priest, who hath an unchangeable priesthood, by which he is able to save to the uttermost all that come unto God by Him. Thus the Levitical economy directed the pious Hebrews to behold " the Lamb of God which taketh away the sin of the world!"

The Epistle to the Hebrews is an inspired commentary upon the book of Leviticus, from which we learn that the Hebrew ritual was the gospel of Christ exhibited in symbols or shadows to the Israelites.

That which is most remarkable in the Levitical ceremonies, is the ordinance of the daily and yearly sacrifices, as atonements for the sins of the nation. The daily sacrifice was a lamb; one in the morning for the sins of the night, and another in the evening for the sins of the day, Exod. xxix. 38—42, at which time the priest offered incense upon the golden altar, with prayers for the whole Israelitish people. The annual sacrifice, on the day of atonement, was two goats: after the sins of the nation had been confessed over their heads, which was the custom at the daily sacrifice, one of them was offered in sacrifice as a burnt-offering; and the other was led into the wilderness to be seen no more, as if it bore away for ever the guilt of the whole community, Lev. xvi. 15—21. See Chapter XII. HEBREW FESTIVALS.

The most remarkable fact recorded in Leviticus, is

the judgment of God upon Nadab and Abihu, sons of Aaron.

Probably nothing was ever written, in so small a compass, so accurately to express the typical and evangelical nature of the Levitical ordinances of religion, as the following verses of the poet Cowper.

>Israel in ancient days,
> Not only had a view
>Of Sinai in a blaze,
> But learned the gospel too·
>The types and figures were a glass,
>In which they saw a Saviour's face.
>
>The paschal sacrifice,
> And blood-besprinkled door,
>Seen with enlightened eyes,
> And once applied with power,
>Would teach the need of other blood,
>To reconcile the world to God.
>
>The lamb, the dove, set forth
> His perfect innocence;
>Whose blood of matchless worth
> Should be the soul's defence;
>For he who can for sin atone,
>Must have no failings of his own.
>
>The scape-goat on his head
> The people's trespass bore,
>And, to the desert led,
> Was to be seen no more:
>In him our Surety seemed to say,
>Behold, I bear your sins away.
>
>Dipt in his fellow's blood,
> The living bird went free:
>The type well understood,
> Expressed the sinner's plea;
>Described a guilty soul enlarged,
>And by a Saviour's death discharged.
>
>Jesus, I love to trace,
> Throughout the sacred page,
>The footsteps of thy grace,
> The same in every age:
>O grant that I may faithful be
>To clearer light vouchsafed to me!

CH. XIV.—ANALYSIS OF NUMBERS.

References in Leviticus.

Ch. iv. 21, 22.	Heb. xiii. 11.	Ch. xix. 15.	James ii. 1.
— xii 6.	Luke ii. 21-24.	— — 17.	Matt. xviii 15.
— xiv. 4.	Matt. viii. 3, 4	— — 18.	Gal. v. 14
— xvi. 14-16.	Heb. ix. 13.	— xx. 10.	John viii. 5.
— — 17.	Luke i. 10.	— xxiii. 34-36.	— vii. 2-37.
— xviii. 5.	Rom. x. 4, 5.	— xxvi. 12.	2 Cor. vi. 16.

NUMBERS.

Numbers is the fourth book in the Bible; and it derives its title from its relating the numberings of the several tribes of the Israelites, and their various marches and encampments in the wilderness, for the space of about thirty-nine years. Numbers was written by Moses. It is divided into thirty-six chapters, and contains four principal sections.

Section I. Relates the numbering of the Israelites; the forming of them into a regular camp, and the appointment of the Levites to the performances of religious services and the instruction of the people, ch. i.—iv.

Sec. II. The ordination of various ceremonies, civil and religious, ch. v.—x.

Sec. III. The journeying of the Israelites from Mount Sinai to the country of the Moabites, ch. xi.—xxi.

Sec. IV. The encampment of the Israelites on the plains of Moab, ch. xxii.—xxxvi.

Among the most remarkable things related in the book of Numbers, are,

1. The miraculous manner in which the Israelites were supplied with food and drink during forty years in the deserts; prefiguring the spiritual blessings of the gospel by Jesus Christ, furnished to believers on their pilgrimage to heaven.

2. The frequent murmuring of the unbelieving people.

3. The awful judgments of God upon them, punishing their rebellions as examples to us.

4. The miraculous healing of the dying camp of Israel when bitten by fiery serpents, by looking to the serpent of brass, according to the appointment of God.

5. The vain attempts of Balak, king of Moab, to curse

the people of Israel, by means of the wicked prophet Balaam.

The most celebrated persons mentioned in the book of Numbers, are—Joshua, the pious and upright minister of Moses, and who, on the death of his master, was divinely ordained to be the conductor of the Israelites into the promised land of Canaan: Korah, Dathan, and Abiram, who, with their company, were swallowed up by a miraculous earthquake, on account of their rebellion against God, in a conspiracy against Moses and Aaron: and Balaam, the wicked prophet, who, for the love of money, eagerly attempted to serve the superstitious king of Moab, in cursing the people of Israel.

In the book of Numbers, God appears every where in a series of the most astonishing providences and events: and yet there is no circumstance or occasion, the evident character of which does not justify those signal displays of his judgment and mercy, and exhibit in every relation the consistency of the Divine intentions, and the propriety of the law which he established among the Israelites.

References in Numbers.

Ch. viii. 16.	Luke ii. 23.	Ch. xxi. 5, 6.	1 Cor. x. 9.
— ix. 17-19.	1 Cor x. 1.	— — 9.	John iii. 14.
— x. 10.	Acts x 4	— xxii. 21-28.	2 Pet. ii. 15;
— xi. 4.	1 Cor. x. 6.		Jude 11.
— xii 7.	Heb iii. 2.	— — 23.	2 Pet. ii. 16.
— xiv. 27.	1 Cor. x. 10.	— xxiv. 14.	Rev. ii 14.
— — 29.	Heb. iii. 17.	— xxv. 9.	1 Cor. x. 8.
— xix. 3.	— xiii. 11.	— xxvi. 65.	— — 5.
— xx. 8.	1 Cor. x. 4.	— xxviii. 9.	Matt. xii. 5.

DEUTERONOMY.

Deuteronomy signifies the second law; the fifth book in the Bible is so called, because it contains a repetition of the moral law, with various and particular explanations of that and other institutions of Israel. Deuteronomy was written by Moses, as it appears, during the last month of his ministry, and finished just before he went up to die after viewing the land of Canaan from Mount Nebo. It is divided into thirty-four chapters, containing four principal sections.

CH. XIV.—ANALYSIS OF DEUTERONOMY.

Section I. Presents a review of the LORD's dealings with the Israelites, from the time of their leaving Egypt, during almost forty years, ch. i.—iv.

Sec. II. A repetition and explanation of the various laws which had been given to the fathers of the generation about to enter Canaan, ch. v.—xxvi.

Sec. III. The confirmation of the moral law, with many affecting exhortations to obedience, ch. xxvii.—xxx.

Sec. IV. The ordination of Joshua, as the successor of Moses; and the farewell addresses of that faithful prophet and devoted servant of God, ch. xxxi.—xxxiv.

The most remarkable things recorded in the book of Deuteronomy, are,

1. The striking prophecy concerning the coming of the Messiah, ch. xviii. 15—19.

2. The prophetic song, which Moses composed for the use of the people of Israel, designed to remain as a perpetual admonition to them against forsaking the Lord their God and his instituted worship.

3. The eminently amiable character and extraordinary death of Moses the man of God.

These first five books in the Bible were written by Moses, with the exception of the last chapter, and a few remarks, or verses, added by later writers. The last chapter of Deuteronomy was added to complete the history: the first eight verses, it is supposed, immediately after his death by Joshua; and the latter four by a later writer, probably either Samuel or Ezra. These books embrace a period of 2553 years, and bring down the history of the world to the year before the birth of Christ, 1451.

References in Deuteronomy.

Ch. vi. 13.	Matt. iv. 10.	Ch. xviii. 18.	John i. 45; Acts iii. 22; vii. 37.
— — 16.	—— — 7.	— xxiv. 1.	Matt. v. 31; xix. 7; Mark x. 4.
— viii. 3.	—— — 4.		
— x. 17.	Acts x. 34; Rom. ii. 11; Col. iii. 25; Eph. vi. 9.	— xxv. 4.	1 Cor. ix. 9.
		— xxvii. 26.	Gal. iii. 10.
— xvii. 6.	Heb. x. 28.	— xxx. 12-14.	Rom. x. 6—9.
— xviii. 1.	1 Cor. ix. 13.	— xxxii. 9.	Eph. i. 18.

Thus ends the Law of Moses, frequently called The Pentateuch, signifying The Five Books: it is a work in every respect worthy of God, who inspired his servant to write it, for the instruction of Israel, and of the church in all ages: it is next in importance to the New Testament, the law and gospel of our Lord and Saviour Jesus Christ. Its antiquity places it at the head of all the writings in the world; and the various subjects it embraces render it of the utmost value to every part of the civilized world. Its philosophy, history, geography, and chronology, entitle it to the respect of the whole human race; while its system of theology and religion, designed for the instruction and salvation of men, demonstrably proves it to be a revelation from God.

The twelve following books, from Joshua to Esther, record the history of the Israelites for about 1006 years, from the death of Moses to the national reformation under Nehemiah: from the year before Christ 1451 to 445.

JOSHUA.

The book of Joshua is so called, because it is a record of the affairs of the Israelites under the government of Joshua, the successor of Moses. It comprises the history of about twenty-six years, from the death of Moses to the death of Joshua, and must be regarded as a most necessary and valuable continuation of the national records of Israel. It is to the books of Moses what the Acts of the Apostles are to the Gospels. It is believed to have been written by Joshua, except a small addition to the last chapter by a later prophet; and it was designed to show the faithfulness of God, in the perfect accomplishment of the promises made to the patriarchs; and the avenging justice of God, in destroying the very guilty, corrupt, and abominable nations of Canaan. Joshua is divided into twenty-four chapters, and contains three principal sections.

Section I. Relates the conquest of Canaan by Joshua, ch. i.—xi.

Sec. II. The division of the country among the several tribes of Israel, ch. xii.—xxii.

Sec. III. The affecting farewell admonition, and the pious and happy death of the upright and venerable Joshua, ch. xxiii. xxiv.

In the book of Joshua there are five things particularly remarkable and worthy of special notice.

1. The river Jordan dividing to allow the priests and the people a passage into the midst of the land, ch. iii.

2. The appearing of Jesus Christ to Joshua, as the Captain of the LORD's host, to encourage Joshua in the conquest of Canaan, ch. v.

3. The falling down of the walls of Jericho at the appointed sounding of the rams' horns, ch. vi.

4. The standing still of the sun and moon for a whole day at the word of Joshua, ch. x.

5. The character of Joshua as typical of Jesus Christ. The Hebrew word Joshua is the same as the Greek word Jesus, both signifying Saviour; Joshua is, therefore, called Jesus, Acts vii. 45; Heb. iv. 8: and as Joshua conducted the Israelites through all opposition to the promised land of Canaan; so Jesus Christ, as the Captain of our salvation, brings all his people through every difficulty, and even death, to the heavenly glory.

References in Joshua.

Ch. i. 5.	Heb. xiii. 5.	Ch. vi. 20.	Heb. xi. 30
— ii. 1.	—— xi. 31; Jas.	— — 23.	—— — 31.
	ii. 25.	— xiv. 1, 2.	Acts xiii. 19.
— — 19.	Matt. xxvii. 25.	— xxii. 6.	Luke xxiv. 50.
— iii. 14.	Acts vii. 44, 45.	— xxiv. 32.	Acts vii. 16.

JUDGES.

The book of Judges is so named on account of its recording the history of the Israelites under thirteen supreme rulers, their deliverers, called Judges. This book includes a period of 400 years, according to Dr. Hales, from the death of Joshua to the death of Samson. The judges were persons whom God at different times raised up from the several tribes, and endowed with extraordinary courage, wisdom, and piety, qualifying them to be deliverers and governors of the people of Israel. The

book of Judges is divided into twenty-one chapters, having three principal sections.

Section I. Contains a short account of the Israelites, during the lifetime of the elders who survived Joshua, and the wickedness of the next generation, ch. i. ii.

Sec. II. A record of the oppressions of the Israelites by their enemies, whom God suffered to afflict them, when by their idolatry they sinned against him: also of their several wondrous deliverances on their repentance before the LORD, by their judges, from Othniel to Samson, with whom the regular history closes, ch. iii.—xvi.

Sec. III. The last five chapters contain several particulars relating to the times of the former part of the book. They relate the establishment of idolatry among the people of Israel, their corruption soon after the death of Joshua, and the dreadful calamity brought upon themselves, especially the tribe of Benjamin, by their support of wicked doers, ch. xvii.—xxi.

The book of Judges exhibits, in an affecting manner, the dreadful consequences of national wickedness; and the grievous calamities which are inseparable from anarchy in a country where little or no regard is paid to the worship of God.

It is a most remarkable history of the long-suffering of God towards the Israelites, in which we see the most signal instances of his justice and mercy alternately displayed: the people sinned, and were punished; they repented, and were forgiven. These things are written for our warning: none should presume, for God is just; none need despair, for God is merciful. Among the most remarkable things recorded in this book, are the accounts of Gideon, Barak, Jephthah, and Samson.

References in Judges.

Ch. ii. 16. Acts xiii. 20.
Actions of the Judges generally, Heb. xi. 32, 40.

RUTH.

The book of Ruth is so called, because it contains the history of a woman of that name. She was a native of

the country of Moab, whither an Israelitish family retired in a season of famine, which was increased by the ravages of the Midianites, who were overcome by Gideon, Judg. vii. Ruth was married into this family; but on the death of her husband, influenced by affection for her mother-in-law, and love of true religion, she forsook her own country to unite with the people of God in Israel. The book of Ruth is supposed to have been written by the prophet Samuel: it must be regarded as a necessary supplement to the book of Judges, to which it was appended by the ancient Jews as a part of that book; and it is a proper introduction to the books of Samuel.

The book of Ruth has four chapters; the design of which appears to be twofold.

1. To point out some particulars of a Gentile extraction in the genealogy of the Messiah, in the line of Judah to David.

2. To show the watchful care of Divine Providence over those who truly fear the Lord, and put their trust in him.

Ruth has been considered as both a type and a pledge of the calling of the Gentiles into the church of Christ. May every reader of this book be a follower of the Saviour, as Ruth was of Naomi, ch. i. 16, 17.

References in Ruth.

Ch. iv. 5, 6. Matt. xxii. 24.
Ch. iv. 18.   Matt. i. 5; Luke iii. 31, 32.

1 SAMUEL.

The books of Samuel are called also the First and Second books of Kings, because they relate the origin of monarchy in Israel. They are called Samuel because that prophet commenced them, and wrote twenty-four chapters of the first book. They are supposed to have been completed by the prophets Nathan and Gad; see 1 Chron. xxix. 29. These books are parts of the national records of the Israelites, for about one hundred and forty years, and preserved by the several prophets whom God raised up for the instruction of the people.

CH. XIV.—ANALYSIS OF 1 SAMUEL.

The first book of Samuel embraces a period of about one hundred years, from the birth of Samuel to the death of Saul. It relates to the last two of the judges of Israel, Eli and Samuel, and the first two of their kings, Saul and David. It is divided into thirty-one chapters, and contains three principal sections.

Section I. Records an account of Eli, who was both priest and judge; of his degenerate sons, and of the birth of Samuel, ch. i.—iv.

Sec. II. The history of Samuel, and of his being divinely called to the offices of both prophet and judge, ch. v.—xii.

Sec. III. The history of Saul, who was divinely appointed to be the first king over Israel, ch. xiii.—xxxi.

The first book of Samuel abounds with interesting narratives; but the most remarkable details are the early histories of Samuel and of David. The apostacy of Saul from the sincere worship of God,—his misguided and bitter persecutions of David, and his own fatal overthrow and death, with the ruin of his family, are deeply affecting and instructive to the young.

What a contrast do we behold between the characters of Eli's sons and Samuel! between Saul and David! How vast the difference which genuine godliness produces in the principles and habits of men! We see exemplified in the sons of Eli, in Saul, and in Nabal, that in this world disgrace, misery, and death are the bitter fruits and hard-earned wages of sin, with terrible intimations of torment in a future state.

David has always been considered an illustrious type of Christ, not only as a prophet, but in the various persecutions he endured on his way to the throne, and in his final exaltation above all his enemies, as king of Israel. May we confide in the Son of David, our adorable King and Lord, and enjoy the imperishable blessings of his eternal kingdom!

References in 1 Samuel.

Ch ii. 1.	Luke i. 46.	Ch. xvi. 7.	2 Cor. x. 7.
— viii. 3.	1 Tim. iii 3.	— xxi. 6.	Matt. xii. 3, 4;
— xiii. 14.	Acts xiii. 22.		Mark ii. 25;
— xv. 22.	Mark xii. 33.		Luke vi. 4.

2 SAMUEL.

The second book of Samuel embraces a period of about forty years, during the reign of David: it is a continuation of the national records of Israel under David, who was elevated to the throne on the death of Saul, as king over the tribe of Judah, and seven years afterwards as king over the whole people of Israel on the assassination of Ishbosheth, Saul's son. The book is divided into thirty-four chapters, and it contains three principal sections.

Section I. Relates the triumphs and prosperity of David's government, ch. i.—x.

Sec. II. The troubles of David, occasioned by his sinning against God, after having been favoured with the most distinguishing manifestations of the Divine kindness, ch. xi.—xix.

Sec. III. The re-establishment of David on his throne after his sincere repentance before the LORD: and a record of the last years of his extended reign, ch. xx.—xxxiv.

The most remarkable things recorded in the second book of Samuel are, David's sinning against God in the affair of Uriah and his wife; his deep repentance and humiliation; the unnatural rebellion of Absalom, the favourite son of David, and the ignominious death of that young prince, while seeking to take away the life of his indulgent and affectionate father!

In the dreadful fall of David we see the power of human corruption, even in holy men of God, unless kept by his almighty hand, and the sovereign efficacy of divine grace in his renewal and restoration. These things are recorded for our special instruction, teaching us to walk watchfully in the ways of holiness, humbly depending on the Spirit of God.

References in 2 Samuel.

Ch. iii. 39.	2 Tim. iv. 14.	Ch. xii. 24.	Matt. i. 6.
— vii. 12.	Acts xiii. 36.	— xv. 23.	John xviii 1.
— — 16.	John xii. 34.	— xx. 9.	Luke xxii. 47.

KINGS.

The books of the Kings contain the national records of the Israelites, continued during the reigns of their sovereigns after the decease of David, and embracing a period of about 426 years, from the anointing of Solomon to the destruction of Jerusalem. They describe the glory of Israel under Solomon; the division of the nation under Rehoboam; the decline of the two kingdoms; the total destruction of Israel, and the subversion and captivity of Judah.

It is supposed that David, Solomon, and Hezekiah wrote histories of their own reigns; that the prophets Nathan, Gad, Isaiah, Iddo, and others, were the historians of their respective times; and that the whole were arranged in their present form and order by the inspired priest and scribe, Ezra, after the return of the Jews from their captivity in Babylon.

1 KINGS.

The first book of Kings comprises the history of the Israelites for about 126 years, from the anointing of Solomon, 1015 years B. C., to the death of Jehoshaphat; 889 years B. C. It is divided into twenty-two chapters, which include two principal sections.

Section I. Contains a detailed account of Solomon's succession to the throne of Israel while David his father was yet living; and of his great prosperity and magnificence as sovereign monarch of Canaan, ch. i.—xi.

Sec. II. The division of the people of Israel into two kingdoms, through the weak pride and foolish conduct of Rehoboam, son of Solomon; with the history of both kingdoms until the death of Jehoshaphat, king of Judah, ch. xii.—xxv.

In the first book of Kings there are many remarkable things recorded; among which are especially to be noticed for our instruction,

1. The building and dedication of Solomon's temple, erected in the most sumptuous manner, according to a pattern given immediately from God, and under the di-

rection of superior workmen, specially and divinely endowed with suitable abilities for the work.

2. The flourishing reign of Solomon, which was typical of the peaceful and prosperous reign of the Messiah.

3. The division of the nation into two kingdoms.

4. The speedy fall of the grandeur of Israel, when the city of Jerusalem was taken by Shishak king of Egypt; and the temple and the royal palace were pillaged of their gold and treasures. This calamity happened when Rehoboam had reigned only five years; and it was appointed by the holy, sin-avenging God, as a righteous punishment for his wickedness and abomination in forsaking, with the nation of Judah generally, the worship of Jehovah, and setting up idolatry, 1 Kings xiv. 21, 28; 2 Chron. xii. 1—9.

5. The extraordinary ministry of the prophet Elijah, and the slaughter of the idolatrous priests of Baal.

References in 1 *Kings.*

Ch. ii. 10.	Acts ii. 29; xiii. 36.	Ch. x. 1.	Luke xi. 31.
		— xiii. 6.	Acts viii. 24.
— vii. 6—12.	John x. 23; Acts iii. 11.	— xvii. 1—5.	Luke iv. 25, 26.
		— xviii. 42.	Jas v. 17, 18.
— viii. 46.	1 John i. 8—10.	— xix. 10—18.	Rom. xi 3, 4.
— x. 1.	Matt. xii. 42.	— xxi. 10.	Acts vi. 11.

2 KINGS.

The second book of Kings is a continuation of the national records of the Israelites, including both kingdoms, of Israel and of Judah, and embracing a period of about 303 years, from the death of Jehoshaphat, 889 years B. C., to the destruction of Jerusalem and its splendid temple by Nebuchadnezzar, king of Babylon, 586 years B. C. It is divided into twenty-five chapters, which include two chief sections.

Section I. Contains a continued history of the two nations, Israel and Judah, until the kingdom of Israel was destroyed in a total captivity of the people by the Assyrians, ch. i.—xvii.

Sec. II. The remaining history of the kingdom of Judah, until the conquest of Judea by Nebuchadnezzar,

and the destruction of Jerusalem; when the surviving people, except some of the peasantry, were led away captive into Babylon, ch. xviii.—xxv.

The most remarkable things recorded in the second book of Kings are,

1. The close of the ministry of Elijah by his translation to heaven in a chariot of fire.

2. The ministry of Elisha the prophet.

3. The total ruin of the kingdom of Israel on account of its irreclaimable wickedness.

4. The destruction of the temple and city of Jerusalem.

5. The captivity of the Jews in Babylon on account of their forsaking the true God to worship idols, and committing the abominations of the heathen.

It is also worthy of the most serious remark, that the nation of the ten tribes had nineteen sovereigns, all of whom were irreligious and wicked men. Through their impious policy the national guilt was increased, and at length the people was brought to ruin. Judah also had many wicked sovereigns; but there were several of their kings who truly feared the LORD; and by their endeavours to reclaim and reform the people, the Divine judgments were for a time averted, until their national crimes occasioned their overthrow by the Chaldeans under Nebuchadnezzar.

References in 2 Kings.

Ch. i. 8.	Matt iii 4.	Ch. iv. 42.	Luke ix. 13—17.
—— 10.	Luke ix 54.	— v. 14.	—— iv. 27.
— iv. 29.	—— x. 4.	— vi. 22.	Rom. xii. 20.
—— 34.	Acts xx. 10.	— viii. 4.	Luke xxiii. 8.

CHRONICLES 1 and 2.

The two books of Chronicles are registers of the times, which their title signifies; they were compiled, as is believed, by Ezra, from the national records. These registers contain an abstract, in order of time, of the whole sacred history, and records of the whole Bible, from the creation down to the Babylonish captivity, embracing a period of 3468 years.

CH. XIV.—ANALYSIS OF CHRONICLES 1 AND 2.

The design of the Chronicles is to furnish a continued course of ancient authentic history; and to supply many important matters relating both to persons and things, which are omitted in the other inspired historical books. They afford an affecting illustration of the dispensations of God towards his highly favoured, yet ungrateful people Israel: they show the unspeakable advantages to nations arising from pious sovereigns, as seen in the cases of David, Jehoshaphat, and Hezekiah; and the various dreadful evils which spring from national depravity and irreligion.

The two books of Chronicles contain four principal sections.

Section I. Contains genealogical tables from Adam down to the time of Ezra, 1 Chron. i.—ix.

Sec. II. Histories of Israel under their first kings, Saul and David, ch. x.—xxviii.

Sec. III. The history of the united kingdom in its flourishing state under Solomon, ch. xxix. to 2 Chron. ix.

Sec. IV. The history of Judah under its several kings, from the secession of the ten tribes to the Babylonish captivity, 2 Chron. x.—xxxvi.

The things most remarkable in the books of Chronicles are the genealogical tables, particularly those which show that Jesus Christ according to the flesh, was of the seed of Abraham.

References in 1 Chronicles.

Ch. xvii. 14.	Luke i. 33.	Ch. xxix. 11.	Matt. vi. 13;
xxiii. 13.	Heb. v. 4.		1 Tim. i. 17;
xxix. 2.	Rev. xxi. 18.		Rev. v. 13.
9.	2 Cor. ix. 7.	12.	Rom. xi. 36.

References in 2 Chronicles.

Ch. iii. 14.	Matt. xxvii. 51;	Ch. xix. 7.	Rom. ii. 11.
	Heb. ix. 3.	xxviii. 15.	Luke vi. 27, 28;
xii. 6.	Jas. iv. 10.		Rom. xii. 20.
xv. 6.	Matt. xxiv. 7.	xxxi. 21.	Matt. vi. 33.
xvi. 14.	John xix. 39, 40.	xxxvi. 15-17.	xxiii. 34.

EZRA.

The book of Ezra is so called from the name of the priest who wrote it. It is an important continuation of

the Jewish history, after the return of that people from their seventy years' captivity in Babylon; embracing a period of about 100 years; from the decree of Cyrus, 536 years B. C., to the reformation by Ezra, 456 years B. C.

The book of Ezra is divided into ten chapters, and contains two principal sections.

Section I. Relates the return of the Jews to Judea, under their prince Zerubbabel, and the rebuilding, after various hinderances, of the temple of Jerusalem, ch. i.—vi.

Sec. II. The arrival at Jerusalem of Ezra the priest, and his reformation in the ordinances of religion, according to the laws of Moses, ch. vii.—x.

The Jewish captives returned from Babylon by the proclamation of Cyrus the Persian conqueror, he having succeeded to the throne of his uncle Darius as king of Persia and Babylon. The most remarkable circumstance related in the book of Ezra, is the sovereign influence of Divine Providence, by which Cyrus was led to grant deliverance to the captive Jews; and at the same time to restore the whole of the sacred vessels of gold and silver which had been pillaged from the temple of God at Jerusalem.

The means by which Providence brought about the emancipation of the Jews, and the restoration of the consecrated vessels, was the influence of Daniel. The wisdom, integrity, and piety of this prophet were acknowledged at the court of Babylon; on account of them he had been promoted to the highest office in the state. And having triumphed over the iniquitous conspiracy of his enemies, when, in the absence of Cyrus, he was miraculously preserved in the den of lions, his uprightness still more recommended him to the confidence of the king. Improving his familiar intercourse with Cyrus, who had succeeded his uncle Darius, for the advancement of the cause of religion, he showed to the king the prophecies of Jeremiah and Isaiah, in which the deliverance of the Jews is specifically predicted, and Cyrus, the conqueror of Babylon, mentioned by name. That Cyrus saw these divine predictions is manifest from the words

of his proclamation of liberty to the Jews; for in that edict he says, "The LORD God of heaven hath given me all the kingdoms of the earth, and he hath commanded me to build him a house at Jerusalem," Ezra i. 2.

The zeal and piety of Ezra are eminently conspicuous in all his works; and his memory has always been reverenced by the Jews, who regard him as a second Moses. Ezra was divinely employed to restore religion to its ancient purity; he disposed the books of Scripture into their proper order, after having carefully revised them. He collected and arranged the materials for the books of Chronicles, to which he added the history of his own times, which was finished by Nehemiah. Ezra died at the advanced age of about 120 years.

References in Ezra.

Ch. i. 5.	Phil. ii. 5.	Ch. ix. 6.	Rev. xviii. 5.
— iii. 7.	Acts xii. 20.	— — 14.	John v. 14.
— viii. 22.	Rom. viii. 28.	— — 15.	Rom. iii. 19.

NEHEMIAH.

The book of Nehemiah is a valuable record of the improvements in the city of Jerusalem, and of the reformation among the people, which were promoted and carried on by an inspired ruler of that name. This eminent man was one of the Jewish captives, selected from among them, and retained by the Persian monarch to fill the office of his cup-bearer, a station of great honour and influence in the ancient eastern nations.

The period to which this book relates is several years later than the history of Ezra. Nehemiah arrived at Jerusalem about thirteen years after Ezra; and after he had governed Judea for about twelve years, he returned to Artaxerxes, who granted him a new commission; with this he went again to Jerusalem, and ruled among the Jews in the whole about thirty-four years. This book of Nehemiah closes the Old Testament history at the death of its excellent author, in about the year of the world 3584, and 420 years before the birth of Christ.

The book of Nehemiah is divided into thirteen chapters, containing four principal sections.

Section I. Relates the departure of Nehemiah from Shushan with the royal commission to Jerusalem, ch. i. ii.

Sec. II. The building of the walls of Jerusalem, ch. iii.—vi.

Sec. III. The reformation of the ordinances of religion, and the sealing of the covenant to serve the Lord, ch. vii.—xii.

Sec. IV. The second reformation among the people, ch. xiii.

The most remarkable things recorded in the book of Nehemiah, are his public works and regulations, which manifest the rare and distinguishing excellencies of its renowned author. For disinterestedness, philanthropy, patriotism, prudence, courage, zeal, humanity, and every virtue that constitutes a great mind, and proves a soul to enjoy deep communion with God, Nehemiah will ever stand conspicuous among the greatest men of the Hebrew nation; and as an example which every true patriot should strive to imitate, especially under the influence of Christianity.

References in Nehemiah.

Ch iii. 1.	John v. 2	Ch. ix. 6.	Rev. xiv. 7.
— viii. 6.	1 Cor. xiv. 16;	— — 13.	Rom. vii. 12.
	1 Tim. ii. 8.	— — 19.	1 Cor. x. 1.
— — 2	Luke xxiv. 27.	— — 29.	Gal. iii. 12.

ESTHER.

The book of Esther derives its name from the lady whose history it relates. It records an extraordinary display of Divine Providence, in the elevation of an orphan Jewish captive to the throne, as queen of Persia, and a remarkable deliverance of the Jews by her means. This preservation of the Jews happened in the time of Ezra; and Ahasuerus is supposed to be the same as Artaxerxes mentioned in Ezra.

The book of Esther is divided into ten chapters, and it contains three sections.

Section I. Relates the elevation of Esther from a state of captive degradation, to be queen of Persia; and the great services which her uncle Mordecai rendered to the king, ch. i. ii.

Sec. II. The advancement of Haman, and his wicked contrivance designed to effect the extirpation of the Jews, ch. iii.—v.

Sec. III. The overthrow of Haman's plot, and his own ignominious and deserved punishment, ch. vi.—x.

The feast of Purim, instituted in commemoration of this deliverance of the Jews, has been observed by that people even to our times.

References in Esther.

Ch. iii. 8.   Acts xvi. 20. | Ch. v. 3.   Mark vi. 23.

THE POETICAL BOOKS.

The former books in the Bible, except some small portions, were written in prose; but the five following, and many parts of the prophetical books, are written in Hebrew metre;—Job, Psalms, Proverbs, Ecclesiastes, and Solomon's Song. They are more entirely of a religious character than any of the preceding; and they are in some respects of greater importance to the Christian church, for the special instructions which they convey. The nature of the subjects of which they treat, requires that they be read with devout attention. The book of Job has been particularly distinguished as doctrinal; the Psalms as devotional and prophetical; the Proverbs as practical; the Ecclesiastes as penitential; and the Song of Solomon as experimental.

JOB.

The book of Job derives its name from the person whose history it records. It contains an account of the singular piety, riches, afflictions, and restoration of that extraordinary character, who lived in Idumea, on the borders of Arabia and Egypt. Job is supposed by some learned men to have been the Jobab mentioned Gen.

xxxvi. 33; 1 Chron. i. 44, a great-grandson of Esau, and that he lived several years before, or about the time of Moses. Many commentators, however, place him earlier than the times of Abraham; and, with much probability, consider him to have been a connecting link in the church of God between Noah and Abraham. The book of Job is believed to have originally been written by Job himself, and to have been perfected in the form in which we possess it by Moses. Unless we except the book of Genesis, Job is the most ancient writing in the world.

The book of Job is divided into forty-two chapters, containing five principal sections.

Section I. Contains an account of Job's piety, family, riches, afflictions, and friends, ch. i. ii.

Sec. II. Relates the several discourses in the controversy between Job and his three friends, ch. ii.—xxxi.

Sec. III. The wise discourses of Elihu, a younger friend of Job, ch. xxxii.—xxxvii.

Sec. IV. The awfully sublime address of the Lord to Job, delivered out of a whirlwind, ch. xxxviii.—xli.

Sec. V. Relates the restoration of Job's health, friends, property, and family, and his sacrifice and intercession on behalf of his censorious friends, ch. xlii.

The religious discourses of these good men deserve to be attentively considered. The friends of Job were indeed mistaken in their views of his character; and, supposing that God never afflicts his sincere servants, at least in so grievous a manner as Job was then suffering, they charge him with being a wicked man and a hypocrite in religion; and therefore they reproach him severely as guilty, and exhort him to repentance before God.

Job, in asserting his integrity, and defending the purity of his character, argues that God does sometimes afflict the righteous for the trial of their faith and obedience; but several expressions of Job manifest a spirit of self-justification, not only against his uncharitable friends, but apparently in relation to the dispensations of God.

Elihu, as moderator between the disputing parties, blames the other friends of Job, on account of their un-

righteous censoriousness, while he reproves Job for his rash expressions.

The contents of the book of Job are the more remarkable, as they relate to times so very ancient; and because they evince to us that the principal articles of the Christian faith were maintained at so remote a period.

Among other points of important evangelical doctrine, we learn the following from the book of Job:

1. The creation of the universe by one supreme, almighty, eternal Being.

2. The government of the world, by the powerful, universal, and perpetual providence of the Creator.

3. That the providential government of Almighty God is carried on by the ministry of a superior order of his intelligent creatures.

4. That a part of these glorious beings are fallen from their original loyalty, dignity, and felicity, and are become apostates, the chief of whom is Satan.

5. That these superior creatures, both good and bad, are subject to their Creator; to whom they are required to render an account on stated occasions.

6. That every human being, descending by ordinary generation from Adam, is a partaker of a fallen nature, and born in sin.

7. That Almighty God would be propitious to sinners, by means of a sacrifice of atonement for transgression.

8. That God, sometimes for his own glory, and for their personal benefit, tries the faith and love of his most eminent servants by great afflictions.

9. That an expectation of the promised Messiah was cherished by many who truly feared God, beyond the boundaries of the land of Canaan.

10. That good men derived substantial consolation from the belief of a general resurrection from the dead, and of a future state of felicity for the righteous.

References in Job.

Ch. i. 7.	1 Pet. v. 8; Rev. xii. 9, 10.	Ch. i. 21.	Eph. v. 20; 1 Thess. v. 18.
— — 21.	1 Tim. vi. 7.	— ii. 10.	James v. 10.

Ch. iv. 18.	2 Pet. ii. 4.	Ch. xix. 26, 27. Phil. iii. 20, 21;
— v. 12.	1 Cor. iii. 19.	1 John iii. 2;
— — 17.	Heb. xii. 5.	1 Cor. xiii. 12.
— — 19.	1 Cor. x. 13.	— xxii. 6, 7. Matt. xxv. 42, 43.
— xii. 10.	Acts xvii. 28.	— xxvii. 8. —— xvi. 26.
— xiv. 12.	—— iii. 21.	— xxxiii. 27. Luke xv. 10, 21.
— xix. 25.	2 Tim. i. 12.	— xlii. 8, 12. James v. 11.

PSALMS.

The Book of Psalms is a collection of inspired hymns and songs, meditations and prayers; and the book is so called, because psalms signify holy songs. In the original they are said to present every possible variety of Hebrew poetry. They are commonly called the Psalms of David, because he wrote the largest portion of them. The other writers of the Psalms were Heman, Moses, Asaph, Jeduthun, and some inspired prophets, who lived during the Babylonish captivity; and some even at a later period, including the prophets Daniel and Ezra.

The book of Psalms is considered as containing the sum of the whole Bible, adapted to the purposes of devotion. The design of these compositions is, the instruction of the church, and the assistance of pious men in the acceptable and profitable worshipping of God. For this purpose, they being written in various styles of verse, many of them were set to music, and sung by the Jews, in their public exercises of religion; and they have always been prized by the people of God, as suitable helps in communion with the Father of spirits, both in public and private: they are regarded among the most precious treasures of Christians.

While this book has a literal sense, applying generally to the circumstances of the several writers, one of its main designs is to exhibit the Saviour, and to manifest the varied experience of true believers. David himself was an eminent type of Christ, being an extraordinary king, priest, and prophet of Israel. The Jewish community prefigured the professing people of God under the Christian dispensation; their enemies were typical

CH. XIV.—ANALYSIS OF PSALMS.

of those of the church; and their victories shadowed forth the triumphs of believers.

To read the Psalms with the full measure of profit designed by the Holy Spirit, we should,

1. Obtain a knowledge of the ancient scriptures, particularly the history of David as recorded in the books of Samuel, and in the first book of Chronicles.

2. Give an attentive consideration to the application of passages in the Psalms to Jesus Christ and to the church, by the inspired writers of the New Testament.

3. We should possess a regenerate and spiritual mind; and the more a believer is advanced in experimental godliness, the better will he be prepared to perceive their divine excellences, and to realize the heavenly consolations which are conveyed by the Psalms. The word Selah, found in many of the Psalms, denotes a musical elevation of sound.

In the confession of his sin, the penitent believer will find the most suitable assistance in the 32nd and 51st Psalms; in praising God, his grateful soul will be enlarged by the 103d and 145th; in praying for grace, and adoring God for the Scriptures, his mind will be abundantly furnished by the 19th and 119th; in supplicating for the prosperity of the church, his heart will be inspired by the 87th and 122nd; and in imploring the extension of the church, embracing the heathen in its salvation, the 67th and 72nd will enliven his benevolent devotion.

The number of the Psalms is one hundred and fifty, and they have been classed under six heads.

I. Prayers—
1. For pardon of sin, vi. xxv. xxxviii. li. cxxx. Those called penitential are, vi. xxxii. li. cii. cxxx. cxliii.
2. When prevented attending public worship, xlii. xliii. lxiii. lxxxiv.
3. In affliction, iii. xiii. xxii. lxix. lxxvii. lxxxviii. cxliii.
4. In trouble, iv. v. xxviii. xli. xliv. lv. lxiv. lxxix. lxxx. lxxxiii. cix. cxx. cxl. cxli. cxlii.

II. Thanksgiving Psalms—
1. For personal mercies, ix. xviii. xxx. xxxiv. xl. lxxv. ciii. cviii. cxvi. cxviii. cxxxviii. cxliv. cxlv.

2. For mercies to the church, xlvi. xlviii. lxv. lxvi. lxviii. lxxvi. lxxxi. lxxxv. xcviii. cv. cxvi. cxvii. cxxiv. cxxvi. cxxix. cxxxv. cxxxvi. cxlix.

III. Psalms of adoration—
Of the majesty, glory, and perfections of God, viii. xix. xxiv. xxix. xxxiii. xlvii. l. lxv. lxvi. lxxvi. lxxvii. lxxxix. xciii. xcvi. xcix. civ. cxi. cxiii. cxiv. cxv. cxxxiv. cxxxix. cxlviii. cl.
Of the providential care of God over good men, xxiii. xxxiv. xxxvi. xci-c. ciii. cvii. cxvii. cxxi. cxlv. cxlvi.

IV. Psalms of doctrinal instruction—
The excellency of the Scriptures, xix. cxix.
The vanity of man as mortal, xxxix. xlix. xc.
The characters of good and bad men, i. v. vii. ix. x. xi. xii. xiv. xv. xvii. xxiv. xxxii. xxxiv. xxxvi. xxxvii. l. lii. lviii. lxxiii. lxxv. lxxxiv. xci. xcii. xciv. cxii. cxix. cxxi. cxxv. cxxvii. cxxviii. cxxxiii.

V. Prophetical Psalms—relating especially to Jesus Christ, or Messiah.
ii. viii. xvi. xxii. xl. xlv. lxviii. lxxii. lxxxvii. cix. cx. cxviii.

VI. Historical Psalms—
lxxviii. cv. cvi. cxxxv. cxxxvi.

About fifty Psalms are either quoted or referred to in the New Testament.

References in the Psalms.

Ps. ii. 1.	Acts iv. 25, 26.	Ps. xxii. 18.	Matt. xxvii. 35; Mark xv. 24; Luke xxiii. 34.
— — 7.	—— xiii. 33; Heb. i. 5; v. 5.		
— viii. 2.	Matt. xxi. 16.	— xxxi. 5.	Luke xxiii. 46.
— — 4, 5.	Heb. ii. 6, 7.	— xxxii. 1.	Rom. iv. 6—8.
— xiv. 1, 3.	Rom. iii. 12.	— xl. 6, 8.	Heb. x. 5, 7.
— xvi. 10.	Acts xiii. 35.	— xli. 9.	John xiii. 18.
— xviii. 49.	Rom. xv. 9.	— xliv. 22.	Rom. viii. 36.
— xix. 4.	—— x. 18.	— xlv. 6.	Heb. i. 8.
— xxii. 1.	Matt. xxvii. 46; Mark xv. 34.	— lxviii. 18.	Eph. iv. 7, 8.
— — 7.	Mark xv. 29; Matt. xxvii. 39.	— lxix. 21.	Matt. xxvii. 34; John xix. 29.
		—— 22, 23.	Rom. xi. 9, 10.
— — 8.	Luke xxiii. 35.		
— — 16.	John xx. 25—27; Phil. iii. 2.	— lxxviii. 2.	Matt. xiii. 35.
		— xci. 11, 12.	—— iv. 6, 7.

CH. XIV.—ANALYSIS OF PROVERBS.

Ps. xcv. 7—11.	Heb. iii. 7, 15;	Ps. cxviii. 22.	Matt. xxi. 42;
	iv. 7.		Acts iv. 11;
— cix. 8.	Acts i. 20.		Eph. ii. 20;
— ex. 1.	Matt. xxii. 44;		1 Pet. ii. 4, 7.
	Luke xx. 42.	— cxxxii. 5.	Acts vii. 46.
— cxvii. 1.	Rom. xv. 11.	— cxxxviii. 8.	Phil. i. 6.

PROVERBS.

Proverbs are wise sayings, contained in short sentences, which can be easily remembered: and the book of Proverbs is a collection of wise sayings, given by divine inspiration, and written in the poetic style. They relate to almost every part of moral and religious duty; and they have been always considered by the church as forming a storehouse of practical wisdom, directing us how to walk with God in the way of holiness. Most of the proverbs in this collection were written by Solomon, the wise king of Israel; on which account they are commonly called by his name. The book of Proverbs is divided into thirty-one chapters, which include three principal sections.

Section I. Embraces the first nine chapters, which contain the wisest, most affectionate, and forcible exhortations to engage men to the study of wisdom in the fear of God, ch. i.—ix.

Sec. II. Contains the wise maxims of Solomon; and which are, in a proper sense, proverbs, ch. x.—xxix.

Sec. III. Consists of the last two chapters; the first of which contains the wise and pious sayings and instructions of Agur given to his two disciples Ithiel and Ucal: the other the excellent lessons addressed to king Lemuel by his mother.

The most remarkable things in the book of Proverbs, are the invitations and counsels to mankind given by Christ, under the name and character of Wisdom. See ch. viii.

References in Proverbs.

Ch. i. 20.	John vii. 37.	Ch. x. 12.	1 Pet. iv. 8.
— iii. 11, 12.	Heb. xii. 5, 6.	— xi. 30.	James v. 20.
— — 34.	James iv. 6;	— xvii. 27.	—— i. 19.
	1 Pet. v. 5.	— xviii. 21.	Matt. xii. 37.

Ch. xix. 17.   Matt. xxv. 35, 44. | Ch. xxv. 21, 22.   Rom. xii. 20.
— xx. 9.   1 John i. 8. | — xxvii. 1.   Jas. iv. 13, 14.
— xxii. 6.   Eph. vi. 4. | — xxviii. 5.   1 Cor. ii. 14, 15;
— xxiv. 23.   James ii. 1. | 1 John ii. 20-27.
— xxv. 6, 7.   Luke xiv. 8-10. | — xxx. 8.   Matt. vi. 11.

ECCLESIASTES.

Ecclesiastes signifies preacher; and this book was so called because of its useful doctrines and the wise design of its publication. It was written by Solomon, at the close of his life, after his reformation from the evil courses into which he had been drawn from the ways of holiness in the service of God by his idolatrous wives, 1 Kings xi. 1, 13; and as a monumental expression of his sincere repentance, and of his unfeigned return to the LORD. The book of Ecclesiastes is a continued discourse in twelve chapters. Its design is twofold: 1. To testify and demonstrate, from the experience of a wise and prosperous king, that riches, and honour, and all possessions and gratifications of an earthly kind, are totally insufficient to satisfy the rational soul of man; 2. To draw off men from the pursuit of all worldly objects as their supreme good, directing them to the fear of God, and to communion with him, as the chief end of man, and as his highest happiness and honour.

The things most remarkable in the book of Ecclesiastes, are, besides the confessions of the humble penitent, the beautiful descriptions which it contains, of the appearances of nature, the circulation of the blood, the structure of the human frame, and its humiliating decay.

References in Ecclesiastes.

Ch. i. 2.   Rom. viii. 20. | Ch. viii. 12.   Matt. xxv.
— iii. 17.   2 Cor. v. 10. | 34—41.
— vi. 12.   James iv. 14. | — — 15.   1 Tim. iv. 4; vi. 17.
— vii. 20.   Rom. iii. 23; | — xi. 9.   Rom. ii. 6.
               1 John i. 8. | — xii. 14.   2 Cor. v. 10.

SONG OF SOLOMON.

The Song of Solomon is a sacred poem, composed by the king of Israel.

CH. XIV.—ANALYSIS OF SONG OF SOLOMON.

According to the best commentators on the Bible, this book is a sublime and mystical allegory, referring to Jesus Christ and his union with an uncorrupted church. Under the natural and endearing figure of a bridegroom and bride, it is designed to set forth, as is believed, the affection of Christ towards his church, he being its heavenly bridegroom and husband; ministers of religion are his friends; the bride is the church of true believers; and her companions are all who seek the society of the church. In the character of husband and bridegroom, in similar figures of speech, our Saviour is several times represented to us, both in the Old and New Testaments. See Psa. xlv.; Jer. iii. 12—14; Hos. ii. 14—23; Matt. ix. 16; xxii. 2; xxv. 1—11; John iii. 29; 2 Cor. xi. 2; Eph. v. 23—27; Rev. xix. 7—9; xxi. 2—9; xxii. 17.

It may be remarked, that no unregenerate, sensual person can understand the spiritual application of this book: none but heavenly-minded men, who can truly say of Christ, "This is my beloved, and this is my friend."

References in Solomon's Song.

Ch. i. 4.	John vi. 44; Phil. iii. 12,13.	Ch. iv. 15.	John vii. 38.
— ii. 3.	Rev. xxii. 1, 2.	— v. 2.	Rev. iii. 20.
— iv. 7.	Eph. v. 27.	— vii. 1.	Eph. vi. 15.
— — 15.	John iv. 10, 14.	— viii. 11.	Matt. xxi. 33—43.
		— — 14.	Rev. xxii. 20.

PROPHETS.

The following series of books, sixteen in number, Lamentations being considered as an appendix to Jeremiah, are chiefly prophetical; but including numerous historical notices. Their writers were a class of God's ministers, who were formerly called seers, holy men of God, and prophets. They were the philosophers, divines, and instructors of the Israelites in religion and virtue. Many of the earlier prophets, as Elijah, Elisha, Micaiah, and some others, appear to have committed nothing to writing: but those who were endowed with the spirit of prophecy in its most exalted sense, and who

were commissioned to utter predictions, the accomplishment of which was far distant, were directed to write, or cause them to be written for the instruction of the church, especially of Christians.

In reading the writings of the prophets, we should have especial regard to the apostle Peter's important declaration: "Knowing this first, that no prophecy of the Scripture is of any private interpretation. For the prophecy came not in old time by the will of man: but holy men of God spake as they were moved by the Holy Ghost," 2 Pet. i. 20, 21.

The prophecies in these books embrace a vast range of the most interesting subjects, especially relating to the Jewish nation, to Jesus Christ, and the Christian church; and include notices of the several empires and nations of the world, down to the end of time, as they were, or as they will be, in various ways connected with the church of God.

The style of the prophets is highly poetical and figurative, and the beautiful metaphors and allusions require devout attention. Kings, queens, and magistrates are frequently represented by the sun, moon, and stars; kingdoms and cities, by mountains and hills; the covenant of God, by lawful marriage; and departure from his worship, in the service of idols, is commonly signified by adultery and whoredom.

Acquaintance with general history, especially regarding the ancient nations and countries, is requisite to qualify a person to understand many of the prophecies; and others, which are yet unfulfilled, are necessarily attended with obscurities or difficulties, which time alone can remove, and which should always be studied with deep humility of mind, under the recollection that they are the oracles of God.

ISAIAH.

Isaiah was a prophet of Judah; and he is supposed to have been of the royal family. He began to prophesy in the reign of Uzziah, who died B. C. 758 years; and he continued his ministry till after the death of Heze-

kiah, who died B. C. 698 years: he must, therefore, have prophesied above sixty years. He is thought to have been put to an ignominious and painful death, being "sawn asunder," Heb. xi. 37, by order of Manasseh, when that king was in the height of his enormous wickedness. Isaiah has been called the evangelical prophet, on account of his having plainly foretold so many things concerning the birth, ministry, sufferings, and death of our Lord Jesus Christ; and the glorious times of the gospel. Many parts of this book are most admirably adapted to promote the spiritual edification and consolation of believers, especially the last twenty-seven chapters.

The design of the prophecies of Isaiah was threefold:

1. To declare to the Jewish people the greatness of their wickedness.

2. To exhort all classes among them to repentance, on account of their transgressions.

3. To comfort those who truly feared the LORD, with promises of divine support; to assure them of the coming of Christ; and to encourage their expectation of the future enlargement, and the permanent glory of the church.

The book of Isaiah is divided into sixty-six chapters, and contains six principal sections.

Section I. Contains several discourses and predictions, delivered in the reign of Uzziah, ch. i.—v.

Sec. II. Predictions delivered in the reigns of Jotham and Ahaz, ch. vi.—xii.

Sec. III. Predictions against the Babylonians, Assyrians, and other nations, by whose oppressions or wickedness the Israelites had been injured, ch. xiii.—xxiv.

Sec. IV. Prophecies of great calamities, which should befall the people of God: His merciful preservation o. a remnant of them, and their restoration and conversion to Christ—their enemies and antichrist being destroyed, ch. xxv.—xxxv.

Sec. V. The accounts of the invasion of Judea by Sennacherib, and the destruction of his army, in answer to

the prayer of Hezekiah; and the sickness and miraculous recovery of Hezekiah, ch. xxxvi.—xxxix.

Sec. VI. Contains a series of prophecies, delivered toward the close of the prophet's ministry. This portion of Isaiah's writings constitutes perhaps the most beautiful part of the Old Testament, and the most important for its evangelical contents. The chief subject is the restoration of the church; and the prophet connects the deliverance from Babylon, with the spiritual and eternal redemption of Jesus Christ.

The most remarkable prophecies delivered by Isaiah, relate to three momentous subjects :—

1. The captivity of the Jews in Babylon, on account of their sins; and their certain deliverance from that idolatrous city, by Cyrus the Persian conqueror, whom Isaiah foretold by name, nearly 200 years before his birth, ch. xliv. 28; xlv. 1—4, 13.

2. The circumstantial particulars concerning the birth, ministry, sufferings, and death of Christ as an atonement for sinners: many of which are described by the prophet with the accuracy of a present observer, and eyewitness of their fulfilment, ch. ix. xxxv. liii. lxv.

3. The growing enlargement of the church in the times of the gospel dispensation; increasing in numbers and prosperity, until "the knowledge of the LORD shall cover the earth," in the full millennial glory, ch. ii. ix. xi. lxvi.

In the book of Isaiah there are several facts recorded, which deserve particular remark.

1. The account of the Assyrian army besieging Jerusalem, and their destruction in one night to the number of 185,000, by a commissioned angel of the LORD.

2. The alarming illness and extraordinary recovery of king Hezekiah, and the merciful addition of fifteen years to his life, ch. xxxvi.—xxxix.

References in Isaiah.

Ch. i. 9.	Rom. ix. 29.	Ch. vii. 14.	Matt. i. 23.
— v. 1, 2.	Matt. xxi. 33.	— viii. 14.	1 Pet. ii. 8.
— vi. 9, 10.	John xii. 40, 41;	— — 18.	Heb. ii. 13.
	Mark iv. 11, 12.	— ix. 1, 2.	Matt. iv. 14, 16
— vii. 14.	Luke i. 31, 35.	— — 7.	Luke i. 32, 33.

CH. XIV.—ANALYSIS OF JEREMIAH.

Ch. xi. 10.	Rom. xv. 10-12.	Ch. xlv. 24.	1 Cor. i. 30.
— xiii. 10.	Matt. xxiv. 29; Mark xiii. 24.	— xlix. 6.	Acts xiii. 47.
— xxi. 9.	Rev. xviii. 2.	— li. 6.	2 Pet. iii. 10-13.
— xxii. 22.	—— iii. 7.	— lii. 7.	Rom. x. 15.
— xxv. 8.	1 Cor. xv. 54.	— liii. 1.	John xii. 38.
— xxviii. 16.	Rom. ix. 33; 1 Pet. ii. 6—8.	— — 4.	Matt. viii. 17.
		— — 5.	1 Pet. ii. 24.
		— — 7.	Matt. xxvii. 57.
— xxix. 13.	Matt. xv. 7, 9.	— — 10.	2 Cor. v. 21.
— xxxv. 5, 6.	—— xi. 5 ; xv. 30.	— — 12.	Heb. vii. 25.
		— liv. 1.	Gal. iv. 27.
— xl. 3.	—— iii. 3 ; Luke iii. 4.	— — 13.	John vi. 45.
		— lviii. 7.	Matt. xxv. 35.
— — 6.	1 Pet. i. 24.	— lix. 20.	Rom. xi. 26.
— — 11.	John x. 11.	— lx. 19.	Rev. xxi. 22, 23.
— xlii. 1—4.	Matt. xii. 18, 21.	— lxi. 1.	Luke iv. 18.
— xliv. 3.	John vii. 38, 39.	— lxiii. 1, 2.	Rev. xix. 13.
— xlv. 9.	Rom. ix. 20.	— lxv. 1.	Rom. x. 20.
— — 23.	—— xiv. 11.	— lxvi. 24.	Mark ix. 44.

JEREMIAH.

Jeremiah prophesied for about forty-three years before the destruction of Jerusalem; and during several years after that calamitous event, which took place 588 years before the birth of Christ. After the destruction of Jerusalem, Jeremiah accompanied those Jews who retired into Egypt. There he continued to reprove them on account of their idolatry, and sealed the truth of his ministry by the blood of martyrdom, the Jews having stoned him. In the opposition and cruel treatment which Jeremiah received from his countrymen, we perceive the rooted enmity of the unrenewed mind of man against the faithful preachers and the righteous authority of God.

The book of Jeremiah is divided into fifty-two chapters, containing four collections of prophecies; but they are not arranged in chronological order.

They have been placed in the following order by a learned translator of the book of Jeremiah.

I. Prophecies delivered in the reign of Josiah, ch. i.—xii.

II. Prophecies delivered in the reign of Jehoiakim, ch. xiii.—xx. xxii. xxxv. xxxvi. xlv.—xlviii. xlix. 1—33.

III. Prophecies delivered in the reign of Zedekiah,

ch. xxi. xxiv. xxvii.—xxxiv. xxxvii.—xxxix. xliv. 34—39; l. li.

IV. Prophecies delivered under the government of Gedaliah, from the taking of Jerusalem to the retreat of the people into Egypt; and those which Jeremiah delivered to the Jews in that country, ch. xl.—xliv.

The fifty-second chapter is supposed to have been added by Ezra, as an introduction to the book of Lamentations.

The prophecies of Jeremiah relate to three principal points, designed,

1. To admonish the Jews of the certain and approaching destruction of their glorious temple, on account of its pollution by their idolatries; and of the wasting of their country, as a punishment for their apostacy and wickedness.

2. To invite the people to repentance by the promises of the Divine forgiveness, and of deliverance from Babylon, at the expiration of seventy years.

3. To comfort the pious with renewed assurances of the advent of Messiah, and the blessings of his kingdom.

The most remarkable things related in the book of Jeremiah are,

1. The series of persecutions and sufferings which the prophet endured in the faithful discharge of his ministry, as the messenger of God; on account of which, and of the affecting nature of some of his writings, Jeremiah has been called the Weeping prophet.

2. The instructive character under which the Messiah was foretold—the Righteous Branch, and the LORD our Righteousness, ch. xxiii. 5, 6.

3. The spiritual and eternal blessings of the LORD'S covenant, to be communicated to the church, as the fruits of the righteousness and sacrifice of Christ, ch. xxxi. 31—36; xxxiii. 8, 14—16.

References in Jeremiah.

Ch. ii. 13.	John iv. 14.	Ch. ii. 30.	Acts vii. 52.
— — 21.	Matt. xxi. 33;	— vi. 16.	Matt. xi. 29.
	Mark xii. 1;	— vii. 11.	— xxi. 13.
	Luke xx. 9.	— ix. 23, 24.	1 Cor. i. 29-31.

Ch. xi. 19.	Luke xx.14,15.	Ch. xxxi. 15. Matt. ii. 17, 18.
— xviii. 6.	Rom. ix. 2.	— —— 31,34. Heb. viii. 8-10.
— xxiii. 6.	1 Cor. i. 30.	— —— 33. —— x. 16, 17.
— xxix. 7.	1 Tim. ii. 2.	— xxxiii. 16. 1 Cor. i. 30.

LAMENTATIONS.

The Lamentations are the mournful elegies which Jeremiah composed on beholding the ruins of the destroyed city and temple of Jerusalem. These poems are remarkable both for the plan on which they are written, and for the subjects which they commemorate. The Lamentations consist of five chapters, each having twenty-two stanzas or verses, beginning with the several letters of the Hebrew alphabet in their proper order: the third chapter having sixty-six verses, has three verses together commencing in Hebrew with the several letters in order.

The subject of these Lamentations is the various dreadful calamities of the Jews, in which they were involved through the unfeeling brutality of the Babylonian soldiers; but they are understood to predict the still greater miseries which were brought upon the Jewish people when the city and temple were finally destroyed by the Roman soldiers, the severer judgment of Heaven on account of their crucifying " the Lord of glory."

References in Lamentations.

| Ch. ii. 2. | Matt. xi. 23. | Ch. iii. 45. 1 Cor. iv. 13. |
| — iii. 33. | Heb. xii. 10. | — iv. 13. Matt. xxiii. 31-37. |

EZEKIEL.

Ezekiel was of the sacerdotal race, and among the Jews whom Nebuchadnezzar carried captive with Jeconiah, king of Judah, from Jerusalem to Babylon, 2 Kings xxiv. 12—17. Ezekiel prophesied during the early part of the captivity, commencing his ministry about 590 years before the birth of Christ. The design of his prophecies was the instruction of the captives; for the first multitude who had been carried to Babylon, seeing no appearance of Jerusalem being destroyed, as

Jeremiah had foretold, deplored their condition in having submitted to the Chaldeans. Ezekiel, therefore, was raised up to exercise his ministry, confirming the preaching and denunciations of the former prophets of God.

1. Confirming the truth of what Jeremiah had declared, he gives new predictions concerning the certain and speedy destruction of Jerusalem, on account of the continued idolatry and wickedness of the people.

2. Comforting the pious among the captive Jews, with the assurance of their future restoration, he declares the Divine judgments upon their cruel oppressors.

3. To foreshow the flourishing and happy state of the church in the times of the Messiah.

The book of Ezekiel is divided into forty-eight chapters, containing four principal sections.

Section I. Relates the call of Ezekiel, and his prophetical commission, ch. i.—iii. 21.

Sec. II. Contains various predictions of approaching judgments upon the Jews, on account of their idolatry and wickedness, ch. iii. 22—xxiv.

Sec. III. Records the threatenings of heavy judgments upon the several surrounding nations, that were enemies and oppressors of the Jews, ch. xxv.—xxxii.

Sec. IV. Describes the future restoration of the Jews, with their spiritual prosperity, especially under the reign of Messiah, and the destruction of their enemies, ch. xxxiii.—xlviii.

Among the most remarkable things recorded by the prophet Ezekiel, are his instructive visions; of which two especially have never failed to attract the attention of pious students of this book.

1. The vision of the resurrection of dry bones, assuring the restoration of the people of Israel, ch. xxxvii.

2. The vision of the holy waters, representing the spiritual blessings conveyed by the gospel in its advancing progress through all nations. See ch. xlvii. compared with Rev. xxii.

References in Ezekiel.

Ch. i. 5.	Rev. iv. 6.	Ch. xii. 22—27.	2 Pet. iii. 4.
— — 10.	—— — 7.	— xviii. 7.	Matt. xxv. 35.
— — 13.	—— — 5.	— xxvii. 27.	Rev. xviii. 19.
— — 27.	—— i. 13—15.	— xxxiv. 23.	John x. 11.
— — 28.	—— iv. 3; i. 17.	— xxxviii. 2.	Rev. xx. 8.
— ix. 4.	—— vii. 1—3.	— xlvii. 1—8.	—— xxii. 1, 2.
— — 6.	1 Pet. iv. 17.	.—— — 22.	Eph. ii. 12, 13.

DANIEL.

Daniel was but a youth (in years) when he was carried among the first captives to Babylon in the third year of the reign of Jehoiakim, 2 Kings xxiii. 36; xxiv. 1; Dan. i. 1, 2, and about eight years before the deportation of Ezekiel. He prophesied during the captivity, until after Cyrus succeeded to the throne of his uncle Darius, a period of more than seventy years. Daniel was a person of extraordinary sanctity and wisdom, with which God endowed him, qualifying him to be an eminent instrument in accomplishing the gracious designs of his all-wise providence. His predictions are the most extraordinary and comprehensive of all that are found in the prophetical writings; for they include the general history of the world, as well as that of the church of God under the Jewish and Christian dispensations, from the period in which he lived to the final consummation of all things; and he alone, of all the prophets, foretold the exact time when the Messiah should appear and finish the great work of human redemption, making reconciliation for iniquity by the sacrifice of himself.

The book of Daniel is divided into twelve chapters, and contains two principal sections; the former historical, and the latter prophetical.

Section I. Relates various circumstances in the history of Daniel and the Jews under several kings of Babylon, ch. i.—vi.

Sec. II. Contains several prophecies concerning the future condition of the Jews and of the surrounding nations, the coming of the Messiah, and the design of his

mission " to make reconciliation for iniquity, and to bring in everlasting righteousness:" the conversion of the Jews to Christ, and the general resurrection of the dead, ch. vii.—xii.

In the book of Daniel there are several things truly remarkable; among which are,

1. The extraordinary piety, integrity, and wisdom of Daniel and his three companions.

2. The miraculous preservation of the three pious Hebrews when cast into the burning, fiery furnace.

3. The madness of Nebuchadnezzar, sent as a judgment from God on account of his pride; in which he was driven from the society of men to feed upon the grass with the beasts of the field.

4. The prediction of four universal empires, the rise and fall of which Daniel describes, and the division of the last, which was the Roman, into ten kingdoms.

5. The riotous feasting of Belshazzar, and his daring impiety in drinking to the praise of his idols in the golden vessels which had been pillaged from the temple of God at Jerusalem.

6. The threatening vision from God, against the guilty monarch, in the midst of his midnight revels, when the city was taken, and the king with his nobles was slain.

7. The conspiracy against Daniel, and his miraculous preservation in the den of lions.

8. Daniel's prayer for the restoration of his people to their own land.

9. The prediction of the precise time at which Messiah should appear on earth and die for sinners.

Seventy weeks of years, or 490 years, reckoned from the seventh year of Artaxerxes in the month Nisan, in which Ezra was commissioned to restore the Jewish state and polity, Ezra vii. 9—26, will bring us to the month Nisan, A. D. 33, in the very month and year in which Christ suffered for us.

References in Daniel.

| Ch. ii. 44. | 1 Cor. xv. 24. | Ch. vi. 14. | Mark vi. 26. |
| — iv. 37. | Rev. xv. 3. | — — 23. | Heb. xi. 33. |

CH. XIV.—ANALYSIS OF HOSEA.

Ch. vii. 10.	Rev. v. 11; xx. 12.	Ch. ix. 26, 27.	Luk. xxiv. 32, 44.
— — 13.	Matt. xxiv. 30.	— x. 11.	Rev. i. 17.
— ix. 17.	John xvi. 24.	— xi. 35.	1 Pet. i. 7.
— — 24.	Heb. ix. 12; 2 Cor. v. 21.	— xii. 1.	Luke x. 20; Rev. xiii. 8.
— — 26.	1 Pet. ii. 22, 24; Matt. xxiv. 2, 15; Tit. ii. 14.	— — 2.	Matt. xxv. 46; John v. 28, 29.
		— — 3.	1 Cor. xv. 41, 42.

HOSEA.

Hosea was raised up among the people of Israel after they had sunk into the grossest idolatry, and during the time that Isaiah prophesied in Judah. He began to prophesy somewhat earlier than Isaiah, and exercised his ministry about sixty years, labouring to recall his countrymen to the true worship of God. The prophecies of Hosea were designed,

1. To impress upon the Israelites a deep conviction of the greatness of their wickedness in forsaking the LORD God of their fathers, the Creator of the world, for the worship of senseless idols, the work of their own hands. This the prophet was inspired to represent under the metaphorical description of a wife proving unfaithful to her marriage vows.

2. To admonish them concerning the terrible judgments of God, which he threatened to bring upon them as a punishment for their transgressions.

3. To call the people to sincere repentance before the LORD, with promises of divine forgiveness; and to direct them in what manner they should return to God, from whom they had revolted.

The book of Hosea is divided into fourteen chapters, containing five principal sections.

Section I. Contains solemn reproofs of the idolatry of the Israelites, with promises of pardon to the penitent, ch. i.—iii.

Sec. II. A condemnation of the bloodshed and wickedness of the people, with various evangelical promises, ch. iv.—vi. 3.

Sec. III. The captivity of the nation denounced on

account of their obstinacy in idolatry and wickedness, ch. vi. 4—viii.

Sec. IV. Terrible denunciations of the Divine judgments renewed, ch. ix.—xiii. 8.

Sec. V. Gracious invitations to repentance, with instructions in what manner and with what words to return to the LORD, ch. xiii. 9; xiv.

The sixth, thirteenth, and fourteenth chapters contain the most affecting invitations to sinners to return to God, with his gracious promises of forgiveness. These deserve particular notice, and are designed for our consolation. But one of the most remarkable things in the book of Hosea, is the prediction of the condition of the people of Israel in their present dispersion, ch. iii. 4, 5.

References in Hosea.

Ch. i. 9, 10.	Rom. ix. 25, 26; 1 Pet. ii. 10.	Ch. vi. 6.	Matt. ix. 13.
— ii. 7.	Luke xv. 18.	— x. 8.	Luke xxiii. 30; Rev. vi. 16.
— — 23.	Rom. ix. 26; 1 Pet. ii. 9, 10.	— — 12, 13.	Gal. vi. 7, 8 Matt. ii. 15
— v. 6.	John vii. 34.	— xi. 1.	
— vi. 5.	Heb. iv. 12.	— xiii. 14.	1 Cor. xv. 54—56.

JOEL.

Joel is believed to have exercised his ministry in Judah in the time of Isaiah. The prophecies of Joel are contained in three chapters, which may be considered as so many sections; the design of which was,

1. To exhort the Jews to immediate repentance, by threatenings of famine, which should be occasioned by numerous swarms of locusts, caterpillars, and cankerworms, destructive as an invading army.

2. To direct them in what manner they should return to the LORD by sincere humiliation and prayer.

3. To assure them of the Divine forgiveness on their repentance, and of spiritual prosperity under the gospel dispensation.

The most remarkable thing in the book of Joel, is the promise of the effusion of the Holy Spirit, which was fulfilled on the day of Pentecost, ch. ii. 28—32.

References in Joel.

| Ch. ii. 28, 31. | Acts ii. 16—21. | Ch. iii. 17. | Rev. xxi. 27. |
| — — 32. | Rom. x. 13—15. | — — 18. | —— xxii. 1. |

AMOS.

Little is known concerning Amos, except that he was called to the prophetic office in Judah from being a herdsman in Tekoa. He prophesied during the early part of Isaiah's ministry. The book of Amos is divided into nine chapters, which include three principal sections.

Section I. Relates the threatening of the Divine judgments against the Syrians, Tyrians, Edomites, Ammonites, and Moabites, ch. i. ii. 3.

Sec. II. The denunciations of God against the impenitent Jews, with invitations to them to return to the LORD by sincere repentance, ch. ii. 4—ix. 10.

Sec. III. Evangelical promises to the godly, to promote their consolation, ch. ix. 11, to the end.

References in Amos.

| Ch. ii. 8. | 1 Cor. viii. 10. | Ch. v. 25. | Acts vii. 42, 43. |
| — iii. 7. | John xv. 15. | — ix. 11. | —— xv. 15—17. |

OBADIAH.

It is not certainly known at what period Obadiah lived: some suppose he was that excellent man who was governor of king Ahab's house, and the person who met Elijah, 1 Kings xviii. 3—7, but others think he was contemporary with Jeremiah. The book of Obadiah has only twenty-one verses, which include two sections.

Section I. Contains threatenings against the Edomites, on account of their pride and their cruelty towards the Jews, ver. 1—16.

Sec. II. Proclaims evangelical promises for the consolation of the pious, ver. 17—21.

References in Obadiah.

| Ver. 3. | Rev. xviii. 7. | Ver. 21. | Rev. xi. 15. |

JONAH.

Jonah prophesied in the reign of Jeroboam, son of Joash king of Israel, about eighty years before the time of Isaiah. The subject of the book of Jonah is the mission of that prophet to the populous city of Nineveh, the capital of the Assyrian empire, and his successful ministry among its people. The design of this prophetic record is to show, by the striking example of the Ninevites, the forbearance and long-suffering of God towards sinners, by which they are spared on their sincere repentance.

The book of Jonah is divided into four chapters, containing two sections.

Section I. Relates the first mission of Jonah, his disobedience and punishment, ch. i. ii.

Sec. II. The second mission, and the success of the prophet, ch. iii. iv.

There are four things especially remarkable in the book of Jonah.

1. The disobedience of Jonah to the command of God, through fear of being accounted a false prophet, if the Ninevites repented, and the city should be spared.

2. The account of Jonah being cast into the sea, and his being swallowed by a great fish, which the LORD had prepared for that purpose.

3. The deliverance of the penitent prophet from his watery dungeon in the belly of the fish.

4. The beneficial effects of Jonah's ministry among the Ninevites.

In the deliverance of Jonah from the prison of the fish, the prophet was a type of our Saviour's resurrection from the grave. It appears scarcely worth mentioning, that some persons have objected to the account of Jonah having been swallowed by a fish; as the prophet expressly declares, that "The LORD had prepared a great fish to swallow up Jonah;" and such doubting or incredulous persons forget the omnipotence of Jehovah, the Creator of the universe, and the God of Jonah. Besides, several monstrous fishes of the shark

kind, have, in modern times, been caught, in whose stomachs were found the whole bodies of men having on their clothes; and, in one instance, of a soldier having his military accoutrements and arms.

References in Jonah.

Ch. i. 1—4.	Acts xxvii. 14-18.	Ch. ii. 9.	Heb. xiii. 15.
— — 17.	Matt. xii. 39-41;	— iii. 5.	Matt. xii. 41.
	Luke xi. 30-32.	— — 6.	Luke xi. 32.

MICAH.

Micah was a prophet of Judah, and he exercised his ministry in the time of Isaiah. He was raised up to confirm the predictions of Isaiah, against both the Israelites and Jews, whom he invited to repentance both by threatened judgments and by promised mercies. The book of Micah is divided into seven chapters, which contain three principal sections.

Section I. Contains various prophecies delivered in the reign of Jotham, ch. i.

Sec. II. Prophecies delivered in the reign of Ahaz, ch. ii.—iv. 8.

Sec. III. Prophecies in the reign of Hezekiah, ch. iv. 9—vii.

The book of Micah has been considered the most important single prophecy in the Old Testament; and the most comprehensive respecting the birth-place and the personal character of the Messiah, and the blessings of his kingdom upon earth, ch. iv. 1—4; v. 2—4.

References in Micah.

Ch. ii. 3.	Eph. v. 16.	Ch. v. 2.	Matt. ii. 6; John
— — 10.	Heb. xiii. 13,14.		i. 1; vii. 42.
— iii. 5.	Matt. vii. 15.	— vii. 6.	—— x. 21, 35, 36.
— iv. 7.	Luke i. 33; Rev.	— — 19.	Rom. vi. 14.
	xi. 15.	— — 20.	Luke i. 72, 73.

NAHUM.

Nahum was a native of Elkosh, in Galilee; and he is supposed to have been contemporary with Isaiah. The

prophecy of Nahum is one continued poem, now divided into three chapters: the design of this book was,

First. To minister consolation to the servants of God, by delivering to them various evangelical promises, ch. i.

Second. To denounce the final and inevitable destruction of the magnificent city of Nineveh, on account of its people returning to their former wickedness, after the mission of Jonah, ch. ii. iii.; and especially because of the cruel tyranny of the Ninevites towards the Israelites, after the overthrow of their kingdom by Shalmanezer, 2 Kings xvii. 6, &c.

The approaching ruin of the great city Nineveh, and the measures preparatory for the accomplishment of that awful calamity, are described by the prophet Nahum with awful grandeur and majesty. So perfectly have these predictions been fulfilled, that even the vestiges of the ruins of Nineveh are scarcely to be discerned by the inquisitive traveller. From the ruin of this country, after the ministry of Jonah, we learn how dangerous it is to trifle with the admonitions of God!

References in Nahum.

| Ch. i. 10. | 1 Thess. v. 2, 3. | Ch. iii. 4. | Rev. xviii. 2, 3. |
| — — 15. | Rom. x. 15. | — — 12. | —— vi. 13. |

HABAKKUK.

Habakkuk prophesied in the time of Jeremiah, a short period before the siege and destruction of Jerusalem. The book of Habakkuk is divided into three chapters, which form two sections.

Section I. Records a kind of dialogue prophecy between God and the prophet, concerning the wickedness of the Jews, and their certain punishment by the ferocious army of the Chaldeans, ch. i. ii.

Sec. II. A meditation or hymn of the prophet; in which, with the most beautiful elegance of language, he encourages the pious amongst the Jews still to trust in the God of their salvation.

In Habakkuk we behold a beautiful illustration of a Christian, living by faith on Jehovah as his covenant God and Saviour.

References in Habakkuk.

Ch. i. 5. Acts xiii. 41. | Ch. ii. 4. Rom. i. 17; Heb. x. 37, 38.

ZEPHANIAH.

Zephaniah prophesied in the former period of Jeremiah's ministry; or, as some think, about the close of the reign of Hezekiah. The design of Zephaniah in writing his prophecy was,

1. To denounce the terrible judgments of God, on account of sin, upon the Jews and the surrounding nations.
2. To excite them to repentance.
3. To comfort the pious with evangelical promises.

The book of Zephaniah has three chapters, which include four sections.

Section I. A denunciation against the Jews on account of their idolatry and wickedness, ch. i.

Sec. II. Invitations to immediate repentance, ch. ii. 1—3.

Sec. III. Denunciations against the Philistines, Moabites, Ammonites, and Ethiopians, ch. ii. 4—15.

Sec. IV. Predictions of the deliverances and ultimate prosperity of the people of God under the reign of the Messiah, ch. iii.

References in Zephaniah.

Ch. i. 7, 8.	Rev. xix. 17—19.	Ch. ii. 11.	John iv. 21, 24.
— — 10.	Heb. x. 38.	— iii. 12.	James ii. 5.
— — 11.	James v. 1.	— — 16.	Heb. xii. 12.

HAGGAI.

Haggai prophesied among the Jews after their return from captivity in Babylon. In their work of erecting the second temple at Jerusalem, the Jews were seriously interrupted by the Samaritans, and the Persian governors of the neighbouring provinces, so as to cause them to cease from their labour for a period of about fourteen years; and they were discouraged, supposing the time to complete the building was not yet come. But God disposing Darius the emperor, to renew the

decree of Cyrus, raised up Haggai to encourage them in the work, which was then finished in a few years. The book of Haggai is divided into two chapters or sections.

Section I. Contains a complaint of the Jews' negligence, and an exhortation to them to proceed in building the temple, under the assurance of the Divine assistance in their work, ch. i.

Sec. II. Records consolatory predictions, that the second temple should be more eminently glorious than the first; being distinguished with the presence and ministry of the Messiah, whom the prophet designates as being "The Desire of all nations."

References in Haggai.

Ch. i. 13.   Matt. xxviii. 20; Rom. viii. 31.
— ii. 6, 7.   Heb. xii. 26; Luke ii. 27—46.

ZECHARIAH.

Zechariah was contemporary and a fellow labourer with Haggai in the prophetic ministry; and the design of his writings was the same as that of his inspired colleague. But the discourses of Zechariah are much more extended and particular, for the purpose of encouraging the Jews in completing their temple and re-establishing their national institutions, confirming the predictions of former prophets respecting the expected Messiah.

The book of Zechariah is divided into fourteen chapters, including two principal sections.

Section 1. Contains several discourses and visions, admirably adapted to inspire the Jews with courage in rebuilding the temple, and renewing its public religious ordinances, ch. i.—vi.

Sec. II. A record of various discourses and predictions of things future, particularly concerning the coming of Christ, and the spiritual blessings of his kingdom upon earth, ch. vii.—xiv.

In the book of Zechariah there are three things which deserve particular attention.

1. The prediction concerning the entrance of Christ

into Jerusalem riding upon a colt the foal of an ass. Compare ch. ix. 9, 10, with Matt. xxi. 5.

2. The prophecy of the exact sum of money which Judas would receive for betraying Christ; and the particular appropriation of that money, when brought by the traitor. Compare ch. xi. 13, with Matt. xxvi. 14, 15; xxvii. 3—10.

3. The sublime exhibition which Zechariah gives of the spiritual blessings to be enjoyed by the church from the mediation of the incarnate Son of God. Almost every paragraph in this prophecy refers to the glory of the gospel church.

References in Zechariah.

Ch. i. 8.	Rev. vi. 4.	Ch. ix. 9.	Matt. xxi. 4, 5; John xii. 14, 15.
— ii. 10.	John i. 14.		
— — 11.	2 Cor. vi. 16.	— — 11.	Heb. xiii. 20.
— iii. 1.	Rom. viii. 33; Rev. xii. 9.	— xi. 13.	Matt. xxvii. 3—10.
— — 9.	Rev. v. 6.	— xii. 10.	John xix. 34—37; Rev. i. 7.
— iv. 10.			
— vi. 1—8.	— vi. 2—4.	— xiii. 7.	Matt. xxvi. 31; Mark xiv. 27.
— — 12, 13.	John i. 45; Heb. iii. 1-3; Matt. xvi. 16, 18.	— xiv. 21.	Eph. ii. 19—22.

MALACHI.

Malachi was the last of the inspired prophets under the Old Testament dispensation. He exercised his ministry about a hundred and twenty years after the return of the Jews from captivity in Babylon; and about four hundred and twenty years from the birth of Christ. His faithful testimony was delivered when, as, the temple having been built, and the city being in a prosperous condition, after the death of Nehemiah, the Jews, though retaining the forms of religion, became grossly hypocritical, profane, and corrupt. Malachi was therefore raised up to call them once more to repentance, and to promote a revival of true religion among them.

The book of Malachi is divided into four chapters, including two sections.

Section I. Contains complaints against the Jews, both

priests and people, on account of their profaneness and wickedness, ch. i. ii.

Sec. II. Records several prophecies relating to the coming of Christ, and of his herald prophet, John the Baptist; who, being endowed with the spirit and courage which distinguished the prophet Elijah, should, by his preaching and ministry, prepare the way of his glorious Lord, ch. iii. iv. See Luke i. 76; Matt. xi. 12—14.

The most remarkable thing in the prophecy of Malachi is, the inviting representation of Messiah's advent, as the Sun of Righteousness, communicating abundant spiritual blessings to those who feared God, ch. iv. 2.

References in Malachi.

Ch. i. 2—4.	Rom. ix. 13.	Ch. iv. 2.	Luke i. 78; Eph. v. 14; 2 Pet. i. 19.
— — 14.	1 Tim. i. 17; vi. 15.		
— ii. 15.	Matt. xix. 4, 5.		
— iii. 2, 3.	—— iii. 10—12.	— — 5.	Matt. xi. 14; xvii. 11, 12.
— — 17.	Tit. ii. 14.		

After a period of nearly 4000 years, "the testimony of Jesus, which is the spirit of prophecy," in the divine oracles of the Old Testament, ceased with the predictions of Malachi. He terminated the illustrious succession of those "holy men of God, who spake as they were moved by the Holy Ghost." He sealed up the roll of Old Testament prophecy, by proclaiming the future, but certain and sudden appearance of the Lord, whom the pious sought in his temple, to be preceded by his herald messenger, who should prepare His way before Him. The fulfilment of these predictions, in the preaching of John the Baptist, and the ministry and miracles of Jesus, during the existence of the temple, as recorded in the New Testament, proving Him to be the true Messiah, cannot be read by the pious without gratitude and joy. May every reader attend to these truths with faith and prayer, lest, like the unbelieving Jews, he perish in his sins, neglecting so great salvation!

Chapter XV.

CHRONOLOGICAL ORDER OF THE BOOKS OF THE OLD TESTAMENT.

HISTORICAL, ETHICAL, AND DEVOTIONAL BOOKS.

Names.	Supposed Authors.	Dates in years before Christ.
1. Genesis	Moses	From 4004 to 1635.
2. Job	Do.	2180 or 2130.
3. Exodus	Do.	From 1635 to 1490.
4. Leviticus	Do.	1490.
5. Numbers	Do.	From 1490 to 1451.
6. Deuteronomy	Do.	1451.
7. Joshua	Joshua	From 1451 to 1425.
8. Judges	Samuel	From 1425 to 1120.
9. Ruth	Do.	From 1241 to 1231.
10. 1 Samuel	Compiled by Samuel, Nathan, Gad, and others.	From 1171 to 1055.
11. 2 Samuel		From 1055 to 1015.
12. Psalms	David and others	At various times — Those by David from 1060 to 1015.
13. Solomon's Song	Solomon	About 1010.
14. Proverbs	Do.	About 1000.
15. Ecclesiastes	Do.	About 977.
16. 1 Kings	Nathan, Gad, Ahijah, Iddo, Isaiah, and others	1 Kings from 1015 to 896.
17. 2 Kings		2 Kings from 896 to 562.
18. 1 Chronicles	Ezra and others	From 4004 to 536.
19. 2 Chronicles		
20. Esther	Ezra	From 521 to 495.
21. Ezra	Do.	From 536 to 456.
22. Nehemiah	Nehemiah	From 455 to 420.

CHRONOLOGICAL ORDER OF THE PROPHETICAL BOOKS.

Name.	Before Christ. Between the years	Kings of Judah.	Kings of Israel.
23. Jonah,	856 and 784.	Joash, Amaziah, or Azariah.	Jehu and Jehoahaz, or Joash and Jeroboam II.
24. Amos,	810 and 725.	Uzziah, ch. i. 1.	Jeroboam II. ch. i. 1.
25. Hosea,	810 and 725.	Uzziah, Jotham, Ahaz, Hezekiah.	Jeroboam II. ch. i. 1.
26. Isaiah,	810 and 698.	Uzziah, Jotham, Ahaz, Hezekiah, and Manasseh.	Zechariah, Shallum, Menahem, Pekaiah, Pekah, and Hosea.
27. Joel,	810 and 660, or later.	Uzziah or Manasseh.	Ditto.
28. Micah,	758 and 699.	Jotham, Ahaz, and Hezekiah, ch. i. 1.	Pekah and Hosea.
29. Nahum,	720 and 698.	About the close of Hezekiah's reign.	
30. Zephaniah,	640 and 609.	Josiah, ch. i. 1.	
31. Jeremiah,	628 and 586.	Josiah.	
32. Lamentations,	586.		
33. Habakkuk,	612 and 598.	Jehoiakim.	
34. Daniel,	606 and 534.	During the whole of the captivity.	
35. Obadiah,	588 and 583.	Soon after the siege of Jerusalem by Nebuchadnezzar.	
36. Ezekiel,	595 and 536.	Captivity.	
37. Haggai,	About 520 or 518.	After the return from Babylon.	
38. Zechariah,	520 and 510.		
39. Malachi,	436 and 397.		

CHRONOLOGICAL ARRANGEMENT OF THE PSALMS.

The following Table has been compiled chiefly from the valuable work of the Rev. G. Townsend, compared with the arrangement of Calmet and others, and contains all that is known respecting the authors, occasions, and dates of the several Psalms.

Dates.		Numbers.	Authors supposed.	Probable Occasions.	Scripture Connexion.
A. M.	B. C.				
2473	1531	88	Heman	Affliction of Israel in Egypt	Exod. ii. 23, 25.
2514	1490	90	Moses	Shortening of man's life	Numb. xiv. 26—35.
2941	1063	9	David	Victory over Goliath	1 Sam. xvii. 4, 54.
2942	1062	11	Ditto	Advised to flee to the mountains	—— xix. 2, 3.
		59	Ditto	Saul's soldiers surrounding his house	—— 11.
		56	Ditto	With the Philistines at Gath	—— xxi. 10.
		34	Ditto	Leaving the city of Gath	—— 15.
		142	Ditto	In the cave of Adullam	—— xxii. 1.
		17	Ditto	Priests murdered by Doeg	—— 17, 19.
		52, 100, 35, 140	Ditto	Persecution by Doeg	—— 20—23.
2943	1051	64, 31	Ditto	Persecution by Saul	—— xxiii. 12.
		54	Ditto	Treachery of the Ziphites	—— 19, 23.
		57, 58	Ditto	Refusal to kill Saul	—— xxiv. 4, 11.
		63	Ditto	In the wilderness of Engedi	—— 22.
2946	1058	141	Ditto	Driven out of Judea	—— xxvii. 1.
2956	1048	139	Ditto	Made king of Israel	1 Chron. xii. 40.
2962	1042	68	Ditto	First removal of the ark	2 Sam. vi. 2, 11.
		24, 132, 105, 96, 106	Ditto	Second removal of the ark	{ 1 Chron. xv. 1, 28. xvi. 1—43.
2964	1040	2, 45, 22, 16, 118, 110	Ditto	Nathan's prophetic address	—— xvii. 2, 27.
2968	1036	60, 108	Ditto	Conquest of Syria and Edom by Joab	—— xviii. 13.
2970	1034	20, 21	Ditto	War with the Ammonites and Syrians	2 Sam. x. 6—19.
		6, 51, 32, 38, 39, 40, 41, 103	Ditto	Adultery, and murder of Uriah	—— xii. 13.
2983	1021	3	Ditto	Flight from Absalom	—— xv. 14—30.
		7	Ditto	The reproaches of Shimei	—— xvi. 5, 12.

CHRONOLOGICAL ARRANGEMENT OF THE PSALMS. (Continued.)

Dates A.M.	B.C.	Numbers.	Authors supposed.	Probable Occasions.	Scripture Connexion.
2983	1021	42, 43, 55, 4, 5, 62, 143, 144, 70, 71	David	Near Jordan, in the flight from Absalom	2 Sam. xvii. 24, 29.
2986	1018	18	Ditto	Conclusion of his wars	—— xxii. 1, 51.
2987	1017	30	Ditto	Dedication of Araunah's threshing floor	1 Chron. xxi. 26, 30.
2989	1015	91	Ditto	After his advice to Solomon	—— xxviii. 9, 10.
		72	Ditto	Coronation of Solomon	—— xxix. 10, 23.
		145	Ditto	A review of his past life	—— 26, 27.
		8, 12, 19, 23, 28, 29, 33, 61, 65, 63, 86, 95, 101, 104, 120, 121, 122, 124, 131, 132, 133	Ditto	Occasions and dates unknown.	
3000	1004	47, 97, 98, 99, 100	Solomon	Removal of the ark into the temple	2 Chron. v. 1—13.
		135, 136	Ditto	Dedication of the temple	—— vi. 1—42.
3074	930	78	Asaph	Asa's victory over Israel	—— xvi. 6, 9.
3108	896	82, 115, 46	Asaph and others	The reign of Jehoshaphat	—— xx. 21.
3294	710	44	Hezekiah	The blasphemy of Rab-shakeh	2 Kings xix. 10, 13.
		73, 75, 76	Asaph	Destruction of Sennacherib's army	—— 35.
3416	588	74, 79, 83, 94	Ditto	Burning of the temple at Jerusalem	Jer. xxxix. 2, 10.
3416	588	137, 130, 80, 77, 37, 67, 49, 53, 50, 10, 13, 14, 15, 25, 26, 27, 36, 89, 92, 93, 123	Asaph, Ethan and others	During the Babylonian captivity	Dan. vi. 28.
3466	538	102	Daniel	Near the close of the captivity	—— ix. 2.
3468	536	126, 85	Sons of Korah	The decree of Cyrus for restoring the Jews	Ezra i. 1—4.
3468	536	107, 87, 111, 112, 113, 114, 116, 117, 125, 127, 128, 134	Various	The return of the Jews from captivity	—— iii. 1—7.
3469	535	84, 66	Sons of Korah	Foundation of the second temple	—— 10—13.
3470	534	129	Ezra or Nehemiah	Opposition of the Samaritans	—— iv. 24.
3485	519	138	Haggai or Zech.	Rebuilding of the temple	—— vi. 1—14.
3489	515	48, 81, 146, 147, 148, 149, 150	Various	Dedication of the second temple	Zech. viii. 3, 23.
3560	444	1, 119	Ezra	Manual of devotion	Neh. xiii. 3.

Ch. XVI.—Jewish History between the Times of the Old and New Testament.

Malachi, the last of the sacred prophets of the Old Testament, in closing his ministry, foretold the advent of our Lord and Saviour Jesus Christ, and the coming of his forerunner John the Baptist, about four hundred years before those momentous events. During that interval, various changes took place among the Jews, by which their national character and condition were greatly affected; and the knowledge of these, from the best historical sources, must be desirable and important to every reader of the Bible: a few brief notices, therefore, of that period will be given in this chapter.

Nehemiah was contemporary with Malachi; but how long he lived at Jerusalem after his reformation of the religious and political affairs of the Jews, we have no means of precisely ascertaining: it appears probable that he died some time before the prophet. After his decease, Judea appears to have been added to the prefecture of Syria; and it remained altogether subject to the Persian governor of that province, under whom the high priest prescribed and enforced such laws of general policy as he might think proper, or the state of things required. But though the Jews were thus permitted to regulate their internal affairs, they enjoyed but an imperfect liberty; and even the high priest himself was appointed by the governor.

Alexander the Great, procuring himself to be chosen general of the Grecian forces against the Persians, defeated their army in Cilicia, under Darius their sovereign, b. c. 333. He then subdued all Syria and Phœnicia, and marched into Judea, to punish the Jews for supplying his enemies with provisions, while they refused such assistance to him. Jaddua, the high priest, hearing of his approach, called upon the people to unite with him in sacrifices and prayer, that God would avert the threatening calamity. Having humbled themselves before the Lord, it was communicated to Jaddua in a

dream, that he should go and meet the conqueror, robed in his pontifical habits, and accompanied by all the priests in their sacerdotal garments. Attended by a numerous body of the people dressed in white, they thus marched in solemn procession to an eminence called Sapha, which commanded a view of the temple and of the whole city. The king approached, but was so struck with profound awe at the extraordinary spectacle, that instead of indulging in revenge, he hastened forward and saluted the man of God with religious veneration. All stood amazed at his singular behaviour; and Parmenio, a favourite of the king, asked the reason of this act of unexpected homage. To this Alexander is said to have replied, that the worship was not offered to the priest, but to his God; in grateful acknowledgment for a vision at Dio, in Macedonia; in which this very priest, and in this very habit, appeared to him, promising to give him the empire of Persia.

Having cordially embraced Jaddua, it is said that Alexander entered Jerusalem, and offered up sacrifices in the temple to Jehovah, the God of Israel. The high priest showed him the prophecies of Daniel, which foretold the subversion of the Persian empire by a Grecian king: by reading these, Alexander went against Darius with still greater confidence of success in his expedition; and, at the request of Jaddua, granted the Jews the free exercise of their religion, the observance of their laws, and exemption from the payment of tribute every seventh year, in which the law required that they should neither reap nor sow. Alexander defeated the numerous army of Darius, and the predictions of Daniel were accomplished in his overthrow of the Persians, Dan. ii. 39; viii. 2, 5, 7, 20, 21; x. 20; xi. 2—4.

The Grecian conqueror greatly favoured the Jews; and Egypt having submitted to his power, he built Alexandria, and induced multitudes of that people to settle in the new city, granting them equal privileges with the Macedonians. This mighty conqueror died, aged only thirty-two years, B. C. 323; all his family were murdered, and four of his generals divided among

themselves the vast dominions of their royal master, as foretold by the prophet Daniel, ch. viii. 8, 20, 23; xi. 2, 4.

Egypt fell to the lot of Ptolemy Lagus, who invaded Judea, and led a hundred thousand of its people captives into his country: but treating them liberally, many were glad to follow their brethren, on account of the miserable condition into which wars had plunged their native land.

In the year B. C. 292, Simon, surnamed the just, high priest of the Jews, died. He was a man of singular wisdom and virtue, and the last of the men of the great synagogue, consisting of one hundred and twenty persons, appointed by Ezra for perfecting the restoration of the Jewish church. Simon the just, it is considered, made the last revision of the books of the Old Testament, and completed the sacred canon by adding the books of Chronicles, Ezra, Nehemiah, Esther, and Malachi.

The Jews in Egypt forgetting the Hebrew language, procured the sacred books to be translated into Greek for their use, and a copy of the five books of Moses was placed in the royal library of Ptolemy Philadelphus, about the year B. C. 284, and subsequently a copy of the whole collection. This translation of the Scriptures into Greek, which is called the Septuagint, became commonly used in all the churches of the Jews wherever they were dispersed. "This version, therefore," as Rollin observes, "which renders the scriptures of the Old Testament intelligible to a vast number of people, became one of the most considerable fruits of the Grecian conquests. In this manner did God prepare the way for the preaching of the gospel, which was then approaching, and facilitate the union of so many nations, of different languages and manners, into one society, and the same worship and doctrines, by the instrumentality of the finest, most copious, and correct language that was ever spoken in the world, and which became common to all the countries that were conquered by Alexander."

For more than a century, Judea suffered grievously in the continual wars of Alexander's successors; especially

from Antiochus, king of Syria, surnamed by himself Epiphanes, the illustrious, but by others, Epimanes, the madman. He deposed Onias, the pious high priest of the Jews, and sold the sacred office, for an annual tribute of 360 talents, to his brother Jason. Him he soon deposed, and again sold it to his brother Menelaus for 660 talents. On a false report that Epiphanes was dead, Jason attempted to recover the priesthood; with a thousand soldiers he entered Jerusalem, and by the sword, and with various torments, he put to death all whom he considered his adversaries. Antiochus having heard that the Jews rejoiced at his death, and supposing that all the nation had revolted, took Jerusalem by storm, the year B. C. 170: he slew 40,000 persons, and sold as many more for slaves; and plundered the temple of its splendid furniture to the amount of 800 talents of gold. In contempt of the God of Israel, he entered the holy of holies, and sacrificed a sow upon the altar of burnt offering. Antiochus then returned to Antioch, laden with the riches of his spoils, appointing Philip, a barbarous Phrygian, governor of Judea; Andronicus, a wicked wretch, to preside in Samaria; and the unprincipled Menelaus to the high priesthood.

In his fourth expedition to Egypt, ambassadors from the Roman people arrived, and threatened him with the vengeance of their victorious legions unless he withdrew his forces. Infuriated to madness by their authoritative interference, he led back his army through Palestine, and despatched Apollonius with twenty thousand of his soldiers, with orders to destroy Jerusalem, to put to the sword all the men, and to make slaves of all the women and children. These commands were executed with savage fierceness on the sabbath day, when the people were assembled for public worship; and none escaped but those who could reach the mountains by flight, or who concealed themselves in caverns of the earth. The city was spoiled of its riches by these impious invaders, and set on fire in several places: they broke down its walls and demolished the principal houses; and with the materials they erected a strong fortress on Mount

Acra; which, overlooking the temple, the garrison were ready to sally forth and murder those who dared to approach it as worshippers.

On his arrival at Antioch, Antiochus published a decree, requiring all people in his dominions to conform to the religion of the Greeks; and Atheneus was commissioned to instruct the Jews in the Grecian idolatrous ceremonies, and to put to death with the most grievous torments those who refused compliance with his abominable commands. Arriving at Jerusalem, he obtained the co-operation of some apostate Jews: he put down the daily sacrifice; suppressed all the public and private observances of the Jewish religion; defiled the temple of God itself, and rendered that sacred edifice unfit for sacred worship. He also sought out every copy of the Scriptures, and burnt all that could be found: he dedicated the temple of Jehovah to Jupiter Olympus, erected his statue on the altar of burnt offering, and punished with death all that could be found who had acted contrary to the decree of his sovereign.

Mattathias, a venerable priest of the Asmonean family, with his five sons, John, Simon, Judas, Eleazar, and Jonathan, retired from the persecution at Jerusalem to their native city Modin, in the tribe of Dan. They were followed by Apelles, an officer of the king, who strove to compel them to observe the commands of Antiochus. The people being called together, Apelles addressed Mattathias to engage his compliance with the idol worship, promising him a reward of great honour and riches. The aged priest not only rejected his offers, but slew the first apostate Jew who approached the idolatrous altar. He also rose upon the king's agent, and, with the assistance of his sons, put him to death with all his attendants, demolished the idols and their altars, and then withdrew to the mountains. Being joined by a number of his faithful countrymen, he marched through Judea; broke down the heathen altars in all the cities; restored circumcision; cut off the ministers of the idols, and those Jews who had apostatized to their abominations, and re-established the true

worship of God, B. C. 167. Mattathias died the next year, appointing his son, Judas, surnamed Maccabeus, to succeed him in the command of the army, which was soon joined by many who were zealous for the law of God. He defeated several large armies of Antiochus under his bravest commanders, recovered Jerusalem, purified the temple, restored the appointed worship of God, and repaired the city, which had been reduced to almost a heap of ruins, B. C. 165. Transported with rage at the defeat of his generals, Antiochus threatened to exterminate the whole nation of the Jews, and make Jerusalem their common burial place: but while these proud words were passing over his lips, the judgment of Heaven fell upon him; he was smitten with an incurable disease, with grievous torments in his bowels, and an intolerable ulcer, breeding vermin, by which his guilty life was terminated, B. C. 164. His son Eupator, under Lysias his general, engaged the neighbouring nations to unite in destroying the whole race of the Jews; but Judas, hearing of the alliance, carried the war into the countries of his enemies, and became a terrible scourge to the Syrians, Idumeans, and Arabians. Judas died in battle, B. C. 161, and was succeeded by his brother Jonathan; who, with Simon his brother, continued to manage the affairs of his people with singular bravery and prudence.

Onias, the high priest, having settled in Egypt, Jonathan assumed the sacerdotal office at Jerusalem, uniting it with the honour of civil governor, and formed an alliance with the Romans, B. C. 161. Jonathan being slain at Ptolemais, by the treachery of Tryphon, who had usurped the throne of Syria, Simon was chosen to succeed him, B. C. 144; and after a reformation at Jerusalem, he rendered the Jews independent of foreign nations. Having made a tour through the cities of Judea, for the purpose of promoting their peace and order, his son-in-law, Ptolemy, entertained him in his castle of Dochus, at Jericho, and murdered him, with his sons Judas and Mattathias, B. C. 135.

Simon was succeeded in the government and priest-

hood by his son John Hyrcanus, who extended his authority to several adjacent provinces; he destroyed the Samaritan temple on Mount Gerizim, B. C. 130, after it had stood two hundred years, and compelled the Idumeans to embrace the Jewish religion. He renewed the alliance with the Romans, by which he secured considerable advantages for his nation, and died, B. C. 107, leaving the sovereignty and priesthood to his son Aristobulus. This prince raised Judea again into a monarchy, and was the first after the captivity who assumed to himself the title of king. He was succeeded by his son Alexander Janneus, who compelled the Philistines to embrace the profession of the Jewish faith, B. C. 97. He reigned twenty-seven years, and died through intemperance, B. C. 79.

The Roman alliance was now found to be prejudicial to the interests of the Jews, who suffered much through the civil discords of Rome. The royal and pontifical dignity became a subject of violent contention, and the assistance of the Romans being called in by Aristobulus, against his elder brother Hyrcanus, Pompey seated Hyrcanus on the throne, but made Judea a tributary province of the Roman empire, B. C. 63. Pompey, with some of his officers, impiously entered the holy of holies; and Crassus, governor of Syria, pillaged the temple of ten thousand talents of silver, B. C. 54.

Soon after, Antipater, a crafty nobleman of Idumea, by the favour of Julius Cæsar, was made procurator of Judea, B. C. 47, while Hyrcanus retained the priesthood. Antipater was succeeded by his son Herod the Great; who, being assisted by Antony, the Roman triumvir, through much bloodshed, obtained the royal dignity, B. C. 40. His authority was confirmed by Augustus Cæsar, B. C. 30, and he maintained his dignity with distinguished ability, but also with most atrocious cruelty. During his long reign he built many cities; and to ingratiate himself with the Jews, he almost rebuilt their temple, Mark xiii. 1; John ii. 20. His inhuman barbarity towards the children of Bethlehem, in attempting to murder the infant Jesus, is recorded by the evangelist

Matthew. Herod died soon afterwards, suffering the most dreadful torments. Under the government of his sons, Judea became more fully recognised as a Roman province; "the fulness of the time was come," as determined in the sure purpose of God; "Shiloh," the 'Prince of peace," came, according to the prophecy given by the Holy Spirit from the lips of dying Jacob, Gen. xlix. 10; Messiah finished his work of redemption, "making reconciliation for iniquity, and bringing in everlasting righteousness," Dan. ix. 24, 26, when "the middle wall of partition between Jew and Gentile was broken down," Eph. ii. 14; the Divine dispensation of sovereign mercy to all nations of mankind was introduced by the ambassadors of Christ; and, after being under the direction of Roman procurators for some years, "the sceptre," or tribal government, "departed from Judah," Gen. xlix. 10; the whole Jewish state, with its appointed ceremonial and magnificent temple, was altogether subverted, A. D. 70, by Titus, son of the emperor Vespasian; and the unbelieving Jews were banished from their own land, and scattered throughout the world, living monuments of the truth and divinity of Christianity!

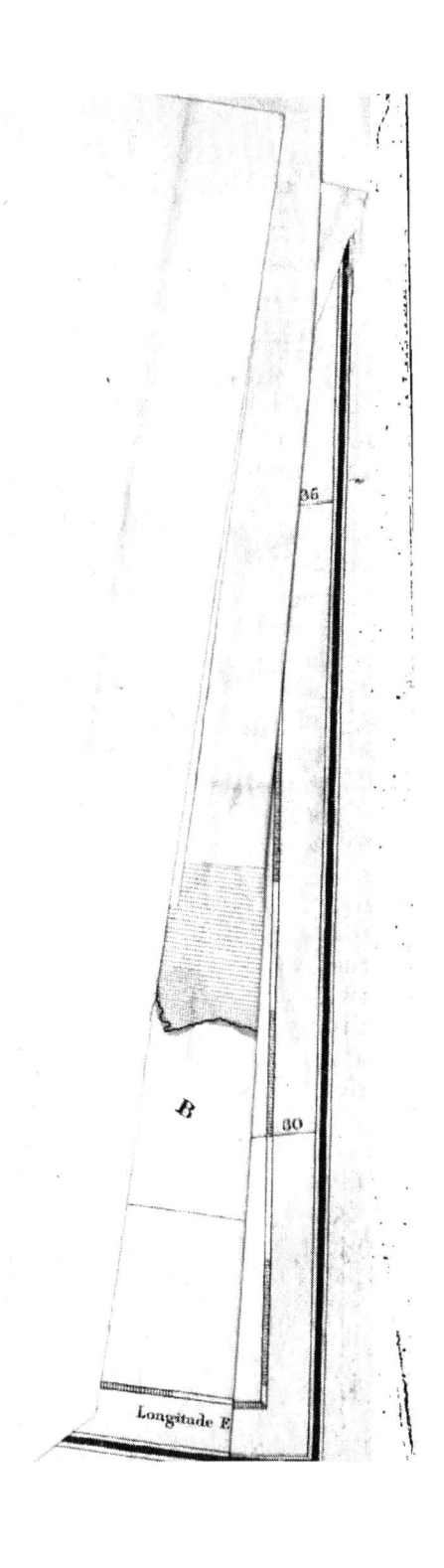

THE NEW TESTAMENT.

Chapter XVII.—Title of the New Testament.

The title Testament, which is given more especially to this latter part of the Holy Scriptures, is taken from a Greek word, which properly signifies covenant. It is translated testament in Matt. xxvi. 28; Heb. ix. 15—17; but covenant, Heb. viii. 7—9, and in most other places. The Christians, in the primitive ages, adopted the present title for this volume of the Scriptures, because it records the free promises of God's covenant mercy and grace to penitent and believing sinners: these promises being ratified by the death of Christ, as a sacrifice for the sin of the world. It is not improperly called the New Testament, because it comprises those sacred writings in which the heavenly inheritance of Christians is sealed to them, as the adopted sons and daughters of God Almighty, through Jesus Christ, Heb. ix. 15—17.

The books of the New Testament are twenty-seven in number; and they are commonly classed in three divisions:—historical, doctrinal, and prophetical. Of the first class are the Gospels according to the records of the evangelists Matthew, Mark, Luke, and John, and the Acts of the Apostles. The second class includes twenty-one Epistles, or letters, which were addressed by the apostles to several of the first churches of Christ, and to individual Christians. The book of the Revelation constitutes the third division of the New Testament.

The term Gospel is more generally applied to the writings of the four evangelists, containing the histories of the life and ministry, the death and resurrection of Jesus Christ our Saviour: but it is sometimes applied to the whole New Testament. The word gospel is formed from two old Saxon words; the first, *god*, signifying good, and *spel*, signifying a speech or tidings; it is intended to denote the glad tidings of divine forgiveness and eternal salvation by Jesus Christ, which God has commanded to be preached and sent to all

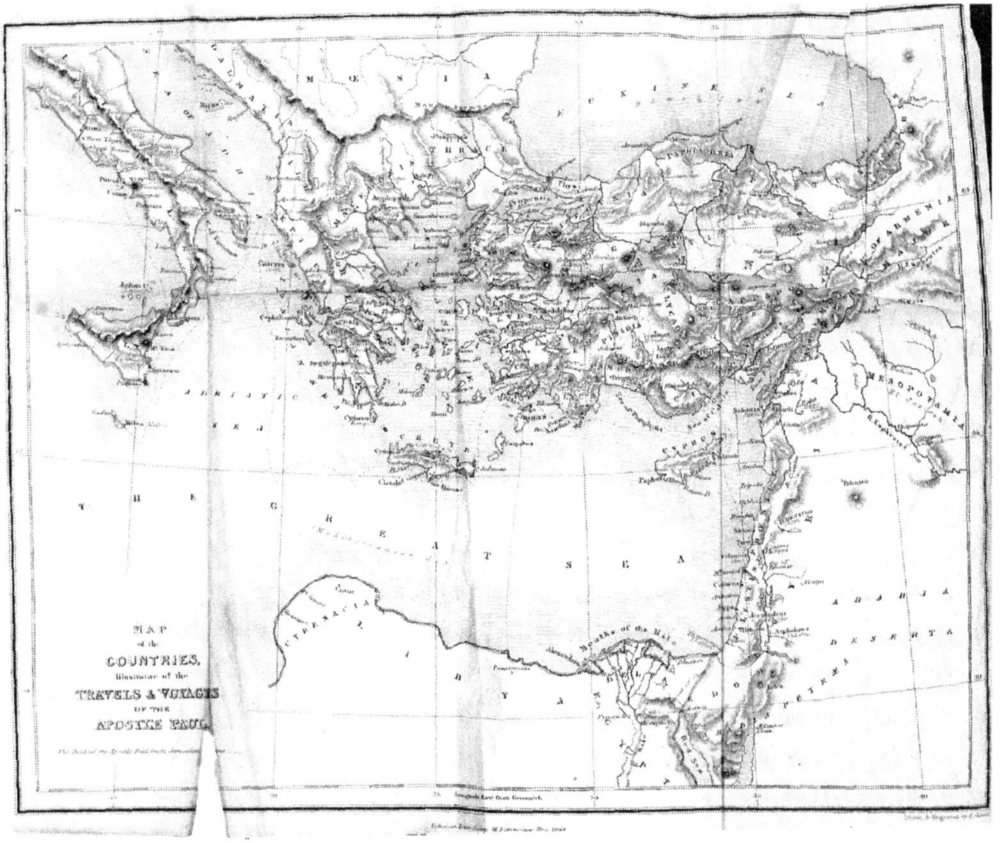
MAP
of the
COUNTRIES,
illustrative of the
TRAVELS & VOYAGES
OF THE
APOSTLE PAUL
M Œ S I A
T H R A C E
A R M E N I A
M E S O P O T A M I A
C Y P R U S
C R E T E
A D R I A T I C
S E A
T H E G R E A T S E A
Mouths of the Nile
C Y R E N A I C A
L I B Y A
A R A B I A
D E S E R T A
Longitude East from Greenwich

nations and people upon the earth, as the doctrine of life everlasting through the Redeemer.

Ch. XVIII.—Biography of the Writers of the New Testament.

To the reader of the New Testament, it will be of no small importance to have present to his mind the chief particulars which may be included in a short sketch of the life and character of those holy men, who were the inspired writers of the sacred books. Their writings, which are the only rule of our faith and practice, convey several points of valuable instruction, in connexion with their personal history, as the founders of the Christian church.

1. MATTHEW.

Matthew, or Levi, which was perhaps his surname, the apostle and evangelist, was the son of Alpheus, and a native of Galilee. Before his call to the apostleship, he was a publican, or tax-collector, in the employ of the Roman government, at Capernaum. This was an office of very bad repute among the Jews, partly because of the covetous exactions of those who were appointed to it, and partly because it was a proof of their being subject to a foreign power. Matthew was a custom-house officer, and his business consisted in collecting the duties on all the merchandise that came by the sea of Galilee to Capernaum, and the tribute payable by passengers who travelled by water. This lucrative post he cheerfully relinquished for the sake of Christ, on whom he became a faithful attendant, and was an eye-witness of his miracles.

Matthew continued with the rest of the apostles till after the ascension of Christ; but little is known of him subsequently to that event. It is related of him, that for eight years he preached the gospel in Judea, and then went to promulgate the faith of Christ among the Gentiles. He laboured to evangelize Ethiopia, Persia, and

Parthia, and at length suffered martyrdom at Nadabbar, in Asiatic Ethiopia, being slain by a halbert, A. D. 62. His only writings are the evangelical history, which bears his name.

2. MARK.

Mark, the evangelist, whose Hebrew name was John, was the son of a pious woman of Jerusalem, at whose house the apostles and first Christians frequently met for prayer, Acts xii. 12. He is supposed to have been converted by the ministry of Peter, who, therefore, calls him his son, 1 Pet. v. 13. Mark accompanied Paul and Barnabas in their missionary labours through several countries: but, declining to attend them through their whole progress, he returned to the apostles at Jerusalem, Acts xiii. 5—13. We find him afterwards at Antioch, Acts xv. 37, whence he went with Barnabas to Cyprus. He subsequently was with Peter at Babylon, which is supposed to have been the chief settlement of the Jews dispersed in the East, 1 Pet. v. 13. Afterwards he visited Paul at Rome, Col. iv. 10, and thence took another missionary journey, returning with Timothy to the apostle Paul at Rome, 2 Tim. iv. 11. He is said to have written his Gospel at Rome.

Mark is said to have been sent by Peter to advance the cause of Jesus Christ in Egypt. His ministry was eminently successful in Libya, Marmorica, and Pentapolis. He returned to Alexandria, where he suffered various severe persecutions from the idolatrous rabble, at the time of celebrating one of the great festivals of Serapis, an Egyptian divinity, and died of the wounds his enemies inflicted on him, as they were repeating their torments after a night of imprisonment.

3. LUKE.

Luke, the evangelist, was a native of Antioch, and by profession a physician. Some suppose he was one of the seventy disciples of Christ, but this appears incorrect from his own statement at the beginning of his Gospel. He was the faithful and constant companion of Paul in

his various travels, labours, and sufferings. He wrote his Gospel in Achaia, about A. D. 63, and the Acts of the Apostles about A. D. 64. Both these books were dedicated particularly to a Christian of distinction named Theophilus, as is supposed, an Egyptian. By some, Luke is said to have suffered martyrdom under the Roman emperor Nero; but others affirm that he was hanged upon an olive tree in Greece by a party of pagans.

4. JOHN.

John, the evangelist and apostle, was the son of Zebedee, a fisherman of Bethsaida, a town of Galilee. He and his brother James were called by Christ to be his apostles; and, on account of their powerful eloquence, they were surnamed by him, Boanerges, or sons of thunder. John was pre-eminently beloved by his Lord; and to his affection, when on the cross, he committed the care of his mother. Leaving Judea before the destruction of Jerusalem, he laboured chiefly in Asia Minor, particularly at Ephesus. The churches in Pergamos, Thyatira, Philadelphia, and Laodicea, are believed to have been founded by him. In the persecution under Domitian, the Roman emperor, John is said to have been put into a caldron of boiling oil, in which he stood four hours unhurt. Being taken out, he was banished to labour in the mines, in the desolate and rocky isle of Patmos, where he was favoured with the glorious visions of the exalted Saviour, and was inspired to write the book of the Revelation. From this island he returned the next year, and resided chiefly at Ephesus, until about A. D. 100, when, beloved by all, and at the advanced age of about a hundred years, he died in peace among his fellow Christians. The three Epistles, and the Gospel, which bear the name of John, were written by this apostle.

5. PAUL.

Paul was an Israelite of the tribe of Benjamin, and a Hebrew of the Hebrews, as both of his parents were Hebrews. He was a native of Tarsus, in Cilicia, and by

birth a free citizen of imperial Rome. Before his call to the apostleship, he was known by his Hebrew name Saul; but he used Paul, his Roman name, among the Gentiles. His parents sent him early to Jerusalem, to study the Jewish law under the direction of Gamaliel, the most celebrated doctor of his nation. The improvement of the pupil corresponded with the fame of his master, and all his influence and talents were devoted to preserve the Jewish traditionary corruptions, to destroy the church of Christ, and to extirpate even the name of Christian. But in the very midst of his murderous career, while "breathing out threatenings and slaughter against the disciples of the Lord," sovereign grace and mercy arrested him in his progress, and renewed his heart, when he consecrated all his powers to the service of Christ! Never, perhaps, was any man so entirely devoted to glorify God, and to promote the best interests of mankind; never, probably, did any disciple of the Saviour exhibit so eminent an example of Christian virtues and benevolent labours, as this chosen vessel of the Lord. It has been said, that the consideration of the conversion and apostleship of Paul alone, must leave every infidel without excuse for his rejection of Christianity. After being the instrument of inestimable blessings to the church of God, by his preaching, example, and writings, he sealed the truth of the gospel with his blood, being beheaded at Rome, June 29, A. D. 66, by order of the emperor Nero. The fourteen Epistles of the apostle Paul are a treasure of inestimable value to the church of Jesus Christ.

6. JAMES.

James was called the Less, to distinguish him from James the brother of John, who was put to death by Herod, Acts xii. He was the son of Alpheus Cleophas, and he is called the Lord's brother, because he was of the kindred of the virgin Mary. On account of the admirable holiness of his life, he was surnamed the Just. He is mentioned as having been the first bishop of the Christian church at Jerusalem, where he was venerated

even by the Jews for his sanctity. However, Ananias the high priest, with the scribes and Pharisees, called him, at the passover, to stand upon the porch of the temple, to satisfy the doubting minds of the people concerning the faith of Christ; but being enraged that his doctrine was received by many, they threw him down from the battlements; and, while he was praying for his barbarous murderers, some of them beat him on the head with a fuller's club, and killed him on the spot. Thus he was martyred by the lawless Jews, while the Roman governor was absent from Jerusalem, A. D. 62. This apostle wrote the Epistle which bears the name of James.

7. PETER.

Peter, son of Jonas, and brother of Andrew the apostle, was a native of Bethsaida. His original name was Simon, but Jesus called him Cephas, or, as it is interpreted, Peter, both words having the like signification, denoting a stone or rock, and intimating the great necessity of stability in faith and duty. Peter was among the most faithful and zealous of the disciples of Christ: but his zeal, on some occasions, led him even to precipitancy and rashness, which occasioned his dreadful fall and criminal denial of his Lord, and brought a foul blot upon his memory. His repentance, however, was equally remarkable, and his subsequent life and labours prove him to have been one of the most eminent of the disciples, and most useful of the apostles of Jesus Christ. Very little is known for certain of this distinguished minister of the gospel, besides what is mentioned in the New Testament, until the admission of the Gentiles into the church of Christ, Acts xv. The Roman catholics assert that he was bishop of Rome for twenty-five years; but we have no evidence of this as fact, nor any thing beyond contradictory tradition, that he ever was at Rome, much less that he was bishop of the Christian church in that city. Tradition reports that he came to Rome during the persecution under Nero; and that he was apprehended and put to death about three miles from the city. It is also said, that being sentenced to be crucified,

and remembering his shameful denial of his Saviour, he requested that he might be allowed to suffer with his head downwards, as unworthy to die in the same position as his Master, which was the manner of his punishment, A. D. 66. We possess two Epistles written by this devoted apostle of Christ.

8. JUDE.

Jude, or Lebbeus, the apostle, surnamed Thaddeus, was the brother of James the Less, and the writer of the Epistle which bears his name. At the commencement of his ministry he preached the gospel in Judea, Samaria, Galilee, and Idumea, and afterwards in Arabia, Syria, Mesopotamia, and Persia, confirming his doctrine with miracles. We have no certain information as to the place where he terminated his ministry, though it is related by some that the magi put him to death in Persia.

Ch. XIX.—Analysis of the Books of the New Testament.

MATTHEW.

MATTHEW wrote his Gospel for the use of the Hebrew Christians, and, as is supposed by some, in their own language, about five years after the ascension of Christ. This book is the only part of the New Testament which is believed to have been written in Hebrew: but as it existed very early both in Hebrew and Greek, it is concluded by the most learned and judicious critics that it was translated into Greek while Matthew was living, either by himself, or under his own immediate direction, about A. D. 60.

Matthew is divided into twenty-eight chapters, containing five principal sections.

Section I. Contains two chapters, which relate the genealogy of Christ from Abraham, and some particulars of his birth and infancy. In this section two things are remarkable.

1. The coming of the wise men to worship the child Jesus, and to offer gifts to him as the promised Messiah.

2. The special providence of God in frustrating the wicked designs of king Herod, while seeking to destroy the infant King and Saviour, ch. ii.

Sec. II. Includes two chapters, containing an account of John the Baptist, and of the entrance of Christ upon his public ministry, ch. iii. iv. In this section there are two things worthy of remark.

1. The character and ministry of John, ch. iii.

2. The baptism and temptation of Christ, ch. iii. iv.

Sec. III. Contains a record of the discourses and miracles of Christ, until his transfiguration, ch. v.—xvii. The most remarkable things in this section are,

1. Our Lord's sermon on the mount, ch. v.—vii.

2. A record of a series of miracles performed by Christ, ch. viii. ix.

3. The commission of the twelve apostles to preach the gospel, ch. x.

4. The confession of faith made by the apostles, ch. xvi.

5. The transfiguration of Christ, when Moses and Elijah appeared conversing upon the manner and design of his death, at Jerusalem, for our redemption, ch. xvii.

Sec. IV. Relates various discourses and miracles of Christ, from his transfiguration to the date of two days before his crucifixion, ch. xviii.—xxv. The most remarkable things recorded in this section are,

1. The entrance of Christ into Jerusalem, ch. xxi.

2. The Saviour's prophecy of the destruction of the city and temple, on account of the infidelity and wickedness of the Jews, ch. xxiv.

3. The description of the general judgment, ch. xxv.

Sec. V. Relates the sufferings, death, and resurrection of Christ. The most remarkable things contained in this affecting section are,

1. The awful wickedness of Judas, in betraying his Master with a kiss, ch. xxvi.

2. The sinful weakness of Peter, in denying his Lord, ch. xxvi.

CH. XIX.—ANALYSIS OF MARK.

3. The dreadful criminality of the Jews and of Pilate, in condemning and crucifying Christ, ch. xxvii.

4. The remorse of Judas, and his testimony to the innocency of Jesus, ch. xxvii.

5. The resurrection of Christ, the miracles by which it was attended, the proofs of its reality, and his commission to his apostles, ch. xxviii.

As Matthew wrote his Gospel for the confirmation of the Hebrew Christians, it was with peculiar propriety that he was directed to show how Christ, as the promised Messiah, descended from Abraham, by David; and that he was born at Bethlehem as foretold by the prophet Micah. Those passages also in the prophetical writings, which refer to the various offices and works of the Messiah, are more particularly noticed by this evangelist than by either of the others, especially for the satisfaction of the converted Jews.

References in Matthew.

Ch. i. 23.	Isa. vii. 14.	Ch. xii. 42.	2 Chron. ix. 1.
— ii. 2.	Num. xxiv. 17.	— xiii. 14.	Isa. vi. 9.
— — 6.	Mic. v. 2.	— — 35.	Psa. lxxviii. 2.
— — 15.	Hos. xi. 1.	— xv. 7.	Isa. xxix. 13.
— — 17.	Jer. xxxi. 15.	— — 30.	—— xxxv. 5, 6.
— — 23.	Judg. xiii. 5;	— xix. 7.	Deut. xxiv. 1.
	1 Sam. i. 11.	— xxi. 4.	Zech. ix. 9.
— iii. 3.	Isa. xl. 3.	— — 13.	Isa. lvi. 7.
— iv. 4.	Deut. viii. 3.	— — 42.	Psa. cxviii. 22.
— — 7.	—— vi. 16.	— xxii. 4.	Prov. ix. 2.
— — 14.	Isa. ix. 1, 2.	— — 24.	Deut. xxv. 5.
— x. 35.	Mic. vii. 6.	— — 44.	Psa. cx. 1.
— — 36.	Psa. xli. 9.	— xxiv. 15.	Dan. ix. 27.
— xi. 10.	Mal. iii. 1.	— xxvii. 9.	Zech. xi. 12, 13.
— xii. 3.	1 Sam. xxi. 6.	— — — 34.	Psa. lxix. 21
— — 5.	Num. xxviii. 9.	— — — 35.	— xxii. 18.
— — 7.	Hos. vi. 6.	— — — 38.	— liii. 12.
— — 42	1 Kings x. 1.	— — — 60.	Isa. — 9.

MARK.

The Gospel according to Mark is supposed to have been written about A. D. 61, under the direction of the apostle Peter, especially for the use of the Gentiles; to

whose conversion the ministry of that apostle had been effectual. It records most of the things contained in Matthew, with some few additional particulars, but in a more concise form. Considering the simplicity and perspicuity of the writing, and the momentous subjects which it narrates, this Gospel has been called "the shortest and clearest, the most marvellous, and at the same time the most satisfactory history in the world."

Mark is divided into sixteen chapters, containing three principal sections.

Section I. Records an account of the ministry of John the Baptist, and of the baptism and temptation of Christ, ch. i. 1—13.

Sec. II. Relates the miracles and discourses of Christ, from the commencement of his public ministry, to his last visit to Jerusalem at the passover, ch. i. 14—x. In this section some of the most remarkable things recorded are,

1. Some particulars relating to John the Baptist, ch. vi.

2. The account of the young ruler, who sacrificed his interest in the kingdom of heaven from his attachment to his worldly wealth, ch. x.

Sec. III. Contains an account of the triumphal entry of Christ into Jerusalem, his parables and discourses there, and his condemnation, death, resurrection, and commission to his apostles, all of which are most important and remarkable, ch. xi.—xvi.

References in Mark.

Ch. i. 2.	Mal. iii. 1.	Ch. ix. 3.	Dan. vii. 9.
— — 3.	Isa. xl. 3.	— — 11.	Mal. iv. 5.
— — 8.	Isa. xliv. 3.	— xi. 9.	Psa. cxviii. 26.
— ii. 25, 26.	1 Sam. xxi. 6;	— xii. 10.	— —— 22.
	Exod xxix.	— xiii. 26.	Dan. vii. 13, 14.
	32, 33.	— xiv. 25.	Joel iii. 18.
— vii. 35.	Isa. xxxv. 5, 6.	— xv. 28.	Isa. liii. 12.

LUKE.

The Gospel according to Luke, was written principally for the use of the Gentile Christians, and dedicated to

Theophilus, a nobleman of Egypt converted to the faith of Christ. It is divided into twenty-four chapters, containing four principal sections.

Section I. Relates the particulars of the birth of John the Baptist, and of Jesus, and of their early history until the baptism of Christ, ch. i.—iii. The things most remarkable in this section are,

1. The appearance of the angel Gabriel to the father of John, and afterwards to the virgin Mary, ch. i.

2. The birth of John, after which his father's speech was restored, ch. i.

3. The birth of Jesus, which an angel announced to the shepherds, ch. ii.

4. The wisdom of Jesus in conversation with the Jewish doctors in the temple, when he was only twelve years of age, ch. ii. 40—52.

Sec. II. Records many of the discourses and miracles of Christ, during the three years of his ministry, until he went into Judea, to his last passover, ch. iv.—ix. The things most remarkable in this section are,

1. The first discourse of Jesus Christ in the synagogue of Nazareth, where he had been brought up, ch. iv.

2. The coming of John's disciples to Christ when he was performing many miracles, ch. vii.

3. The healing of the man who had been possessed by a legion of devils, ch. viii.

Sec. III. Relates the discourses, parables, and works of Christ in Judea and at Jerusalem, until he was betrayed, ch. x.—xxi. The most remarkable things in this section are,

1. The commission of the seventy disciples to preach the gospel, ch. x.

2. The parables of the prodigal son, the rich man and Lazarus, and the Pharisee and publican, ch. xv. xvi.—xviii.

3. The conversion of the publican Zaccheus, ch. xix.

Sec. IV. Contains an account of the sufferings, death, resurrection, and ascension of Christ, ch. xxii.—xxiv. Besides the particulars of the Saviour's sufferings, which

are related by the other evangelists, the things most remarkable in this section are,

1. The conversion of the dying malefactor on the cross, ch. xxiii.
2. The conversation of Christ, after his resurrection, with the two disciples on the road to Emmaus, ch. xxiv.
3. The manner of Christ's ascension, ch. xxiv.

References in Luke.

Ch. i. 5.	1 Chron. xxiv. 10—19.	Ch. vii. 22.	Isa. xxxv. 5.
— — 9.	2 Chron. viii. 14.	— ix. 54.	2 Kings i. 10—12.
— — 32.	2 Sam. vii. 11,13; Isa. ix. 6,7.	— x. 27.	Deut. vi. 5; Lev. xix. 18.
— — 33.	Psa. cxxxii. 11.	— xi. 31.	1 Kings x. 1.
— — 55.	Gen. xvii. 19.	— — 50.	2 Chron. xxiv. 20, 21.
— — 79.	Isa. ix. 2.		
— ii. 34.	—— viii. 14.	— xiii. 6.	Isa. v. 2.
— — 42.	Exod. xxiii. 15—17; Deut. xvi. 1—16.	— — 34.	Mic. iii. 11, 12.
		— xvii. 26.	Gen. vii. 7—14.
		— — 28.	—— xix. 14.
— iii. 4.	Isa. xl. 3.	— xix. 38.	Psa. cxviii. 26.
— — 6.	—— lii. 10.	— xx. 17.	— —— 22.
— iv. 8.	Deut. vi. 13.	— xxi. 22.	Dan. ix. 26, 27.
— — 10.	Psa. xci. 11.	— xxiii. 11.	Isa. liii. 3.
— — 25.	1 Kings xvii. 9.	— xxiv. 46.	—— l. 6; liii. 2, etc.
— — 27.	2 Kings v. 1, 14.		

JOHN.

The precise year in which John wrote his Gospel is not agreed among the learned; some supposing it to have been written A. D. 69, before the destruction of Jerusalem; while others, among whom are some of the ancients, conclude it was written after his return from exile, A. D. 98. The particular reasons for the writing of this Gospel were, to preserve several of the most important and edifying discourses of Christ, not recorded by the other evangelists,—to destroy some pernicious heresies which had been promulgated by false teachers respecting the person and death of Christ,—and especially to establish the primitive Christians in their be-

lief of the proper Deity and humanity of their redeeming Lord and Saviour.

The Gospel of John is divided into twenty-one chapters, including five principal sections.

Section I. Relates several particulars concerning John the Baptist, and the first acts of Christ after his entrance upon his public ministry, ch. i. In this section it is especially worthy of remark, how plainly and fully the apostle declares that Jesus is the Son of God, that he was the Creator of all things, and that he was made man to take away the sin of the world, ver. 1—3, 14—29.

Sec. II. Records several discourses and actions of Christ until his last public appearance at Jerusalem, ch. ii.—xii. In this section the things most remarkable are,

1. The miracle of water being turned into wine, ch. ii.

2. The Saviour's discourse with Nicodemus respecting regeneration or the new birth, ch. iii.

3. The conversion of the woman of Samaria, ch. iv.

4. The important discourses of Christ with the Jews, ch. v.—x.

5. The wonderful narrative of Lazarus and his being raised from the dead, ch. xi.

Sec. III. Contains the affectionate discourses of Christ with his apostles before his death, ch. xiii.—xvii. In this section the most remarkable things recorded are,

1. The lesson of humility which the Saviour taught, by washing the feet of his disciples, ch. xiii.

2. The repeated promise of the Holy Spirit, as an extraordinary Comforter to the apostles, infallibly to instruct them for their mission, and as the abiding Comforter of the church, ch. xv. xvi.

3. The Saviour's prayer for his apostles, and for all believers in his name, ch. xvii.

Sec. IV. The account of Christ being betrayed, condemned, and crucified, ch. xviii. xix. That which is most remarkable in this section, in addition to the things recorded by the other evangelists, is—the affectionate care of his mother, shown by Jesus; who, when on the cross, committed her to the protection of John his beloved disciple, ch. xix.

Sec. V. Records some particulars of Christ's resurrection, and of his last discourses with his apostles, ch. xx. xxi. In this section the most remarkable things are,

1. The condescending kindness of Christ, in satisfying the doubts of the apostle Thomas, ch. xx.

2. The Saviour's affectionate discourse with repentant Peter, ch. xxi.

References in John.

Ch. i. 1.	Prov. viii. 22, 23—30.	Ch. vii. 37.	Isa. lv. 1.
— — 12.	Isa. lvi. 5.	— — 42.	1 Sam. xvi. 1-4.
— — 21.	Mal. iv 5; Deut. xviii. 15—18.	— x. 11.	Isa. xl. 11.
— — 23.	Isa. xl. 3.	— — 12.	Ezek. xxxiv. 12.
— — 45.	Deut. xviii. 18; Mic. v. 2.	— xii. 13.	Ps. cxviii. 25, 26.
— iii. 13.	Prov. xxx. 4.	— — 15.	Zech. ix. 9.
— iv. 5.	Gen. xxxiii. 19; Josh. xxiv. 32.	— — 34.	Ps. lxxix. 36, 37; Ezek. xxxvii. 25; Dan. vii. 13, 14.
— — 9.	2 Kings xvii. 24.	— — 41.	Isa. vi. 1—10.
— — 25.	Gen. iii. 15; xlix. 10.	— xiii. 18.	Psa. xli. 9.
— vi. 14.	Deut. xviii. 18.	— xix. 24.	— xxii. 18.
— — 31.	Exod. xvi. 15.	— — 28.	— lxix. 21.
— — 45.	Isa. liv. 13; Jer. xxxi. 34.	— — 31.	Deut. xxi. 23.
		— — 36.	Exod. xii. 46.
		— — 37.	Ps. xxii. 16, 17; Zech. xii. 10.
— vii. 35.	Isa. xi. 12.	— xxi. 25.	Amos vii. 10.

THE ACTS OF THE APOSTLES.

The book of the Acts of the Apostles is a kind of history of the ministry and actions of the apostles of Christ, and from which it derives its name. It forms a most desirable supplement to the four Gospels, and a necessary introduction to the several Epistles. It commences with relating the ascension of Christ, and declares the miraculous endowments of the apostles with requisite qualifications for the fulfilment of their extraordinary commission, and continues its records to the event of Paul's imprisonment at Rome, A. D. 65, including a period of more than thirty years. It shows the first planting of Christianity, and the gathering of Christian churches among both the Jews and Gentiles; the spread

of the gospel in several parts of the world; the patience and courage of some of the apostles under the various sufferings which they endured for the sake of it, and the marvellous success which attended them, all uniting to demonstrate the truth and divinity of Christianity.

Luke does not give a universal or general account of the first Christian churches, as he is silent concerning the labours of most of the apostles, and of the planting of Christianity in most of the eastern nations, in Egypt, and many other places in which it had been received. There are two things eminently conspicuous in the design of this book; first, to show the miraculous establishment of Christianity, by the gifts and graces of the Holy Spirit, both upon the apostles and the churches, agreeably to the promises of Christ: and, secondly, to develope the gracious purposes of the God of mercy, in bringing the Gentiles into his church, according to the Old Testament predictions. Considered merely as a human witness, Luke, the writer of this book, was better qualified than any other to draw up an authentic history of the apostles, as he was the faithful companion of Paul in many of his labours and journeys. Besides, as he was a physician, and a man of superior education, Luke was capable of forming a sound judgment upon the various miracles which were wrought by Paul; and from his testimony, so direct and circumstantial, we have convincing proofs of their divine reality.

The Acts of the Apostles is divided into twenty-eight chapters, containing six principal sections.

Section I. Relates the proceedings of the apostles during ten days at Jerusalem, until the feast of Pentecost, ch. i. In this section there are to be remarked,

1. The particulars relating to the ascension of Christ.
2. The unanimity of the first Christian church in the exercises of devotion.
3. Their election of a qualified disciple to be an apostle in the room of the traitor Judas.

Sec. II. Relates the first publication of Christianity as the gospel of salvation to all nations; and the rise

and progress of the church at Jerusalem, until the murder of Stephen, ch. ii.—vii. In this section the most remarkable things are,

1. The miraculous qualification of the apostles, by the gifts of the Holy Spirit, to prepare them to execute their apostolical commission, by preaching the gospel in all languages, ch. ii.

2. The addition to the church of about three thousand persons, as the effect of Peter's sermon in their conversion to Jesus Christ, ch. ii.

3. The healing of the man born a cripple, by Peter and John, ch. iii.

4. The addition to the church of several thousand more converts, ch. iv.

5. The vain threatenings of the Jewish council against the apostles, ch. iv.

6. The extraordinary liberality of the primitive believers, the effect of their eminent personal godliness, ch. iv.

7. The awful death of Ananias and of his wife Sapphira, as a judgment upon them for their hypocrisy and lying, ch. v.

8. The imprisonment of the apostles, ch. v.

9. The election of the seven deacons to manage the temporal affairs of the church, ch. vi.

10. The iniquitous condemnation, and the martyrdom of pious Stephen, ch. vii.

Sec. III. Records the persecution of the church at Jerusalem, the dispersion of the disciples, and the establishment of churches among the Gentiles, ch. viii.—xii. In this section the most remarkable things are,

1. The formation of a Christian church at Samaria, ch. viii.

2. The conversion of the Ethiopian nobleman, ch. viii.

3. The extraordinary conversion of the blood-thirsty persecutor Saul, ch. ix.

4. The preparation of Peter, by means of a divine vision, to welcome and invite the Gentiles into the church of Christ, ch. x.

5. The conversion of the Roman centurion Cornelius, and the establishment of a Christian church at Cesarea, ch. x.

6. The martyrdom of the apostle James, ch. xii.

7. The imprisonment of Peter, and his deliverance by an angel, ch. xii.

8. The judgment of God upon the impious king Herod, ch. xii.

Sec. IV. Narrates the labours of Paul and Barnabas until their separation, ch. xiii.—xv. In this section the things most remarkable are,

1. The special designation of Paul and Barnabas to labours among the Gentiles, ch. xiii.

2. The infliction of blindness upon Elymas the sorcerer, ch. xiii.

3. The preaching of the gospel to the Gentiles at Antioch, ch. xiii.

4. The healing of the cripple at Lystra, where Paul was stoned to death, and miraculously restored to life, ch. xiv.

5. The decision of the apostles, with the assembled church, concerning the Levitical ceremonies being of no obligation upon the Gentiles, ch. xv.

Sec. V. Contains an account of the labours of Paul among the Gentiles, from whom he gathered many Christian churches, ch. xvi.—xx. The most remarkable things in this section are,

1. The introduction of the gospel into Europe, ch. xvi.

2. The conversion of Lydia and the jailor at Philippi, and the formation of a church in that place, after Paul and Silas had been shamefully treated by the multitude and the magistrates, ch. xvi.

3. The formation of another Christian church in Europe, at Thessalonica, ch. xvii.

4. The preaching of the gospel at Athens, ch. xvii.

5. The conversion of much people at Corinth, and the formation of a church in that city, ch. xviii.

6. The conversion of those who used secret arts, or divinations, a sort of conjurors, at Ephesus, and the establishment of a church in that city, ch. xix.

7. The tumult excited by the silversmith Demetrius, in favour of the worship of the pretended goddess Diana, ch. xix.

8. The bringing to life of Eutychus, who had fallen from a window, when asleep, while Paul was preaching, ch. xx.

9. Paul's affectionate counsel and farewell address to the elders of Ephesus, ch. xx.

Sec. VI. Relates Paul's journey to Jerusalem, his persecution by the Jews, his appeal to Cæsar, and his being sent prisoner to Rome, ch. xxi.—xxviii. Among the most remarkable things in this section are,

1. The restless malignity of the Jews against the name of Christ, and their contrivances to kill Paul, ch. xxi.

2. Paul's address to the Jews from the castle stairs, ch. xxii.

3. Paul's defence of himself against the accusations of the Jews, before the Roman governor Felix, ch. xxiv.

4. Paul's defence of himself before the Roman governor Festus, ch. xxv.

5. Paul's declaration of his conversion to Christianity, before king Agrippa, who confesses himself almost persuaded to become a Christian, ch. xxvi.

6. Paul's dangerous voyage towards Rome, his shipwreck on the island of Malta, his arrival at Rome, and his being allowed to reside two years in his own hired house, preaching the gospel, even while wearing the badge of imprisonment, ch. xxvii. xxviii.

Every reader of the Acts of the Apostles must perceive the abundant and satisfactory evidence which this book affords of the truth and divinity of Christianity. The historical details of the advancement, progress, and triumphs of the gospel, among both Jews and Gentiles, prove that its establishment was the result, not of human policy, but of the power and grace of God accompanying the ministrations of the holiest, most benevolent, and most self-denying preachers that ever professed to seek the welfare of mankind. Their miraculous endowments, and their singleness of purpose, their perse-

verance amidst the greatest difficulties, and the fruit of their labours, in the recovery of multitudes from ignorance, superstition, and sin, to holiness and obedience to the laws of Christ, manifest their character as the servants of God. And the whole contents of the book, as a history of the planting of Christianity in the world, indicate it to be one of the most important and valuable portions of Holy Scripture.

References in Acts.

Ch. i. 3.	1 Cor. xv. 5.	Ch. iv. 8.	Luke xii. 11, 12.
— — 5.	See ch. ii. 2—6; Matt. iii. 11.	— — 25, 26.	Psa. ii. 1, 2.
		— vii. 42,43.	Amos v. 25, 26.
— — 9.	Luke xxiv. 51.	— — 52.	2 Chro. xxxvi 16.
— — 16.	Psa. xli. 9.	— ix. 40, 41.	1 Kings xvii. 21—23.
— — 20.	— cix. 8.		
— ii. 4.	Mark xvi. 17.	— xiii 34.	Isa. lv. 3.
— — 17, 39.	Joel ii. 28, 32.	— — 35.	Psa. xvi. 10.
— — 25, 28.	Psa. xvi. 8, 11.	— — 41.	Isa. xxix. 14.
— — 30.	2 Sam vii. 12,13	— — 47.	— xlix. 6.
— — 34.	Psa. cx. 1.	— xv. 16.	Amos ix. 11, 12.
— iii. 22.	Deut. xviii. 15—18.	— xxi. 11.	See ver. 33.
		— xxviii.26.	Isa. vi. 9.

EPISTLE TO THE ROMANS.

Rome was the metropolis of the world at the time this Epistle was written. By whom Christianity was introduced into that imperial city cannot be ascertained. Some of the ancient writers, however, supposed that the Roman church was planted by Peter and Paul. That Peter ever was at Rome there exists no satisfactory historic evidence; and it is plain that Paul had not been at Rome when he wrote this Epistle to the Christian church in that city, about A. D. 58; yet the faith of that church was spoken of throughout all the world, Rom. i. 8. It seems most probable that some of those " strangers of Rome, Jews and proselytes," who received the gospel at Jerusalem, Acts ii. 10, on their return laid the foundation of that flourishing Christian society. Paul had for a long time purposed to visit the Roman church, but being prevented, he was

CH. XIX.—ANALYSIS OF ROMANS.

inspired to write this Epistle for their instruction, exhibiting to them fully the whole gospel economy. The Epistle to the Romans is "a writing which, for sublimity and truth of sentiment, for brevity and strength of expression, for regularity in its structure, but above all for the unspeakable importance of the discoveries which it contains, stands unrivalled by any mere human composition, and as far exceeds the most celebrated productions of the learned Greeks and Romans, as the shining of the sun exceeds the twinkling of the stars." *Macknight*.

Clearly to understand this Epistle, it will be necessary to consider, 1. The general character of those who composed the Roman church; they consisted partly of converted heathens, and partly of Jews, who, with much remaining prejudice, had embraced the gospel of Christ; and that while the Gentile converts claimed equal privileges with the Jewish, they refused to concede these rights, unless the Gentiles would submit to circumcision. 2. The erroneous notions of the Jews concerning justification. Of this they assigned three grounds:

1. The extraordinary piety and merits of their ancestors, especially Abraham, and the covenant that God had made with those holy men.

2. The knowledge which they had of God through the law of Moses, and their diligent study of that law.

3. The works of the Levitical law, especially sacrifice and circumcision, which were to expiate sin.

The Epistle to the Romans is divided into sixteen chapters, or four parts.

Part I. Contains the introduction to the Epistle, ch. i. 1—15.

Part II. Is doctrinal, ch. i. 16; ii.—xi. The important doctrines taught at large in the Epistle to the Romans, may be summarily expressed in the following order.

1. That all the children of men, whether Gentiles or Jews, are guilty before God.

2. That no works of man, whether ceremonial or moral, can justify a sinner in the sight of God.

3. That Jesus Christ, the Son of God, by the unspotted holiness of the human nature which he assumed, by his perfect obedience in heart and life, and by the propitiatory sacrifice of his death, is become the Saviour of all who trust in his name.

4. That true faith in Jesus Christ is necessarily connected with the sanctification of the soul, and its reality is demonstrated by the life being consecrated to the service of God.

5. That the mission of the Son of God to our world, to be made man, so that he might become the Redeemer and Saviour of sinners, and the gift of all the blessings of the gospel to believers, are the fruits of the sovereign love of God to mankind.

6. That in the last days, the Jews and all the Gentile nations, shall be effectually called to embrace the gospel of Christ, and be brought into his church.

These divine principles are stated and proved, illustrated, defended, and enforced, in a manner singularly edifying in this extended part of the Epistle. The plan of the apostle, in the several steps of his developement of the gospel, is very remarkable. An outline of his method is contained in twelve sections.

Section 1. The apostle's declaration of the gospel of Christ, ch. i. 16, 17.

Sec. 2. The awful criminality of all mankind, proved from the atheistical wickedness of the Gentiles, and from the infidel wickedness of the Jews, ch. i. 18—32; ii. iii. 1—20.

Sec. 3. The gospel method of divine grace more fully stated, as necessary for the redemption and salvation of both Jews and Gentiles, ch. iii. 21—28.

Sec. 4. The universality of this salvation by grace through faith: Abraham, David, and all believers, being saved only by grace, through faith, their minds being led to the promises of God in Christ, ch. iii. 29—31; iv.

Sec. 5. The elevated privileges and blessed experience of believers, ch. v. 1—11.

Sec. 6. As all mankind are involved in sin and death by virtue of their natural relation to Adam, so all

believers are interested in the Redeemer's righteousness, and the eternal blessings of abounding grace, by virtue of their spiritual relation to Christ, the Surety of the new covenant, ch. v. 12—21.

Sec. 7. The recovery of sinners from a state of alienation of heart, to a state of grace, is necessarily productive of a life of holiness, and inseparably connected with eternal life, ch. vi.

Sec. 8. The renewal of the mind to a state of fruitfulness to God, which renders it alive to the spirituality and holiness of his law, and deeply sensible of the more secret sins of the heart; thus, while grieved with a consciousness of the radical corruption of nature, and from principles of grace delighting in the law after the inner man, the believing soul anticipates full salvation through Jesus Christ, ch. vii.

Sec. 9. The Christian's triumph of faith, from the completeness of the mediatorial work of Christ,—from his possession of the Spirit of God,—from his privilege of divine adoption,—from the co-operation of all things in favour of those who love God, according to the eternal purpose of mercy in Christ Jesus, by which the calling, justification, glorification, and salvation of the people of God are effectually secured, ch. viii.

Sec. 10. The righteous sovereignty of God vindicated from Jewish cavils, which were raised against the admission of the Gentiles into the church of Christ, ch. ix. 1—24.

Sec. 11. The calling of the Gentiles a subject of ancient prophecy; as also the rejection of the Jews on account of their unbelieving self-righteousness, ch. ix. 25—33; x.

Sec. 12. Further illustration concerning the partial rejection of the infidel Israelites, and the partial incorporation of the Gentiles into the church, with a view to engage all believers to cherish a spirit of faith, humility, and gratitude, ch. xi.

Part III. Contains the application of the doctrinal part, in various exhortations to believers, ch. xii.—xv. 1—14. In this part there are four sections.

Section 1. Exhortations to devote themselves to God in all the duties of a holy life, as members of Christ, from a consideration of the sovereign mercies of God, ch. xii.

Sec. 2. Exhortations to obey rulers and the magistrates, as the appointed ordinances of God, ch. xiii.

Sec. 3. Exhortations to cultivate a tender spirit towards those brethren who are weaker in the faith, ch. xiv. xv. 7.

Sec. 4. Exhortations and prayers that even as Gentile believers they may cherish and express habitual joyfulness in God their Saviour, ch. xv. 8—14.

Part IV. Contains the conclusion of the Epistle, in which the apostle notices various particulars relating to his labours and his delay in visiting Rome, and sends salutations to many persons, ch. xv. 15; xvi.

Christianity had evidently made great progress at Rome, as appears from the long list of eminent believers whom the apostle salutes at the close of the Epistle: for though he might personally know some of them, many others he had probably only heard of in connexion with their reported profession of the gospel of Jesus Christ.

References in Romans.

Ch. i. 17.	Hab. ii. 4.	Ch. x. 6, 7.	Deut. xxx. 12, 13.
— iii. 2	Deut. iv. 7, 8.		
— — 10.	Psa. xiv. liii.	— — 11.	Isa xxviii. 16.
— iv. 3.	Gen. xv. 6.	— — 15.	— liii. 7.
— — 7.	Psa. xxxii. 1, 2.	— — 19.	Deut. xxxii. 21.
— — 13, 17.	Gen. xvii. 4, 5.	— — 21.	Isa. lxv. 2.
— v. 15.	Isa. liii. 11.	— xi. 3.	1 Kings xix. 10—14.
— vii 15.	Gal. v. 17.		
— viii. 15.	Isa. lvi. 5.	— — 7, 8.	Isa xxix. 10.
— — 26.	Zech. xii. 10.	— — 9.	Psa. lxix. 23.
— — 36.	Psa. xliv. 22.	— — 26.	Isa. lix. 20.
— ix 13.	Mal. i. 2, 3.	— xii. 19.	Deut. xxxii 35.
— — 15.	Exod. xxxiii. 19.	— xiv. 6.	1 Cor. x. 31.
— — 25.	Hos. ii. 23.	— xv. 9.	Psa. xviii. 49.
— — 29.	Isa. i. 9.	— — 12.	Isa xi. 1—10.
— — 33.	— viii. 14.	— xvi. 26.	2 Pet. i. 20.

FIRST EPISTLE TO THE CORINTHIANS.

Corinth was the capital of Achaia, a province of ancient Greece: it was situated on the isthmus which

separates the Peloponnesus from Attica, and the most celebrated of all its cities; exceeding every other in the magnificence of its public buildings, the extent of its commerce, and the opulence of its inhabitants. Their learning and ingenuity were equally celebrated, and the city was called, "The Light of all Greece," and "The Ornament of Greece." The Corinthians were no less distinguished for the corruption of their morals, and their licentious profligacy was proverbial; yet a gospel church was collected among them by the ministry of Paul, who laboured in preaching the doctrines of Christ at Corinth with considerable success for nearly two years, Acts xviii. This church appears to have been numerous, and remarkably distinguished for spiritual endowments: yet, through the shocking impurity of manners in their city, and the ambition of some erroneous teacher, the Corinthian professors were led into many disorders. This Epistle was written A. D. 57, about two years after the apostle left them; the design of it was twofold. First, to correct their improprieties, by healing their divisions, by engaging them to gospel holiness, and by establishing the doctrine of the resurrection. Second, to satisfy their inquiries on several points concerning which they had written to the apostle; especially respecting marriage, meats offered to idols, and spiritual gifts.

The Epistle is divided into sixteen chapters, and contains six principal sections.

Section I. Contains an introduction to the Epistle, with a general review of the doctrines and privileges of the gospel, as it had been embraced by the Corinthians, stated with a view to their edification, ch. i.—iv. In this section we should remark,

1. The estimation in which the apostle declares the gospel of salvation by the sacrifice of Christ, was held by different characters—by unbelievers it was regarded as foolishness, by believers it was esteemed as the wisdom and the power of God, ch. i.

2. The declared necessity of the Holy Spirit's illuminating and sanctifying influences, to prepare the heart

of man to receive with enlightened affection the things of God, ch. ii.

Sec. II. Contains reproofs and instructions for the removal of the various scandals and corruptions, with which some of the members of this church were disgracing it, ch. iii.—vi. The more remarkable points in this section are, the admonitions relating to incest, fornication, and litigiousness, ch. v. vi.

Sec. III. Embraces the consideration of the questions proposed by the Corinthians to the apostle, ch. vii.—x. The things more particularly remarkable are,

1. The instructions concerning marriage, and the influence of Christianity on the civil condition of believers, ch. vii.

2. Concerning the flesh of animals which had been offered to idols, ch. viii.

3. The right of ministers of the gospel to a liberal maintenance for their labours, ch. ix.

4. The review which the apostle takes of the rebellions of Israel, with their punishment as a warning to Christians generally, ch. x.

Sec. IV. Contains instructions concerning the manner of women worshipping in public, the decent and profitable reception of the Lord's supper, and the design and exercise of spiritual gifts, ch. xi.—xiv. In this section the most remarkable things are,

1. The directions for the proper and intelligent commemoration of our blessed Redeemer's sacrifice, in the ordinance of the Lord's supper, ch. xi.

2. Instructions concerning the desiring and using of the extraordinary spiritual gifts, for the establishment of the first Christian churches, ch. xii. xiv.

3. The surpassing excellence of the Christian graces, faith, hope, and especially charity, above all miraculous gifts, ch. xii.

Sec. V. Treats at large on the doctrine of the resurrection of believers in Christ, ch. xv. In this section the things most remarkable are,

1. The various and abundant proofs of the resurrection

of Christ, as the first-fruits and security of the resurrection of believers, ver. 1—34.

2. The manner of the resurrection of believers, ver. 35—49.

3. The transformation to glory of those who shall be alive at the coming of Christ, ver. 50—55.

4. The inspiring use of the doctrine of the resurrection to Christians, ver. 56—58.

Sec. VI. Closes the Epistle; with directions concerning a contribution for the saints at Jerusalem; a promise of a visit to them; commendations of several ministers; and salutations to several members of the church, ch. xvi.

References in 1 Corinthians.

Ch. i. 19.	Isa. xxix. 14.	Ch. x. 4.	Exod. xvii. 6.
— — 20.	—— xliv 25.	— — 5.	Num. xiv. 29—32.
— — 30.	Jer. xxiii 5, 6.	— — 6.	—— xi. 4—34.
— — 31.	—— ix. 23, 24.	— — 7.	Exod. xxxii. 6.
— iii. 11.	Isa. xxviii. 16.	— — 8.	Num. xxv. 1—9.
— — 19.	Job v. 13.	— — 9.	—— xxi. 6, 9.
— vi. 2.	Dan. vii. 22.	— — 10.	—— xiv. 2—29;
— ix. 7.	Deut. xx. 6.		xvi. 49.
— — 10.	—— xxv. 4.	— — 18.	Lev. ii. 3; vii. 14.
— x. 1.	Exod. xiii. 21;	— — 20.	Deut. xxxii. 38.
	xiv. 22; Ps.	— xv. 3.	Isa. liii; Dan.
	cv. 39.		ix. 24—26.
— — 3.	Exod. xvi.	— — 4.	Psa. xvi. 10.
	15—35; Neh.	— — 54.	Isa. xxv. 8.
	ix. 20.	— — 55.	Hos. xiii. 14.

SECOND EPISTLE TO THE CORINTHIANS.

The Second Epistle to the Corinthians is supposed to have been written about a year after the First. The former having been made useful to promote a reformation in that church, especially in many of its members whose conduct had been scandalous or disorderly, some false teachers were offended with the apostle, and blamed him for interfering in their affairs. This Epistle was intended to minister comfort to the penitents, and to justify the character of the apostle, as fully commissioned

for his office by Jesus Christ. It is divided into thirteen chapters, and contains five principal sections.

Section I. Contains the apostle's salutation to the Corinthians, and his affectionate introduction to the chief subject of the Epistle, ch. i.

Sec. II. Comprises instructions to the church to show a tender benevolence towards penitents; a defence of his apostolic character, from the superior excellency of his ministry above that of the law, and from his faithful discharge of its duties, being supported by the consolations and prospects of the gospel, ch. ii.—vii. In this section we should remark,

1. The apostle's commendation of the gospel as the ministration of the Spirit and of righteousness, in contradistinction from the law, as the ministration of death and of condemnation, ch. iii.

2. The soul-inspiring influence of the gospel, in those who receive it by faith under the gracious influences of the Spirit, ch. iv. v.

3. The distinguishing peculiarity of the gospel constitution, in the imputation of the guilt of men to Christ as the Surety of the covenant, and the imputation of his righteousness, to all who truly believe, ch. v. 18—21.

4. The application of the gospel doctrines in exhortations to universal holiness, ch. vi. vii. 1.

Sec. III. Gives exhortations and directions to make a liberal contribution, for the relief of the poor and persecuted brethren in Judea, ch. viii. ix. That which is most remarkable in this section is, the apostle's argument taken from the unexampled grace of our Lord Jesus Christ, in that though he was rich in his Divine nature, as the Son of God, became poor in human form, that we might be enriched with eternal glories, ch. viii. 9.

Sec. IV. Contains the apostle's defence of his apostolic character and authority, ch. x.—xii. In this section we should remark,

1. The confidence of the apostle in the goodness of his cause, and of the power of God to support and defend him against a powerful and sagacious party, whose

reputation and authority were deeply interested in overthrowing his claims to an apostolical commission from Christ, ch. xi.

2. The enumeration of the apostle's sufferings in fulfilling his ministerial commission, ch. xi.

3. The vision of Paradise, with which the apostle had been favoured, ch. xii.

Sec. V. Concludes the Epistle, with exhortations to self-inspection and watchfulness, and prayers for the spiritual prosperity of the Corinthians; the apostle closes with a memorable benediction, ch. xiii.

References in 2 Corinthians.

Ch iii. 3.	Jer. xxxi. 33; Ezek. xi 19; xxxvi. 26.	Ch. vi. 16.	Lev. xxvi. 12; Ezek. xxxvii. 26, 27.
— — 7.	Exod. xxxiv. 1, 28, 29, 35.	— — 18. — vii. 1.	Jer. xxxi. 1—9. Psa. li. 7—10.
— — 15.	Isa. xxv. 7.	— viii. 15.	Exod. xvi. 18.
— vi. 2.	—— xlix. 8.	— xii. 7.	Ezek. xxviii. 24.
— — 16.	Exod. xxix. 45.	— xiii. 5.	1 John iii. 20, 21.

EPISTLE TO THE GALATIANS.

The Galatians were a people inhabiting a large district of Asia Minor, among whom Christianity was planted by the ministry of Paul, Gal. i. 6; Acts xvi. 6; xviii. 23. These churches consisted of both Jewish and Gentile converts, many of whom, in a short time, were drawn away from the simplicity of Christian doctrine, and the great essentials of the gospel, by some judaizing or false teachers, who insinuated that Paul was not properly an apostle of Christ, but only a missionary deputed from the church at Jerusalem. To refute their errors, and to establish the Galatians in that principal article of Christian doctrine, the free justification of sinners in the sight of God, only by faith in the righteousness and atonement of Jesus Christ, the apostle was directed to write this Epistle, about A. D. 53. It is divided into six chapters, having three parts.

Part I. Contains Paul's vindication of himself and the

doctrines he preached, ch. i. ii. In this part there are four sections.

Section 1. Contains the introduction, ch. i. 1—5.

Sec. 2. Proves that he was not a missionary sent by the other apostles; but that he derived his commission immediately from Christ: he was, therefore, not inferior to any of them, ch. i. 6—24.

Sec. 3. Shows that he preached the same gospel as the other apostles, ch. ii. 1—10.

Sec. 4. That his practice was agreeable to his doctrine, ch. ii. 11—21.

Part II. Contains a defence of the doctrine of free justification by faith, in a series of proofs taken from the Old Testament, ch. iii.—v. 1—12. In this part there are five sections.

Section 1. Justification by faith proved from the covenant made with Abraham, ch. iii. 1—18.

Sec. 2. The same doctrine proved from the Mosaic law, which was not to disannul the promise, but to prepare men to embrace the gospel, ch. iii. 19—29; iv. 1—7.

Sec. 3. Affectionately reproves the Galatians for their defection from the gospel, ch. iv. 8—20.

Sec. 4. The pupilage of the Jewish church illustrated by an allegory taken from the family of Abraham, ch. iv. 21—31.

Sec. 5. Shows the folly of departing from the gospel, by submitting to circumcision, thereby becoming indebted to keep the whole ceremonial law, ch. v. 1—12.

Part III. Contains the practical application of the doctrines of grace, in various suitable exhortations to a life of devotedness to God, in the strength of the Holy Spirit, and under his promised guidance, ch. v. 13—26; vi. In this part we should especially remark,

1. The instructive statement respecting the abominable works of the flesh in the ungodly: and, in contrast,

2. The blessed fruits of the Spirit in the temper and lives of genuine Christians, ch. v. 13—24.

References in Galatians.

Ch. iii. 6.	Gen. xv. 4, 6.	Ch. iii. 16.	Gen. xvii. 7.
— — 8.	—— xii. 3; xviii. 18.	— iv. 4.	Dan. ix. 24.
		— — 14.	Zech. xii. 8.
— — 10.	Deut. xxvii. 26.	— — 24.	Deut. xxxiii. 2.
— — 13.	—— xxi. 23	— — 30.	Gen. xxi. 10—12.
— — 16.	Gen. xii. 3—7.	— vi. 8.	Prov. xi. 18.

EPISTLE TO THE EPHESIANS.

Ephesus was a city of great note in Asia Minor. It was celebrated on account of its magnificent temple dedicated to the fabulous goddess Diana, and which was esteemed one of the wonders of the world. The Ephesians were deplorably sunk in degrading superstition and idolatry, and consequently addicted to the grossest impurities. Among these people, however, the ministry of Paul was eminently blessed to the conversion of many, some particulars of which we have recorded, Acts xviii. 19—21; xix. The church at Ephesus was formed about A. D. 54, and this Epistle was written when the apostle was prisoner at Rome, about A. D. 62, on hearing of their constancy in the faith, and of their flourishing in the Christian virtues.

The Epistle to the Ephesians is divided into six chapters, which include two principal parts.

Part I. Is doctrinal; embracing the first three chapters. In this part there are six sections.

Section 1. The inscription, ch. i. 1, 2.

Sec. 2. The elevated thanksgiving to God, for the gracious purposes of his sovereign mercy, in securing the blessings of adoption, redemption, and eternal salvation to sinners by Jesus Christ, ch. i. 3—14.

Sec. 3. Praise and prayer on behalf of the Ephesian believers as forming a part of the body of Christ's church, ch. i. 15—23.

Sec. 4. The apostles admonition to the Ephesians, concerning their former degraded condition, while heathen, and their blessed state, as created anew in Christ Jesus, as by his blood of atonement brought nigh to

God, and as fellow citizens with the saints and of the family of God, ch. ii.

Sec. 5. The declaration of the mystery of Divine mercy, to bring Gentiles into the church of God according to his eternal purpose, ch. iii. 1—12.

Sec. 6. The apostle's prayer for the establishment of believers in the knowledge and love of Christ, ch. iii. 13—21.

Part II. Is practical, comprising the last three chapters, in which are seven sections.

Section 1. A general exhortation to the Ephesians to walk in a manner becoming their high vocation, ch. iv. 1—3.

Sec. 2. The exhortation enforced from a consideration of the unity of the Spirit, and the diversity of his gifts for the benefit of the church, ch. iv. 4—16.

Sec. 3. The exhortation enforced from a reflection upon the renovation of their minds by his effectual grace, ch. iv. 17—24.

Sec. 4. An exhortation to avoid various specified vices, with a commendation of the opposite virtues, ch. iv. 25; v. 1—21.

Sec. 5. The relative duties enjoined, from the consideration of believers being alike redeemed by Christ, and heirs of heaven, ch. v. 22; vi. 1—9.

Sec. 6. The final exhortation to contend in the spiritual warfare, furnished with the armour of God, ch. vi. 10—20.

Sec. 7. The conclusion of the Epistle, ch. vi. 21—24.

In this Epistle to the Ephesians, we should remark,

1. The origin of the salvation of sinners by Christ, as described by the apostle, ch. i.

2. The mystery of grace to include the Gentiles in the church, ch. iii.

3. The manner of the Christian's conflict with his spiritual enemies, ch. vi.

References in Ephesians.

Ch. i. 11.	Isa. xlvi. 10, 11.	Ch. iv. 4.	Isa. xxviii. 9, 13.
— ii. 12.	Ezek. xiii. 9.	— v. 8, 14.	——lx. 1, 19.
—— 17.	Zech. ix. 10.	— vi. 2.	Deut. v. 16; Jer.
—— 20.	Isa. xxviii. 16.		xxxv. 18, 19.

EPISTLE TO THE PHILIPPIANS.

Philippi was a city of Macedonia, and a Roman colony. It was the first place in Europe in which the gospel appears to have been preached by an apostle of Christ. To this city the apostle Paul appears to have been directed by a vision sent from God, about A. D. 50, and it is memorable for the conversion of Lydia and the jailor, Acts xvi. The apostle wrote this Epistle while a prisoner at Rome, about A. D. 62, in acknowledgment of a liberal contribution, sent by the Philippian church for his relief and support, while in confinement for the cause of Christ: it was also designed to instruct and encourage the believers in their profession of the gospel, to guard them against judaizing teachers, and to direct them in the ways of holiness after the example of Christ. The Epistle is filled with the loftiest sentiments, and the most affectionate exhortations to all the members of the Philippian church. It is divided into four chapters, containing seven sections.

Section I. The inscription, ch. i. 1, 2.

Sec. II. Expresses the apostle's thanksgiving to God for their stedfastness in the faith, and in the assurance of their continuance, prays for their spiritual improvement, ch. i. 3—11.

Sec. III. Declares the effects of the apostle's imprisonment at Rome, and the extension of the gospel, even in the imperial palace; so that though he was desirous of enjoying the beatific vision of Christ, he was willing to continue in the body for the service of the church, ch. i. 12—26.

Sec. IV. Contains various exhortations to the Philippians, expressed in the most affecting terms, to cherish a temper and behaviour becoming the gospel, enforced by the example of our divine Redeemer, ch. i. 27; ii. 1—16.

Sec. V. The apostle's care for the Philippians in sending Timothy and Epaphroditus to them, ch. ii. 17—30.

Sec. VI. Contains solemn cautions against the cavilling, judaizing teachers, who pretended to preach the gospel; proposing to them his own example of rejecting

all supposed excellences and attainments in righteousness, and declaring his superlative attachment to the gospel of Christ, and to the righteousness which is of God by faith, ch. iii.

Sec. VII. Contains various general exhortations to joyfulness, moderation, and prayer, recommending every virtue which could adorn the Christian character. The apostle acknowledges their benevolent contribution, and assures them of a rich supply from his covenant God, according to the riches of his glory, ch. iv. 1—20.

Sec. VIII. Is the conclusion of the Epistle, ch. iv. 21—23.

The most remarkable thing in this Epistle is the argument drawn from the love and condescension of Christ, who, though equal with God the Father in his essential Divine nature, assumed the nature of man, that he might obey the law for sinners, and die for their redemption, ch. ii. 5—11.

References in Philippians.

Ch. ii. 7.	Psa. xxii. 6;	Ch. iii. 2.	Isa. lvi. 10.
	Dan. ix. 26.	— — 8.	Jer. ix. 23, 24.
— — 10.	Isa. xlv. 23.	— iv. 6.	Psa. lv. 22.

EPISTLE TO THE COLOSSIANS.

Colosse was one of the chief towns in Phrygia, in Asia Minor: it was built on the river Lycus, and at an equal distance between Laodicea and Hierapolis. By whose ministry this church was gathered is not certainly known, unless it were Epaphras or Philemon. This Epistle to that church was written about the same time as those to the Ephesians and Philippians, when the apostle was a prisoner at Rome. The occasion of this Epistle was the visit of Epaphras their minister, to Rome, to consult Paul on some novelties of doctrine, which had been published among them by false teachers, respecting the worshipping of angels as mediators with God, and the observance of various ceremonies. The design of this Epistle was to show, that all hope of the salvation of guilty man is founded on the Divinity and

all-sufficient merits of Jesus Christ, our glorious Redeemer; to caution the Colossians against the speculations of vain men, who boasted of their deceitful philosophy; and to excite them to a life of universal holiness, with a temper becoming their Christian profession.

For the purpose of seeing more clearly the beauties of this Epistle, and of understanding more fully its divine and saving doctrine, it should be compared with the Epistle to the Ephesians. It is divided into four chapters, containing nine sections.

Section I. The introduction, ch. i. 1, 2.

Sec. II. The apostle's thanksgiving and prayer on behalf of the Colossians, ch. i. 3—14.

Sec. III. Declares in the most exalted terms the personal Divinity of Jesus, as the Son of God and Creator of all things, and of the mediatorial glories of Christ, by whose reconciliation the Gentiles are to be brought into the church of God, ch. i. 15—29.

Sec. IV. Assures the Colossians of Paul's solicitude and prayers for their establishment and advancement in Christian knowledge and grace, ch. ii. 1—7.

Sec. V. Admonishes them to beware of the philosophical speculations of vain men, to abide by the pure doctrine of Christ, in whom dwells all the fulness of the Godhead bodily, who is the Head of the church, and of all the heavenly powers, and by whom all the Levitical ceremonies have been for ever abolished, ch. ii. 8—17.

Sec. VI. Warns them against worshipping angels, and neglecting Christ, ch. ii. 18—23.

Sec. VII. Exhorts them to set their affections on things above, from the consideration of their security in Christ at the right hand of God, and to the practice of various moral and evangelical duties, agreeably to their character as the disciples of Christ, ch. iii. 1—17.

Sec. VIII. Gives suitable instructions concerning the relative duties, ch. iii. 18; iv. 1.

Sec. IX. Contains various exhortations, instructions, salutations, and the conclusion, ch. iv. 2—18.

The most remarkable part of this Epistle, is the testi-

mony of the apostle concerning the proper Deity of the Son of God, and his manifestation in human nature, to become the Head of the church, and the Redeemer of sinners, ch. i. 13—22; ii. 9—14.

References in Colossians.

| Ch. i. 16. | John i. 1—3; 1 Cor. viii. 6; Eph. iii. 9; Heb. i. 2; Rom. viii. 38, 39. | Ch. ii. 11. — — 15. — — 18. — iv. 6. | Deut. xxx. 6. Psa. lxviii. 18. Ezek. xiii 3. Eccles. x. 12. |

FIRST EPISTLE TO THE THESSALONIANS.

Thessalonica, now called Salonichi, is in Turkey in Europe: it is a large sea-port town, situated in the Thermaic Gulf, the metropolis of Macedonia, the ancient kingdom of Alexander the Great. Here Paul preached the gospel immediately after leaving Philippi; and his ministry was blessed of God to the gathering of a Christian church, Acts xvii. The unbelieving Jews being inflamed with indignation at his success, and persecuting him, he was compelled to flee from the city: he escaped to Berea, and thence to Athens, whence he sent Timothy back to ascertain the state of the Thessalonian believers. Timothy having returned to Paul, at Corinth, with so pleasing a report of their stedfastness in the faith, the apostle wrote this Epistle to confirm them in the truth of the gospel, to direct them in the way of salvation, and to encourage them in their Christian course. It is believed that this is the first of the inspired epistles that the apostles wrote, A. D. 52.

The First Epistle to the Thessalonians is divided into five chapters, containing six sections.

Section I. Contains the introduction, expressing the apostle's thanksgiving to God, for the eminent and operative graces of the Thessalonians, ch. i. 1—4.

Sec. II. Expresses the apostle's satisfaction with the Thessalonians, in receiving the gospel with spiritual affection, turning to God from idolatry, and becoming examples to all the churches in the neighbouring provinces, ch. i. 5—10.

Sec. III. Contains the apostle's appeal to the Thessalonians as to the integrity and purity, the disinterestedness and affection, with which he and his colleagues had preached the gospel to them, notwithstanding the persecutions to which they were subjected on that account, ch. ii. 1—16.

Sec. IV. Expresses the affectionate solicitude of the apostle for their preservation from the delusions of the tempter, and for their permanent establishment and advancement in faith and universal holiness, ch. ii. 17; iii. iv. 1—12.

Sec. V. Contains consolatory instructions concerning those who have died in the faith of the gospel, as they sleep in Jesus, with whom they rest until the resurrection: believers are therefore exhorted to prepare for the coming of the Lord, ch. iv. 13—18.

Sec. VI. Comprises various exhortations suitable to their character as the children of light, especially to the cultivation of holiness, brotherly love, respect for their ministers, and godliness, with increasing joyfulness, for all which prayer is offered, and the Epistle closes with the usual benediction, ch. v.

The fifth section of this Epistle is most remarkable, as it so plainly declares what will become of the godly, who may be living at the day of the resurrection, ch. iv. 17.

References in 1 *Thessalonians.*

Ch. ii. 16.	Gen. xv. 16.	Ch. iv. 15, 16.	1 Cor. xv. 22,
— iii. 13.	Zech. xiv. 5;		51, 52.
	Dan. vii. 10.	— v. 8.	Isa. lix. 17.

SECOND EPISTLE TO THE THESSALONIANS.

The First Epistle to the Thessalonians was the means of much consolation to that people; but some expressions in it had been misapprehended by several members of the church. They were in expectation of the near approach of Christ, of the end of the world, and of the day of judgment; by which they were led to neglect their temporal affairs, as inconsistent with the anticipation of that awful event. To correct this misapprehension, the

tendency of which was so injurious to society and to the honour of Christianity, the apostle was inspired to write this Second Epistle soon after the former. It is divided into three chapters, comprising seven sections.

Section I. The salutation, ch. i. 1, 2.

Sec. II. The apostle's commendation of their increase in faith, charity, and patience, under continued persecution, in which he encourages them by the glorious coming of Christ, as universal Judge, for the destruction of unbelievers and the complete salvation of his people, ch. i. 3—10.

Sec. III. The apostle's prayer for their perfect sanctification, ch. i. 11, 12.

Sec. IV. The correction of their error respecting the end of the world; which he declares must be preceded by a great apostacy, in which the "man of sin" would ruin many, and sink himself into perdition, ch. ii. 1—12.

Sec. V. The apostle thanks God for his grace in choosing and calling the Thessalonians unto salvation and the glory of Christ, exhorts them to stedfastness, and prays for them, and entreats their prayers in return, ch. ii. 13; iii. 1—5.

Sec. VI. Contains various exhortations, particularly in relation to those who might be disorderly and busybodies, ch. iii. 6—16.

Sec. VII. The conclusion of the Epistle, ch. iii. 17, 18.

The most remarkable part of this Epistle is the prophecy respecting the Romish antichrist, under the characters of "the man of sin," "the son of perdition," and "the mystery of iniquity."

The succession of popes, with the Romish priesthood, seems to be intended by these titles, on account of the disgraceful lives of many of them; the corruption of Christian doctrine, by the worship of angels, saints, images, the host, &c.; their selling indulgences and pardons for the most shocking crimes; taking the Scriptures from the people, and perverting the instituted worship of God.

"Exalting himself above all that is called God, or is worshipped," denotes the pope's assuming authority

over the ministers of Christ, over kings, and emperors, so as even "to dispose of kingdoms at his pleasure." "Sitting in the temple of God," may denote the inauguration of the pope, which takes place at St. Peter's church, where he is seated on the high altar, and makes the table of the Lord his footstool, in which position he receives adoration. "Showing himself that he is God," intends his affecting divine titles, as "His Holiness," "Our Lord God the Pope." See Bishop Newton's Dissertations on the Prophecies, Diss. XXII. for a particular application of this prophecy.

References in 2 Thessalonians.

Ch. i. 19.	Isa. ii. 9.	Ch. ii. 9.	Deut. xiii. 1;
— ii. 3.	Dan. vii. 25.		Rev. xix. 20.
— — 4.	—— xi.36; Ezek. xxviii. 2.	— — 11.	1 Kings xxii. 22; Ezek. xiv.7—9.
— — 8.	Dan. vii. 10, 11.	— iii. 10.	Gen. iii. 19.

FIRST EPISTLE TO TIMOTHY.

Timothy, the evangelist, appears to have been a native of Lystra, a city of Lycaonia. His father was a Greek: but his mother Eunice, who was a Jewess, and his grandmother Lois, who were excellent persons, took such pious care of his education, that his mind was stored with numerous passages from the Scriptures even from a child. He was brought to a knowledge of the truth as it is in Jesus, when but a youth, by the ministry of Paul; who, on a second visit to the brethren of Lystra, found Timothy in such high estimation by the Christian church at that place, and by the brethren at Iconium, that he chose him as his companion and assistant in his missionary labours. To conciliate the prejudices of the Jews, Timothy, being partly a Jew by descent, submitted to circumcision, and was ordained an evangelist. From this period Timothy accompanied Paul in his journeys, assisting him in his apostolical office, preaching the gospel, and establishing the infant churches; and he never afterwards left him except when sent on some special mission to advance the king-

dom of Christ. To defend and preserve the purity of evangelical doctrine, and to regulate the discipline of the church at Ephesus, Timothy was left by the apostle for a season in that city. To serve as an apostolical warrant for his conduct in opposing the heresies, and perfecting the ecclesiastical offices, the First Epistle was written to Timothy by Paul, about A. D. 64.

How long Timothy continued at that city is not known. Uncertain tradition reports, that he was put to death by clubs and stones, while preaching against idolatry, near the temple of Diana, at Ephesus, A. D. 97. This Epistle is divided into six chapters, containing eleven sections.

Section I. The introduction, ch. i. 1, 2.

Sec. II. Admonitions to Timothy concerning the purpose for which he had been left at Ephesus, especially in relation to the preservation of sound doctrine, ch. i. 3—14.

Sec. III. Encouragements to Timothy, taken from the glorious gospel, of the renovating grace of which the apostle was so eminent an example, ch. i. 15—20.

Sec. IV. Directions as to the subjects and manner of prayer and thanksgiving, ch. ii. 1—8.

Sec. V. Instructions concerning the behaviour of Christian women, ch. ii. 9—15.

Sec. VI. Special instructions relating to the qualifications of bishops and deacons, ch. iii.

Sec. VII. Prophecy of a lamentable apostacy from the purity of the gospel, ch. iv. 1—5.

Sec. VIII. Precepts for the personal conduct of Timothy, ch. iv. 6—16.

Sec. IX. Rules to be observed towards the several classes of persons in Christian communion, especially widows, ch. v.

Sec. X. Instruction concerning servants, false teachers, and riches, ch. vi. 1—10.

Sec. XI. Solemn charge and instructions to Timothy respecting his adherence to the truth, urged by the most affecting and inspiring considerations, ch. vi. 11—21.

This Epistle to Timothy must be regarded as giving

the most convincing evidences of Paul's sincerity, uprightness, and spirituality of mind. For if his secret views and expectations had been different from those which he proposed to the churches and declared to the world, surely he would have given some intimations of them in a letter written to so particular a friend. The perfect portraits which are here drawn of the characters and duties, and necessary qualifications of bishops and deacons, are very instructive to those who fill such offices; and to those who are interested in their ministrations, as the servants of Jesus Christ.

References in 1 *Timothy.*

Ch. ii. 1, 2.	Ezra vi. 10; Jer. xxix. 7.	Ch. iv. 1.	Dan. xi. 35; Rev. ix. 20; xvi. 14.
— — 8.	Mal. i. 11; Isa. i. 15.	— — 16.	Ezek. xxxiii. 9.
		— v. 4.	Gen. xlv. 10, 11.
— iii. 6.	Prov. xvi. 18; Isa. xiv. 12.	— — 19.	Deut. xix. 15.
		— vi. 13.	xxxii. 39.

SECOND EPISTLE TO TIMOTHY.

The Second Epistle to Timothy was written by Paul, while he was, the second time, a prisoner at Rome, and expecting the termination of his life by martyrdom, and, as many suppose, only a few months before that event happened, by order of the cruel emperor Nero. The immediate design of Paul in writing this letter, was to inform Timothy of the circumstances that had befallen him, and to request his presence, that he might receive the apostle's dying instructions. But, being uncertain whether he should be spared to see Timothy, he gave him in this Epistle a variety of advices, injunctions, and encouragements, to persevere in the faithful discharge of his ministerial functions. It was intended further to prepare Timothy for those sufferings to which the apostle foresaw he would be exposed; to inform him of a fatal apostacy which was already commencing among the professors of the gospel of Jesus Christ, and to encourage him by his own example. As this letter was written to Paul's most beloved friend, under the miseries of a prison, and in the prospect of a violent death, it

cannot fail to be instructive to us, as it exhibits the consoling influence of the gospel in the most trying circumstances of a Christian minister. " Imagine a pious father, under sentence of death for his piety and benevolence to mankind, writing to a dutiful and affectionate son, that he might see and embrace him again before he left the world; particularly that he might leave with him his dying commands, and charge him to live and suffer as he had done : and you will have the frame of the apostle's mind during the writing of this Epistle." *Dr. Benson.*

This Epistle is divided into four chapters, containing ten sections.

Section I. The inscription, ch. i. 1, 2.

Sec. II. Paul's affectionate desire to see Timothy, with a commendation of his faith, which had been possessed by his maternal ancestors, ch. i. 3—5.

Sec. III. Exhortations to constancy in the gospel, from the consideration of its glorious provisions which had been experienced, ch. i. 6—14.

Sec. IV. The apostle's deserted condition, with a commendation of the generous faithfulness of Onesiphorus, ch. i. 15—18.

Sec. V. Various exhortations to encourage Timothy in his ministry, in expecting the glory awaiting those who suffer for Christ, ch. ii. 1—13.

Sec. VI. Directions relative to the ministry, and to shun those things by which others have been led to apostacy, ch. ii. 14—26.

Sec. VII. A prediction of a declension and apostacy from the gospel, ch. iii. 1—9.

Sec. VIII. Reminds Timothy of his ministerial duty, by a reference to the apostle's example and to his own knowledge of the Scriptures, ch. iii. 10—17 ; iv. 1—5.

Sec. IX. Paul's triumphant reflections on finishing his course, his prospect of death and anticipations of his crown of glory, ch. iv. 6—8.

Sec. X. Concludes the Epistle with various instructions and salutations, ch. iv. 9—12.

References in 2 Timothy.

Ch. ii. 13.	Num. xxiii. 19.	Ch. iii. 12.	Matt. xvi. 21-24;
— iii. 8.	Exod. vii. 11.		Acts xiv. 22.
— — 9.	—— — 12;	— — 16.	2 Pet. i. 20, 21.
	viii. 18; ix. 11.	— iv. 18.	Psa. lxxiii. 18.

EPISTLE TO TITUS.

Titus, the evangelist, was by descent and birth an idolatrous Gentile; it is supposed, a native of Antioch, in Syria, and he appears to have been a convert to Christianity by Paul's ministry. How highly he was afterwards esteemed by the apostle, is evident from the manner in which he is spoken of to the Corinthians, 2 Cor. viii. 23; and, though his name is not mentioned in the Acts, he was much with Paul, as is plain from the notices in several of the Epistles. Titus was left by the apostle in the island of Crete, as he says, "to set in order the things that were wanting, and to ordain elders in every city." The Epistle to Titus might not improperly be called the Epistle to the Cretans, as it was designed not so much to instruct Titus, as to serve for a divine warrant to lay before them, to which he might appeal as his infallible directory in the regulation of the churches on that island. How long Titus remained among the people is not certainly known; nor how frequent or extensive were his missionary excursions. Ancient tradition affirms that he died in Crete, and was buried there, aged ninety-four years.

This Epistle is divided into three chapters, containing seven sections.

Section I. The introduction, ch. i. 1—4.

Sec. II. Directions concerning the ordination of elders, whose qualifications are enumerated, ch. i. 5—9.

Sec. III. The necessity for caution in relation both to Jews and Cretans, ch. i. 10—16.

Sec. IV. Various exhortations in reference to different classes of believers, to be urged from the consideration of redemption, purity, and glory by Christ, ch. ii.

Sec. V. Obedience to the magistracy, and universal gentleness of behaviour, to be enjoined from the con-

sideration of the sovereign kindness and abundant grace of God, in regeneration, justification, and salvation, ch. iii. 1—7.

Sec. VI. Injunctions to affirm the doctrines of grace constantly, for the maintenance of good works, and to avoid heretical cavilling, ch. iii. 8—11.

Sec. VII. The conclusion of the Epistle, containing requests, directions, and salutations, ch. iii. 12—15.

References in Titus.

Ch. i. 6, 7.	1 Tim. iii. 1 7.	Ch. ii. 14.	1 Pet. ii. 9.
— — 14.	Isa. xxix. 13;	— iii. 5.	Rom. iii. 20, 28;
	Matt. xv. 1—10.		2 Tim. i. 9;
— ii. 14.	Eph. v. 2; Heb.		Ezek. xxxvi. 25;
	ix. 14; Deut.		Acts x. 45;
	vii. 6; xiv. 2.		xv. 7 9.

EPISTLE TO PHILEMON.

Philemon was a resident at Colosse, a citizen of considerable note, and highly exemplary as a Christian. He appears to have become a convert to the faith of the gospel by the ministry of the apostle Paul, and to have been a deacon in the Colossian church, if not its pastor. This Epistle was written by Paul, when a prisoner at Rome, about A. D. 63, for the purpose of reconciling Philemon to his slave Onesimus; who, having robbed his master, and fled to that city, was there converted to the faith of Christ by means of the apostle's ministry. This letter contains only twenty-five verses, but it is commended as the most finished and perfect example of epistolary writing in existence; its usefulness to the Christian church, however, is invaluable in other respects, affording many of the most instructive lessons, of which the following are especially worthy of remark.

1. It shows that liberality to the necessitous servants of Christ is highly ornamental to the Christian, ver. 4—7.

2. It exemplifies the Christian temper in benevolent endeavours to mitigate the resentment of an injured master towards his offending slave, ver. 8—10.

3. It exhibits to the highest in the church, a worthy example of affectionate concern for the souls of even the meanest persons, ver. 10, 11, 13.

4. It shows that all Christians are equal before God: Onesimus, a slave, on becoming a Christian, is spoken of as the apostle's son, and Philemon's brother, ver. 10—16.

5. That Christianity does not interfere with the civil condition of men; Onesimus was still Philemon's servant, ver. 11, 12, 14.

6. That we should never despair of reclaiming the wicked, but still employ means for their conversion, ver. 10—18.

7. That we should forgive offenders, who are penitent, and be heartily reconciled to them, ver. 20, 21.

References in Philemon.

| Ver. 10. | Col. iv. 9; | Ver. 13. | 1 Cor. xvi. 17. |
| | 1 Cor. iv. 15. | — 17. | 2 Cor. viii. 23. |

EPISTLE TO THE HEBREWS.

The Hebrews, to whom this letter was written, were the Jewish believers of the gospel, dwelling in Palestine, A. D. 63. Their circumstances will be evident from a perusal of the Epistle: by which we learn, that they were exposed to grievous suffering on account of their profession of Christ. The infidel Jews continued to employ their power for the purpose of withdrawing their believing brethren from the Christian faith. To ruinous persecution and incessant threats, they added arguments against Christianity derived from the acknowledged divinity of the Jewish religion, observing, that their law was given by the ministry of angels; that Moses was far superior to Jesus of Nazareth, who was put to death upon the cross; that the public worship of God, instituted by their great legislator and prophet, was truly splendid and worthy of Jehovah, while the Christians, on the contrary, had no temple, no priesthood, no altars, and no sacrifices, and the early prejudices of those who had embraced the gospel were

still strong in favour of these things. In refutation of the Jewish reasonings, the apostle shows that the Levitical ordinances, though divine, were only temporary,—a shadow of good things to come. From their own scriptures he fully proves to the Hebrews, that Jesus of Nazareth was the Son of God, manifested in human nature—as a Divine person, infinitely superior to angels, his creatures—as an apostle, far more worthy than Moses—and, as the Messiah, called to that office, and constituted our great High Priest by the oath of God, incomparably more excellent than Aaron; and that, superseding all the ceremonial sacrifices commanded by the law, he made a real atonement for our sins by his own death, through which the blessings of eternal salvation are to be enjoyed by all who come unto God by him. The grand object of the apostle, therefore, in this Epistle is, to set forth the proper Divinity and humanity of Jesus Christ, and the surpassing excellency of the gospel, when compared with the institutions of Moses; to fortify the minds of the Hebrew converts against apostacy under persecution, and to engage them to a deportment becoming their Christian profession.

In some respects the Epistle to the Hebrews is the most important of the New Testament scriptures: it is an invaluable appendix to the Epistle to the Romans, inculcating precisely the same momentous doctrines; but proving and illustrating them in a different manner, upon principles peculiarly suited to the scriptural knowledge possessed by a Jew; while that to the Romans is designed especially for the converted Gentiles. It is an epitome of the dispensations of God to man, from the foundation of the world to the advent of Christ. It contains not only the essence of the gospel, but the sum and completion of the law, of which it is a most luminous commentary. It contrasts the grandeur, the efficacy, and the perpetuity of the new covenant privileges, worship, and promises under the gospel, with the earthly character and temporary nature of the typical economy established by Moses. It was calculated to reconcile the Jew to the destruction of his temple—the

CH. XIX.—ANALYSIS OF HEBREWS.

loss of his priesthood—the abolition of sacrifices—the devastation of his country—and even the extinction of his name; because it exhibits a nobler temple, a better priesthood, the only perfect sacrifice of atonement, a heavenly country, and an eternal memorial in the kingdom of God.

The Epistle to the Hebrews is divided into thirteen chapters, and contains three parts.

Part I. Demonstrates the superiority of Christianity to the Levitical dispensation, ch. i.—x. 18. In this part there are twenty sections.

Section 1. Declares the personal dignity of the mediatorial glory of Jesus, the Son of God, by whom the Father speaks to men in the gospel, ch. i. 1—4.

Sec. 2. Proves, from the Old Testament scriptures, the superiority of Christ to angels, who worship him as their Creator and Lord, ch. i. 5—14.

Sec. 3. Requires devout attention to the gospel of Christ, from the danger of neglecting so great salvation, thus brought to mankind, ch. ii. 1—4.

Sec. 4. Advances further proofs of the superiority of Christ to angels, notwithstanding his temporary humiliation, ch. ii. 5—9.

Sec. 5. Shows the reasons and benefits of his incarnation, sufferings, and death, he being the High Priest and Saviour of his people, ch. ii. 10—18.

Sec. 6. Demonstrates and illustrates the vast superiority of Christ to Moses, ch. iii. 1—6.

Sec. 7. Solemnly admonishes the Hebrews not to fall by unbelief, as their ancestors perished in the wilderness, ch. iii. 7—19; iv. 1, 2.

Sec. 8. Exhibits the certainty and excellency of the heavenly rest, typified by the sabbath, and by the land of Canaan, ch. iv. 3—11.

Sec. 9. Urges the powerful force of the word of God, the omniscience of our Judge, and the compassion of our great High Priest, as motives to stedfastness and prayer, ch. iv. 12—16.

Sec. 10. Demonstrates the superiority of Christ to the Aaronic priesthood, he having been constituted a

High Priest after the order of Melchisedec, ch. v. 1—10.

Sec. 11. Reproves the Hebrews for their small proficiency in Christianity, ch. v. 11—14.

Sec. 12. Leads them forward in the knowledge of Christ, ch. vi. 1—3.

Sec. 13. Shows the awful condition of apostates, illustrated by a simile taken from barren land, which is cultivated in vain, ch. vi. 4—8.

Sec. 14. Expresses hope of the Hebrews, and desires for their perseverance, ch. vi. 9, 10.

Sec. 15. Expatiates on the security of the covenant of grace, as confirmed to Abraham by the promise of God, for the consolation of believers, ch. vi. 11—20.

Sec. 16. Proves the superiority of Melchisedec's typical priesthood to that of Aaron, ch. vii. 1—10.

Sec. 17. Shows that the change of the priesthood, and consequently the change of the law for a better covenant, and a never-dying Priest in the person of Christ, was designed for the complete and eternal salvation of all who come to God by Him, ch. vii. 11—28.

Sec. 18. Proves further the superiority of Messiah's priesthood to that of Aaron's, and the necessary abrogation of the old covenant for a better, through a superior Mediator, ch. viii.

Sec. 19. Exhibits the typical nature of the tabernacle, with its furniture and ordinances, as fulfilled in the covenant, priesthood, and sacrifice of Christ, ch. ix.

Sec. 20. Proves the insufficiency of the legal sacrifices; and their abolition by the substitution of Christ, through whose sacrifice believers obtain eternal remission, ch. x. 1—18.

Part II. Contains the application of the doctrines established, for the consolation of the Hebrews under their trials, ch. x. 19—39; xii. 2. In this part there are three sections.

Section 1. Exhorts the believing Hebrews to faith, prayer, constancy, love, and good works, from the consideration of the blessings of the gospel, and the dreadful consequences of rejecting it, ch. x. 19—39.

Sec. 2. Illustrates the nature, excellency, efficacy, and fruits of faith, by examples of the most eminent saints, from Abel to the close of the Old Testament dispensation, ch. xi.

Sec. 3. Applies the consideration of former worthies, and the example of Christ, by way of exhortation to Christian perseverance, ch. xii. 1, 2.

Part III. Contains practical exhortations to the Hebrews, ch. xii. 3—29; xiii. In this part there are six sections.

Section 1. Exhorts to persevering faith, filial resignation, and universal holiness, ch. xii. 3—17.

Sec. 2. Enjoins an obedient attachment to the gospel, from the consideration of its excellency above the law, and the consequent danger of rejecting it, ch. xii. 18—29.

Sec. 3. Enforces brotherly love, hospitality, compassion, charity, contentment, and confidence in God, ch. xiii. 1—6.

Sec. 4. Enjoins the recollection of the faith and examples of deceased pastors, as the means of establishment in the doctrine of Christ, ch. xiii. 7—15.

Sec. 5. Directs to liberality, obedience to faithful pastors, and to prayer for them, ch. xiii. 16—19.

Sec. 6. Concludes the Epistle with prayer for the Hebrews, a salutation, and a benediction, ch. xiii. 20—25.

References in Hebrews.

Ch. i. 1.	Num. xii. 6—8.	Ch ii 12.	Psa. xxii. 22-25
— — 4, 5.	Psa. ii. 1—8.	— — 13.	Isa. viii. 18.
— — 6.	— xcvii. 7.	— iii. 2.	Exod. xiv. 31; Num. xii. 7, 8.
— — 7.	— civ. 4.		
— — 8.	— xlv. 6, 7.	— — 15.	Psa. xcv. 7, 11.
— — 10.	— cii. 25.	— — 17, 18.	Num. xiv. 22, 29, 30.
— — 11.	Isa. xxxiv. 4; li. 6.		
— — 13.	Psa. cx. 1.	— v. 2, 3.	Lev. ix. 7, 22.
— — 14.	Gen. xxxii. 1, 2; 2 Kings vi. 17; Dan. iii. 28; Acts xii. 7.	— — 5.	Psa. ii. 7.
		— — 6.	— cx. 4.
		— vi. 13.	Gen. xxii. 16, 17.
		— vii. 1, 2.	— xiv. 18, etc.
— ii. 2.	Num. xv. 30, 31.	— — 27.	Lev. xvi. 6—11.
— — 6, 7.	Ps. viii. 4; cxliv. 3; 1 Cor. xv. 27.	— viii. 5.	Exod. xxv. 40.
		— — 8, 12.	Jer. xxxi. 31—34.

CH. XIX.—ANALYSIS OF JAMES.

Ch. viii. 8, 12.	Isa. liv. 13; Zech. viii. 8.	Ch. xii. 5, 6.	Prov. iii. 11, 12.
— ix. 1, 2.	Exod. xxv. xxvi. xl.	— — 9.	Num. xvi. 22.
— — 7.	Lev. xvi. 2, 11, 12.	— — 12.	Isa. xxxv. 3, 4.
		— — 16.	Gen. xxv. 33, 34.
— — 19.	Exod. xxiv. 6—8.	— — 17.	—— xxvii. 34-38.
— x. 4.	Mic. vi. 6, 8.	— — 18.	Exod. xix. 12-18.
— — 5, 7.	Psa. xl. 6, 8	— — 24.	Gen. iv. 10, 11.
— — 16.	Jer. xxxi. 33, 34.	— — 26.	Hag. ii. 6, 7.
— — 28, 29.	Deut xvii. 2—6.	— xiii. 11	Exod. xxix. 14; Lev. xvi. 27.
— xi.	Gen. Exod. Jud. etc.	— — 20.	Ezek. xxxiv. 23; Dan. ix 24, 27; Zech. ix. 11.

THE EPISTLE OF JAMES.

This Epistle of James is called catholic or general, because it was not written to any particular church, but to the whole Jewish nation then dispersed abroad. It also addresses Christians in some passages, and in others those who did not believe on Christ while they yet possessed the Scriptures. On that account this Epistle, in the mode of its address, is entirely different from all the others; and the general style of it is more like that of a prophet of the Old Testament, than of an apostle of the New. Our blessed Lord is mentioned but twice in the whole Epistle: it begins without any apostolical salutation, and it closes without any apostolical benediction. It may be regarded as a kind of connecting link between Judaism and Christianity, as the ministry of John the Baptist was between the Old and the New Testament. The elegant and beautiful simplicity of the sacred writers is, however, eminently conspicuous in this Epistle of James; and it is commended as one of the most finished productions in the New Testament. Its excellence and value are indeed clearly apparent. It was written about A.D. 61, and was designed,

1. To comfort the Christians under their various tribulations.

2. To correct their notions and confirm their minds in the doctrine of justification, by describing a fruitful faith.

3. To prevent believers from falling into those evil tempers and practices which prevailed among the unbelieving Jews.

4. To warn the ungodly of their approaching visitations in judgment.

The Epistle of James is divided into five chapters, containing eighteen sections.

Section I. Exhorts believers to rejoice under afflictions, ch. i. 1—4.

Sec. II. Directs to seek wisdom from God, firmly believing his promise, ch. i. 5—8.

Sec. III. Counsels both rich and poor believers to expect eternal life at the end of their trials, ch. i. 9—12.

Sec. IV. Shows that sin is the fruit of men's lust, and not from God, who is the gracious author of every gift and blessing, ch. i. 13—18.

Sec. V. Admonishes to receive the word of God with meekness, so as to reduce it to practice, ch. i. 19—27.

Sec. VI. Cautions against partiality to the rich and contempt of the poor, as contrary to the law of love, ch. ii. 1—9.

Sec. VII. Shows that the transgression of one commandment violates the whole law, ch. ii. 10—12.

Sec. VIII. Shows that faith without works is dead; and that therefore such a faith cannot save the soul, ch. ii. 13—26.

Sec. IX. Cautions against a haughty conduct, and the fatal evils of an unbridled tongue, ch. iii. 1—12.

Sec. X. Contrasts the nature and effects of earthly and heavenly wisdom, ch. iii. 13—18.

Sec. XI. Exhibits the bad effects of the lusts and passions of ungodly men, ch. iv. 1—6.

Sec. XII. Exhorts to submission unto God and repentance before him, ch. iv. 7—10.

Sec. XIII. Cautions against slander, censoriousness, and carnal security, from the consideration of the shortness of human life, ch. iv. 11—17.

Sec. XIV. Denounces dreadful judgments on wicked rich men, and oppressors, ch. v. 1—6.

Sec. XV. Exhorts believers to patience under trials, in the hope of deliverance, ch. v. 7—11.

Sec. XVI. Cautions against swearing, and enjoins prayer and praise, ch. v. 12, 13.

Sec. XVII. Instructs for visiting the sick, the mutual acknowledgment of offences, and the efficacy of prayer, ch. v. 14—18.

Sec. XVIII. Encourages to seek the recovery of offending brethren, and the conversion of sinners, as the greatest of benefits, ch. v. 19, 20.

References in James.

Ch. i. 5.	1 Kings iii. 9, 11, 12; Jer. xxix. 12, 13.	Ch. ii. 25.	Josh. ii 1, 21.
		— iii. 2.	1 Kings viii. 46.
— — 17.	Mal. iii. 6; Num. xxiii. 19.	— v. 11.	Ps. xciv. 12; Job i. 21, 22; xlii. 10, 17.
— — 18.	Jer. ii. 3.	— — 16.	Gen. xx. 17, 18; Deut. ix. 18-20.
— ii. 8.	Lev. xix. 18.		
— — 21—23.	Gen. xv. 6; xxii. 9—12; Isa. xli. 8.	— — 17, 18.	1 Kings xvii. 1; xviii. 42—45.
		— — 20.	Prov. x. 12.

FIRST EPISTLE OF PETER.

This First Epistle of Peter appears to have been written in a time of grievous persecution, by which Christians were scattered abroad. It is called general, because it was addressed to all believers in their dispersion; the converts both from among the Jews and those from idolatry. It was written in the reign of the emperor Nero, about A. D. 64, and sent by Peter from Babylon, ch. v. 13; by which some have understood Rome, as the mystical Babylon, Rev. xviii. 2: but most regard it as the proper name of that ancient city or its province, where was the principal eastern settlement of the dispersed Jews. It is evidently the design of this Epistle to comfort believers under their fiery trials, by the noblest considerations which the gospel could suggest, especially by the sure prospect of a glorious reward, an inheritance incorruptible, undefiled, and that fadeth not away, reserved in heaven for the faithful. In this

admirable Epistle are the principles of our most holy religion inculcated in perfect accordance with the analogy of faith, as taught in the Epistles of Paul, and in the other parts of the New Testament. They are levelled against all manner of immorality in practice, and every corrupt affection, and Christians are urged by the purest motives to all those virtues and graces which constitute our conformity to God, and the true glory of our nature. How excellent, therefore, how elevated, how divine, how worthy of all acceptation, is the religion of Jesus Christ!

This Epistle is divided into five chapters, containing sixteen sections.

Section I. Salutes the brethren as the elect, sanctified, and obedient; and blesses God for his abundant mercy, and for the inestimable blessings bestowed upon them both for time and eternity, ch. i. 1—5.

Sec. II. Shows the necessity of their trials, to prepare them for the full enjoyment of that salvation by Christ, which was foretold by prophets, confirmed by the Spirit, and contemplated by angels, ch. i. 6—12.

Sec. III. Exhorts believers to holiness, as worshippers of God, and redeemed by the precious blood of Christ, ch. i. 13—20.

Sec. IV. Enjoins upon them brotherly love, as the regenerate children of God, ch. i. 21—25.

Sec. V. Exhorts believers to a devout study of the word of God, as a spiritual priesthood, resting upon Christ the rock of ages, the precious corner-stone on which the church is built, ch. ii. 1—8.

Sec. VI. Declares the character of believers as the children of God, ch. ii. 9, 10.

Sec. VII. Beseeches believers to abstain from fleshly lusts, to glorify God, and to practise the various duties of life, whether as subjects or as servants, ch. ii. 11—18.

Sec. VIII. Exhorts to patience under persecution, after the example of Christ, by whose sufferings we obtain salvation, ch. ii. 19—25.

Sec. IX. Enjoins upon husbands and wives their respective duties, ch. iii. 1—7.

CH. XIX.—ANALYSIS OF 1 PETER. 163

Sec. X. Exhorts to the duties of brotherly love, and to stedfastness under persecution, so as with a well-furnished mind, and in the most proper temper, to be able to defend the gospel, ch. iii. 8—16.

Sec. XI. Shows that the destruction of the antediluvians was an emblem of the perdition of the wicked at the day of judgment, and the preservation in the ark was an emblem of salvation signified in baptism, through Christ our risen Redeemer, ch. iii. 17—22.

Sec. XII. Exhorts to conformity to Christ, who redeemed us from iniquity, and to preparation for a speedy judgment, ch. iv. 1—6.

Sec. XIII. From the approaching end of all things in the Jewish state, believers are urged to watchfulness, prayer, charity, hospitality, and a right use of spiritual gifts, ch. iv. 7—12.

Sec. XIV. Gives various encouragements to patience and confidence, under the sufferings for Christ which are to be expected, ch. iv. 13—19.

Sec. XV. Exhorts the ministers of the churches to feed the flock of Christ, expecting a crown of glory, and the people to suitable behaviour in hope of eternal life, ch. v. 1—9.

Sec. XVI. Concludes with prayers, salutations, and benediction, ch. v. 10—14.

References in 1 Peter.

Ch. i. 7.	Isa. xlviii. 9, 10; Zech. xiii. 9.	Ch. ii 9.	Exod. xix. 5, 6; Deut. vii. 6.
— — 10, 11.	Dan. ii. 44; vii. 28; viii. 13; Hag. ii. 7, 15; Isa. liii.; Dan. ix. 26; x. 1—3.	— — 10.	Hos. i. 9, 10.
		— — 23, 24.	Isa. liii. 4—12.
		— iii. 6.	Gen. xviii. 12.
		— — 20.	— vi. 5—22.
		— iv. 11.	Jer. xxiii. 22, 28.
— — 12.	Isa. ii. 2, 3; Dan. xii. 8, 9, 13.	— — 17.	Isa. x. 12; Ezek. ix. 6, 9.
— — 24, 25.	— xl. 6—8.	— v. 3.	Ezek. xxxiv. 2, 10.
— ii. 5.	— lxi. 6; lxii. 12.		
		— — 5.	Isa. lvii. 15.
— — 6.	— xxviii. 16.	— — 10.	Zech. x. 6, 12.

SECOND EPISTLE OF PETER.

The Second Epistle of Peter was addressed to the same persons as the former, and was written, as is believed, about a year later. It was evidently written in the prospect of a violent death, ch. i. 14, and it is supposed by some to have been drawn up at Rome; where, on the authority of uncertain tradition, it is believed, the apostle had been summoned to answer charges against him as a disturber of the government, by his preaching the doctrine of Christ, and suffered there for the gospel. The general design of this Epistle was to confirm the doctrines and instructions contained in the former, to establish converts in the truth and profession of the gospel, to excite them to adorn their heavenly calling; to caution them against the artifices of false teachers, whose tenets and practices he describes; to warn them against the inveterate enemies of the gospel, who scoffingly mocked at the coming of Christ to judgment, and to prepare them for that event by a holy and unblamable conversation. The Epistle is divided into three chapters, including nine sections.

Section I. Contains the salutation, showing the inestimable blessings to which the brethren had been called by the grace of God, ch. i. 1—4.

Sec. II. Exhorts to diligence in Christian duties, in order to make their calling and election sure to themselves, and to secure a triumphant entrance into heaven, ch. i. 5—11.

Sec. III. Declares his approaching martyrdom to be a special reason of his affectionate admonition, ch. i. 12—15.

Sec. IV. Urges the evidence of what the apostle had seen and heard, in confirmation of his testimony concerning the glory of Christ, and enjoins regard to the inspired word of God in the Scriptures, ch. i. 16—21.

Sec. V. Foretells the coming of false teachers, their corrupt tenets and practices, and the Divine judgments against them, ch. ii.

Sec. VI. Warns believers against scoffers and impostors, who would ridicule their expectation of Christ's coming, ch. iii. 1—7.

Sec. VII. Shows the reason why that great day is delayed, and describes its awful circumstances and consequences, as a powerful argument for personal holiness, ch. iii. 8—14.

Sec. VIII. Declares the agreement of Paul's doctrine with that of this Epistle, ch. iii. 15, 16.

Sec. IX. Concludes with warnings against seducers, and exhortations to grow in grace and in the knowledge of Christ, ch. iii. 17, 18.

In this Epistle there are two things especially remarkable:

1. The character of false teachers as described by the apostle, and the dreadful judgments of God denounced as certain to fall upon them; as the apostate angels, the old world of ungodly men, and Sodom and Gomorrha were overwhelmed, ch. ii.

2. The terrible sublimity and solemn grandeur with which the awful dissolution of the heavens and the earth is described, ch. iii. 11, 12.

References in 2 Peter.

Ch. i. 13.	Josh. xxiii. 14.	Ch. iii. 4.	Isa. v. 19, 21.
— — 16, 17.	Matt. xvii. 1—5.	— — 5, 6.	Gen. i. 6—9; vii. 11—22.
— — 21.	2 Sam. xxiii. 2; 2 Tim. iii. 16.	— — 10.	Psa. cii. 26, 27.
— ii. 5.	Gen. vii. 1, 7, 16, 23.	— — 13.	Isa. lxv. 17—19; Rev. xxi. 1; xxii. 5.
— — 6, 7.	—— xix. 15, 24, 25.		
— — 15, 16.	Num. xxii. 5, 7, 21, 23, 28.	— — 16.	2 Thess. ii. 10—12.

FIRST EPISTLE OF JOHN.

The name of John is neither prefixed nor subscribed to this Epistle, yet, from the earliest times, it has always been attributed to the beloved apostle of Christ. The peculiar style and spirit of the writing seem strongly to indicate it to have been the work of John. It begins without a salutation, and ends without a benediction,

and, therefore, some have doubted the propriety of calling it an Epistle, addressed to any church or body of Christians. " It is, indeed, a didactic discourse upon the principles of Christianity, both in doctrine and practice; and whether we consider the sublimity of its opening, with the fundamental topics of God's perfections, man's depravity, and Christ's propitiation; the perspicuity with which it propounds the deepest mysteries of our holy faith, and the evidences of the proof which it brings to confirm them: whether we consider the sanctity of its precepts, and the energy of argument with which they are enforced; the dignified simplicity of language in which both doctrines and precepts are delivered: whether we regard the importance of the matter, the propriety of the style, or the general spirit of ardent piety and warm benevolence, united with a fervent zeal, which breathes throughout the whole composition—we shall find it, in every respect, worthy of the holy author to whom the constant tradition of the church ascribes it, the disciple whom Jesus loved." *Bishop Horsley.*

This Epistle was written about A. D. 68; or, as some think, A. D. 96;* the design of it was to guard the Christians against the doctrines of certain heretics, or antichrists, supposed by learned men to be the Cerinthians and Gnostics, the earliest corrupters of the gospel among the Gentiles; to excite all who profess to know God and Jesus Christ, to walk in the light of holiness and love, and not in the darkness of sin and ungodliness; to live in holy communion with one another, and with the Father and his Son Jesus Christ, and to rejoice in hope of eternal felicity in heaven.

This Epistle has five chapters, including sixteen sections.

Section I. Declares the proper Divinity and humanity of the Saviour, for the purpose of promoting Christian communion and fellowship with the Father, and with his Son Jesus Christ, ch. i. 1—4.

* The date of A. D. 96 has been assigned for the three Epistles of John. See *Townsend.*

Sec. II. Shows that those who have fellowship with God walk in the light of holiness; and that God, in faithfulness and righteousness, through Christ, is engaged to pardon and purify penitents confessing their sins; while those who say they have no sin, are deceived or deceivers, ch. i. 5—10.

Sec. III. Warns believers not to sin, yet directs to Christ as our Advocate in heaven, the universal propitiation for sin, ch. ii. 1, 2.

Sec. IV. Shows that the knowledge of Christ, and union with him, must be evidenced by obedience to his commands, by imitating his example, and by love to the brethren, ch. ii. 3—11.

Sec. V. Warns believers against attachment to the perishing things of the world, from the consideration of their sins being forgiven, and their matured knowledge and victorious faith, ch. ii. 12—17.

Sec. VI. Cautions against apostates from their profession denying that Jesus was the Christ, they being so many antichrists, and it declares the unction of the Holy Spirit as the only effectual preservative, ch. ii. 18—23.

Sec. VII. Exhorts to cherish the influences of the Holy Spirit as effectual to instruct the mind, and to preserve in the ways of holiness, by which regeneration is evinced, ch. ii. 24—29.

Sec. VIII. Expresses admiration at the sovereign love of God in the adoption of sinners, who knowing their privileges, anticipate eternal glory, and labour after holiness in heart and life, ch. iii. 1—3.

Sec. IX. Shows how men may be distinguished, as being the children of God, or the children of the devil, ch. iii. 4—10.

Sec. X. Exhorts to cherish brotherly love, as the means of demonstrating our regeneration or new birth, and of enjoying confidence towards God, ch. iii. 11—24.

Sec. XI. Warns against false teachers, who denied that Christ was come in the flesh, and instructs how to distinguish between the spirit of truth and the spirit of error, ch. iv. 1—6.

Sec. XII. Exhorts further to brotherly love, from the

example of God giving his Son as a propitiation or satisfaction for sinners; from its being a proof of our union with God; from its giving confidence in looking forward to the day of judgment; and from its happy influence on the mind, ch. iv. 7—21.

Sec. XIII. Shows the connexion between regeneration, love to God, universal obedience, and victory over the world, ch. v. 1—5.

Sec. XIV. States the manifold testimonies by which the doctrine of Christ is proved, declaring the inseparable union between true faith and eternal life, ch. v. 6—13.

Sec. XV. Declares the readiness of the Lord to hear prayer, and that there is a sin unto death, ch. v. 14—17.

Sec. XVI. Concludes the Epistle, strongly marking the difference between the regenerate who are taught of God, and the world which lieth in wickedness, ch. v. 18—21.

References in 1 John.

Ch. i. 8.	1 Kings viii. 46; Eccles. vii. 20.	Ch. iii. 1.	Isa. lvi. 5.
— — 9.	Job xxxiii. 26, 28; Isa. lv. 7.	— — 2.	Job xix. 26, 27; Psa. xvi. 11.
— ii. 2.	John i. 29; Rom. iii. 25; 1 Tim. ii. 6.	— — 5.	Isa. liii. 4, 12; Dan. ix. 24.
		— — 12.	Gen. iv. 3—8.
		— — 22.	Psa. cxlv. 18, 19.
— — 19.	Deut. xiii. 13; Psa. xli. 9.	— v. 3.	Mic. vi. 8.
		— — 16.	Job xlii. 8.
— — 27.	Isa. lxi. 1; Jer. xxxi. 33, 34.	— — 20.	Isa. ix. 6; liv. 5.

SECOND EPISTLE OF JOHN.

The elect lady, or, according to some, Lady Electa, to whom this Epistle was addressed, appears to have been an honourable Christian matron, probably a widow, well known to the churches, but where she resided we have no certain information; perhaps it was in the vicinity of Ephesus. Though this Epistle does not bear the name of the author, it was evidently written by John the apostle, and, as many suppose, about A. D. 69, for the purpose of comforting this lady and her family, and

of establishing them in the true doctrine of Christ. It is divided into thirteen verses, including five sections.

Section I. Addresses the lady and her children, with apostolical salutation commending their love in the truth, ver. 1—3.

Sec. II. Congratulates the family on their stedfastness in the truth, and exhorts them to perseverance in faith and love, ver. 4—6.

Sec. III. Declares that many antichrists had arisen, and, therefore, watchful diligence and adherence to the doctrine of Christ were indispensable to the obtaining a full reward, ver. 7—9.

Sec. IV. Admonishes to have no intercourse with those who disseminate false doctrines, ver. 10, 11.

Sec. V. Concludes the Epistle, ver. 12, 13.

Ignorant as we are of the abode and history of this worthy lady, we cannot but rejoice that her children had obtained like precious faith, through the righteousness of our God and Saviour Jesus Christ, with their mother; and that by their walking in the truth they proved the reality of their personal religion, while they delighted the benevolent soul of the apostle John. The lovely picture of family religion drawn in this short Epistle affords much encouragement to Christian mothers in seeking the salvation of their children; and it is highly instructive to the young, inviting them to receive the truth of Christ in the love of it, and to follow the example of their pious parents in the service and ways of God.

References in 2 John.

Ver. 7.	1 John iv. 1.	Ver. 9.	John xv. 6.
—— 8.	Phil. iii. 16;	—— 10.	Gal. i. 8, 9.
	Heb. ii. 1.	—— 11.	1 Tim. v. 22.

THIRD EPISTLE OF JOHN.

Gaius, of Macedonia, is mentioned, Acts xix. 29, Gaius, of Derbe, Acts xx. 4, and Gaius, of Corinth, Rom. xvi. 23; 1 Cor. i. 14. The latter of these was the excellent person to whom, in a declining state of health, this Epistle is thought to have been addressed. He

appears to have been a wealthy member of the church at Corinth, and a valuable friend to religion and to mankind, in furthering the work of Christian missions, by the generous support he afforded to the laborious ministers of the gospel, ver. 6—8.

The design of this Epistle to Gaius, was to encourage him, commending the stedfastness of his faith and his kind hospitality, especially to those who, in great peril and self-denial, laboured as the missionaries of Christ to the Gentiles; to caution him against the ambitious turbulence of one Diotrephes; to recommend Demetrius to his friendship, and to intimate the intended visit of the apostle.

This Epistle was written about the same time as the Second: it is divided into fourteen verses, including five sections.

Section I. Expresses affection to Gaius in the bonds of the gospel, and desires health equal to the prosperity of his soul, ver. 1, 2.

Sec. II. Congratulates him on the testimony borne by the brethren to his stedfastness in the faith, ver. 3, 4.

Sec. III. Commends his generous hospitality to the missionaries, so necessary to those self-denying men, who were consecrating all their powers to the ministry of the gospel among the Gentiles, ver. 5—8.

Sec. IV. Complains of Diotrephes, whose ambitious violence wasted the church, and cautions against so evil an example, ver. 9—11.

Sec. V. Recommends Demetrius, promises a visit, and concludes with salutations, ver. 12—14.

References in 3 John.

Ver. 3.	2 John 4.	Ver. 7.	1 Cor. ix. 15, 18.
—— 4.	Prov. xxiii. 23, 24.	—— 9.	Matt. xxiii. 2—8.
—— 5.	1 Pet. iv. 9, 10.	—— 10.	Isa. lxvi. 5.

EPISTLE OF JUDE.

The Epistle of Jude was written about A. D. 65. The design of it was to guard believers against the corrupt principles and the licentious practices of the false teach-

ers who had arisen in the church during the apostolic age. By describing their character, and pointing out the Divine judgments which such persons had reason to expect, the apostle cautions Christians against listening to their insinuations, and being thereby perverted from the faith and purity of the glorious gospel. In this Epistle we see the holy indignation with which the bosom of this man of God glowed in writing against every form of vice; and the benevolent solicitude with which he exhorts the Christians, "to keep themselves in the love of God, looking for the mercy of our Lord Jesus Christ unto eternal life."

This Epistle is divided into twenty-five verses, containing seven sections.

Section I. After the general salutation to believers, the apostle exhorts them to a vigorous and holy contention for the purity of the faith once delivered to the saints, especially because of the errors of licentious apostates, ver. 1—4.

Sec. II. Reminds them of some awful instances of the Divine vengeance on sinners; the unbelieving Israelites; the apostate angels; and Sodom and Gomorrha, ver. 5—8.

Sec. III. Declares that these false teachers—filthy dreamers, and despisers of magistracy—being greedy of gain and sunk in corruption, were preparing themselves for the blackness of eternal darkness, ver. 9—13.

Sec. IV. Shows the certainty of those punishments on the wicked, from a noted prophecy of Enoch concerning the coming of Christ to judgment, ver. 14, 15.

Sec. V. Further describes these corrupters of doctrine and morals, ver. 16—19.

Sec. VI. Exhorts to seek their own edification by the gracious influences of the Holy Spirit in their devotions, ver. 20, 21.

Sec. VII. Directs to pity and restore those in danger; and concludes with a doxology to God our Saviour, ver. 22—25.

It is generally regarded as most probable that the apostle took the account concerning "Michael, the arch-

angel," and that remarkable passage of the prophecy of Enoch, from ancient traditions preserved and well known among the Jews.

References in Jude.

Ver. 5.	Num. xiv. 29; xxvi. 64, 65.	Ver. 11.	Num. xvi. 1, 3; xxii. 7—21.
—— 7.	Gen. xix. 24; Deut. xxix. 23.	—— 13.	Isa. lvii. 20.
—— 9.	Dan. x. 13; Zech. iii. 2.	—— 14, 15.	Gen. v. 18; Zech. xiv. 5.
—— 11.	Gen. iv. 5, 8.	—— 19.	Ezek. xiv. 7.
		—— 24.	Zech. iii. 4, 5.

THE BOOK OF THE REVELATION.

The title of this book is contained in its first verse. It is called The Revelation, from the signification of Apocalypsos, its Greek title. This book may be regarded as the most sublime of all that are contained in the New Testament. What is here recorded was made known to, and was written by, the apostle John, during his banishment in the isle of Patmos, the body of its revelations being imparted to him especially to exhibit the prophetic history of the church of Christ down to the end of the world. Some mistaken persons have objected to the study of this book, because presumptuous men have failed in their interpretations of its difficult passages. But their fault can be no apology for our neglect of duty. Sir Isaac Newton well observes, that " the folly of interpreters has been to foretell times and things by this prophecy, as if God designed to make them prophets."

Many parts of the Revelation are necessarily obscure to us, because they contain predictions of events still future: but enough is sufficiently clear to convey to us what the prophecies of the Old Testament afforded to the Jews under the former dispensation. No prophecy of the Revelation can be more clouded with obscurity to us, than were many of the ancient predictions to the pious Israelite: yet he looked into the holy books of the inspired prophets in which they were contained, with humble hope, patiently waiting for the promised Mes-

siah, as the consolation of Israel. We, in the same manner, look into these prophecies of the Apocalypse for the full discovery regarding the consummation of the great scheme of the gospel; when Christianity shall finally prevail over all the corruptions of the world, and be universally established in its utmost purity. In each case the great end was the main object to be kept in view, not the intervening details.

"It is worthy of notice, in respect of the Revelation, that the views given in it of God and heavenly things, of the kingdom of providence and grace, of the Redeemer's glory, and the happiness and character of his people, with the wickedness and ruin of his enemies, are set forth in so striking and peculiar a manner, that even those who do not at all understand the prophetical meaning, are interested and edified by reading it, in proportion to the degree of their humility, faith, and piety." *Scott.*

The eloquent Saurin remarks, " This is a very mortifying book to a mind greedy of knowledge and science; but one of the most satisfying to a heart solicitous about maxims and precepts."

The Revelation is divided into twenty-two chapters, containing four parts.

Part I. The introduction, contains an address to the seven churches in Asia Minor, ascriptions of glory to God, and a description of the glorious vision of the Lord Jesus Christ, with which John was favoured in his exile, ch. i.

Part II. Contains seven epistles to the churches, ch. ii. iii.

1. To the church at Ephesus, ch. ii. 1—7.
2. ——————— Smyrna, ver. 8—11.
3. ——————— Pergamos, ver. 12—17.
4. ——————— Thyatira, ver. 18—29.
5. ——————— Sardis, ch. iii. 1—6.
6. ——————— Philadelphia, ver. 7—13.
7. ——————— Laodicea, ver. 14—22.

Part III. Describes several wondrous visions which the apostle beheld, ch. iv. v.

174 CH. XIX.—ANALYSIS OF REVELATION.

1. Of the Divine Majesty enthroned in glory, surrounded with angels and the heavenly church, in the exercise of sacred worship, ch. iv.

2. Of the Lamb, who alone was worthy even to look upon the volume of God's decrees, which, as a sealed book, is given to Him; and who, on that account, receives the adoring acclamations of the whole choir of saints and angels, equally with Him who sat on the throne, ch. v.

Part IV. Includes the remainder of the book, from ch. vi. to xxii., referring to the condition of the church in all succeeding ages, to the consummation of blessedness in the world of glory. This part of the book relates to seven distinct parts or periods of the church, which the apostle describes.

I. The opening of the seals of the book, ch. vi.—viii. 1.

1. Seal opened, exhibits a white horse, ch. vi. 1, 2.
2. ———————————— a red horse, ver. 3, 4.
3. ———————————— a black horse, ver. 5, 6.
4. ———————————— a pale horse, ver. 7, 8.
5. ———————————— the souls of the martyrs, ver. 9—11.
6. ———————————— various judgments, ver. 12—17.

Six of the seals having been opened, John beheld the heavenly church of 144,000, sealed, and innumerable multitudes from all nations blessing God and the Lamb for their salvation and immortal glory, ch. vii.

7. Seal opened, exhibits a universal silence, introducing

II. The trumpets, ch. viii. 2—13.—x.

The vision of the intercession of Christ, ch. viii. 3—5.
First angel sounded, ver. 6, 7.
Second ——————, ver. 8, 9.
Third ——————, ver. 10, 11.
Fourth ——————, ver. 12, 13.
Fifth ——————, ch. ix. 1—12.
Sixth ——————, ver. 13—21.

The sixth angel having sounded, John had a wonderful vision, which he relates, of a mighty angel bringing him a little book, as a commission to prophesy to all nations, ch. x.

III. Is distinguished by a series of representations, ch. xi.—xix.

1. The temple, altar, and worshippers of God measured, ch. xi. 1, 2.

2. The two witnesses commissioned to prophesy 1260 days, ch. xi. 3—6.

3. The beast fights against and kills them, but they rise again and ascend to heaven, ch. xi. 7—14.

4. The seventh trumpet sounds, and glorious things follow, ch. xi. 15—19.

5. The church described as a woman clothed with the sun, whose man-child is persecuted by a dragon, ch. xii. 1—6.

6. Michael overcomes the dragon, Satan, and expels him, which causes great joy in heaven, ch. xii. 7—12.

7. The dragon persecutes the church on the earth, ch. xii. 13—17.

8. The vision of a wonderful beast rising out of the sea, to which the dragon gives power, ch. xiii. 1—10.

9. A second beast, rising out of the earth, and by which all are compelled to worship the dragon, ch. xiii. 11—18.

10. A vision of the Lamb, on Mount Zion, with 144,000 of his elect; and the heavenly church celebrates the happiness of the faithful, ch. xiv. 1—5.

11. A vision of an angel flying to preach the gospel to all nations, and to denounce judgments from God on the beast and his worshippers, ch. xiv. 10—20.

12. A vision of the angels with the vials of plagues, and of the heavenly church rejoicing in the righteous government of God, ch. xv.

13. The vials of divine wrath poured forth upon the enemies of God and of his church, ch. xvi.

14. The vision of the mystical Babylon, ch. xvii.

15. The overthrow and utter ruin of Babylon, and the miseries of the wicked, ch. xviii.

16. The triumph of the heavenly host over the desolation of Babylon, ch. xix. 1—10.

17. The conquest of Christ over the enemies of his church, ch. xix. 11—21.

IV. Exhibits an angel binding Satan during the happy millennium of the church, ch. xx. 1—6.

V. Exhibits Satan loosed for a season, and his vain attempts to re-establish his tyranny over the minds of mankind, ch. xx. 7—10.

VI. Exhibits the general resurrection, the universal judgment, and the everlasting misery of the ungodly, ch. xx. 11—15.

VII. Exhibits a vision of the New Jerusalem, with the felicity of the redeemed, described in all the magnificence and grandeur which human language can express, ch. xxi. xxii. 1—6.

1. The angel attests the truth of these things, ch. xxii. 7—9.

2. Christ himself shows the apostle that the state of men will soon be unchangeably fixed; declares who shall enter heaven, and who shall be excluded; urgently calls upon men to accept his salvation, and denounces plagues on those who alter or abridge the words of this prophecy, ch. xxii. 10—19.

3. The apostle closes with a benediction, ch. xxii. 20, 21.

"How delightfully does the canon of Scripture conclude, leaving, as it were, the music of heaven upon the attentive ear! 'O thou blessed bright and morning Star, impress on all our hearts these thy gracious words, to aid our faith in those which thou didst deliver, while in mortal flesh.' Then did the compassionate Saviour proclaim, in the temple, to a crowd, *If any man thirst, let him come unto me and drink*, John vii. 37. And now, from his celestial temple, he points to the fountain of happiness, near the throne of God, and says, *Whosoever will, let him come, let him freely take of this living water:* yea, and not content with this language by his Spirit, he calls on his bride, the church, to publish this kind invitation; and bids every one that hears it to communicate the good tidings to others.

"With what sacred observance should these books be guarded! Of what dreadful curses are they worthy, who presume to add to what is perfect, or to take from that

CH. XIX.—ANALYSIS OF REVELATION.

which is divine! While we are employed in any service which Providence has assigned us, whatever labours may exercise us, difficulties surround us, or sorrows depress us, let us with pleasure hear our Lord proclaiming, 'Behold, I come quickly; I come, and my reward of grace is with me, to recompense, with royal bounty, every work of faith and labour of love; I come, to receive my faithful, persevering people to myself, to dwell for ever in that blissful world, where the sacred volume shall be no more necessary; but knowledge, holiness, and joy, shall be poured in upon their souls in a nobler and more effectual manner.' Even so, come, Lord Jesus." *Dr. Doddridge.*

References in Revelation.

Ch. i. 3.	Prov. viii. 32-34.	Ch. x. 6.	Dan. xii. 6, 7.
— — 4.	Exod. iii. 14.	— — 9.	Ezek. iii. 3.
— — 7.	Dan. vii. 13.	— xi 1, 2.	—— xl. 3, etc.
— — 8.	Isa. xliv. 6.	— — 4.	Zech. iv. 11—14.
— — 12, 20.	Zech iv. 2, 14; Ezek. i. 26.	— — 11.	Ezek. xxxvii. 5, 9, 10, 14.
— — 14, 15.	Dan. vii. 9, 13.	— xii. 7.	Dan. xii. 1, 10.
— — 17.	Ezek. i. 28; Dan. x. 8.	— xiii. 1, etc.	—— vii. 3, etc.
— ii. 7.	Gen. ii. 9; iii. 24.	— xiv. 8.	Isa. xxi. 9; Jer. li. 8.
— — 14.	Num. xxiv. 14; xxv. 1; xxxi. 16.	— — 11.	Isa. xxxiv. 10.
— — 20.	1 Kings xvi. 31; xxi. 25.	— — 14.	Dan. vii. 13.
— iii. 7.	Isa. xxii. 22.	— — 20.	Isa. lxiii. 3.
— — 18.	— lv. 1, 2.	— xvii. 2.	Jer. li. 7.
— iv. 2, 3.	Ezek. i. 26—28.	—— 12.	Dan. vii. 20.
— — 6.	—— — 5, etc.	— xix. 20.	—— — 11, 12.
— v. 11.	Dan. vii. 10.	— xx. 8.	Ezek. xxxviii. 2, etc.
— vi. 2,4,5,8.	Zech. vi. 2—8.	— — 11, 12.	Dan. vii. 9, 10.
— — 15.	Isa. ii. 19—21.	— xxi. 1.	Isa. lxv. 17, 18; lxvi. 22, 23.
— vii. 1.	Dan. vii. 2.	— xxii. 1.	Ezek. xlvii. 1—12.
— — 14.	Isa. i. 16, 18; Zech. xiii. 1.	—— — 17.	Isa. lv. 1, 7.

Ch. XX.—Harmony of the Gospels.

The following concise harmony of the Gospels is revised and corrected from that of the late Rev. John Brown. It is presumed that it will be found useful to the reader of the New Testament. By this means the subjects of the sacred narratives are exhibited at one view, with all their concurrent circumstances, as recorded by the several Evangelists.

		MATT.	MARK.	LUKE.	JOHN.
I.	Luke's preface	. .	. .	i. 1-4.	. .
II.	Christ's Divinity	. .	. .	. .	i. 1-14.
III.	John Baptist's birth, and Christ's foretold	. .	. .	i. 5-80.	. .
IV.	Mary in danger of being put away . .	i. 18, 19.	. .	. .	. .
V.	Christ's birth	. .	. .	ii. 1-20.	. .
VI.	—— pedigree both by Joseph and by his mother	i. 1-17.	. .	iii. 23-38.	. .
VII.	—— circumcision	. .	. .	ii. 21-40.	. .
VIII.	The wise men from the east seek Christ	ii.	. .	. .	. .
IX.	Christ hears and questions the doctors	. .	. .	—— 41-50.	. .
X.	Ministry of John	iii. 1-12.	i. 1-8.	iii. 1-18.	i. 6-8.
XI.	Christ baptized	—— 13-17.	—— 9-11.	—— 21, 22.	. .
XII.	—— tempted	iv. 1-11.	—— 12, 13.	iv. 1-13.	. .
XIII.	John's testimony to Christ . . .	. .	. .	. .	i. 15-36.
XIV.	Christ's first miracle	. .	. .	. .	ii.
XV.	—— discourse with Nicodemus .	. .	. .	. .	iii.
XVI.	John imprisoned	xiv. 3-5.	vi. 17-20.	iii. 19, 20.	. .
XVII.	Christ converts many Samaritans .	. .	. .	. .	iv.
XVIII.	—— preaches in Galilee . .	iv. 17.	i. 14, 15.	iv. 14, 15.	. .
XIX.	—— at Nazareth . .	. .	. .	—— 16-30.	. .
XX.	Christ at Capernaum	{ iv. 13-16. viii. 5-17. }	i. 21-45.	—— 31-44. v. 1-16.	. .
XXI.	—— heals a man sick of the palsy .	ix. 2-8.	ii. 1-12.	—— 17-26.	. .
XXII.	—— calls Peter, etc. . . .	iv. 18-22.	i. 16-20.	—— 1-11.	. .
XXIII.	—— Matthew, and dines with him	ix. 9-17.	ii. 13-22.	—— 27-39.	. .

CH. XX.—HARMONY OF THE GOSPELS.

	MATT.	MARK.	LUKE.	JOHN.
XXIV. Christ asserts his own Godhead				v.
XXV. The disciples pluck the ears of corn	xii. 1-8.	ii. 23-28.	vi. 1-5.	
XXVI. Christ heals many	— 9-16.	iii. 1-12.		
XXVII. —— chooses and ordains his apostles		— 13-19.	— 12-16.	
XXVIII. ——'s sermon on the mount	v. vi vii.		— 20-49.	
XXIX. The centurion's servant healed	viii. 5-13.		vii. 1-10.	
XXX. A widow's son raised			— 11-17.	
XXXI. John's message to Christ	xi 2-19.		— 18-35.	
XXXII. Chorazin, etc. upbraided			x. 13-16.	
XXXIII. A woman anoints Christ	— 20-24.		vii. 36-50.	
XXXIV. Of blasphemy against the Holy Ghost	xii. 22-45.	iii. 22-30.	xi. 14-26. 29-32.	
XXXV. Christ's mother and brethren seek him	— 46-50.	— 31-35.	viii 19-21.	
XXXVI. Parable of the sower	xiii. 1-23.	iv. 1-20.	— 4-15.	
XXXVII. A scribe wishes to follow Christ	viii. 18-22.			
XXXVIII. The disciples in a storm	— 23-27.	— 36-41.	— 22-25.	
XXXIX. Christ heals the possessed	— 28-34.	v. 1-20.	— 26-39.	
XL. Jairus's daughter raised	ix. 18-26.	— 21-43.	— 40-56.	
XLI. Two blind men cured	— 27-31.			
XLII. Christ teaches at Nazareth	xiii. 54-58.	vi. 1-6.		
XLIII. —— journeys again into Galilee	ix 35.			
XLIV. The apostles sent out	x. vi. 1.	— 7-13.	ix. 1-6.	
XLV. John beheaded	xiv. 6-12.	— 21-29.		
XLVI. Herod's opinion of Christ	— 1, 2	— 14-16.	— 7-9.	
XLVII. Five thousand fed	— 13-21.	— 30-44.	— 10-17.	vi. 1-13.
XLVIII. Christ walks on the sea	— 22-33.	— 45-52.		— 15-21
XLIX. —— the bread of life				— 22-71
L. The Jews' impious traditions	xv. 1-20.	vii. 1-23.		
LI. The daughter of the Canaanitish woman healed	— 21-28.	— 24-30.		
LII. A dumb man healed	— 29-31.	— 31-37.		
LIII. Four thousand fed	— 32-39.	viii. 1-9.		
LIV. The leaven of the Pharisees	xvi. 1-12.	— 14-21.		
LV. A blind man healed		— 22-26.		

		MATT.	MARK.	LUKE.	JOHN.
LVI.	Peter's confession of Christ	xvi. 13-28.	viii. 27-38.	ix. 18-27.	vi. 66-71.
LVII.	Christ's transfiguration	xvii. 1-13.	ix. 2-13.	— 28-36.	
LVIII.	Christ cures a lunatic child	— 14-21.	— 14-29.	— 37-45.	
LIX.	Humility enjoined	xviii. 1-4.	— 33-37.	— 46-48.	
LX.	The feast of tabernacles				vii.
LXI.	Christ goes to Jerusalem			ix. 51.	— 10.
LXII.	The seventy sent forth			x. 1-24.	
LXIII.	An adulteress				viii.
LXIV.	A blind man healed				ix.
LXV.	Christ the good Shepherd				x. 1-21.
LXVI.	The efficacy of prayer			xi. 1-13.	
LXVII.	Against hypocrisy, covetousness, etc.			xii.	
LXVIII.	Repentance urged			xiii. 1-9.	
LXIX.	The feast of dedication				x. 22.
LXX.	The strait gate			— 22.	
LXXI.	A dropsical man healed; wedding feast			— 23-30.	
LXXII.	Lost sheep, money, and prodigal son			xiv.	
LXXIII.	Unjust steward and rich voluptuary			xv.	
LXXIV.	Various admonitions, ten lepers, etc.			xvi.	
LXXV.	Unjust judge, and Pharisee and publican			xviii. 1-14.	
LXXVI.	Concerning divorce	xix. 1-12.	x. 1-12.		
LXXVII.	Infants brought to Christ	— 13-15.	— 13-16.	— 15-17.	
LXXVIII.	Rich young ruler	— 16-30.	— 17-31.	— 18-30.	
LXXIX.	Labourers in the vineyard	xx. 1-16.			
LXXX.	Lazarus sick				xi. 1-16.
LXXXI.	Christ foretells his passion	xx. 17-19.	x. 32-34.	xviii. 31-34.	
LXXXII.	The request of the sons of Zebedee	— 20-28.	— 35-45.		
LXXXIII.	Blind man healed, Zaccheus converted, parable, etc.	— 29-34.	— 46-52.	{ — 35-43. / xix. 1-27.	
LXXXIV.	Lazarus raised				xi. 17-46.
LXXXV.	Mary anoints Christ	xxvi. 6-13.	xiv. 3-9.		xii. 1-11.
LXXXVI.	Christ's entrance into Jerusalem	xxi. 1-16.	xi. 1-11.	xix. 28-44.	— 12-19.
LXXXVII.	Some Greeks have an interview with Christ				— 20-22.

CH. XX.—HARMONY OF THE GOSPELS. 181

		MATT.	MARK.	LUKE.	JOHN.
LXXXVIII.	The barren fig-tree cursed	xxi 17-22.	xi 12-26.		
LXXXIX.	Christ's authority questioned	— 23-27.	— 27-33.	xx. 1-8.	
XC.	Parable of the two sons	— 28-32.			
XCI.	Of the vineyard let out	— 33-46.	xii. 1-12.	— 9-19.	
XCII.	Of the marriage feast	xxii. 1-14.		xiv. 16-24.	
XCIII.	Concerning paying tribute, scribes, Pharisees	— 15-16.	xii 13-37.	xx. 19-40.	
XCIV.	Pharisees and scribes accused and threatened		— 38-40.	— 45-47.	
XCV.	The widow and her two mites		— 41-44	xxi 1-4.	
XCVI.	Christ foretells the destruction of Jerusalem	xxiv.	xiii.	— 5-36	
XCVII.	Parable of the virgins and talents; the last judgment	xxv.			
XCVIII.	Christ washes his disciples' feet				xiii.
XCIX.	Preparation for the passover	xxvi. 17-19.	xiv. 12-16.	xxii. 7-13	
C.	Christ institutes the Lord's supper	— 20-30	— 17-26.	— 14-20	
CI.	Christ's consolatory discourses to his disciples				xiv. xv. xvi.
CII.	——— mediatorial prayer				xvii.
CIII.	——— warning to his disciples	xxi. 31-35.	xiv. 27-31.	xxii. 22-20.	xviii. 1, 2
CIV.	——— agony in the garden	— 36-46.	— 32-42.	— 40-46	— 3-11.
CV.	——— apprehension	— 47-56.	— 43-52.	— 47-53.	— 12-24.
CVI.	——— arraignment	— 57-68	— 53-65.	— 54-65.	— 17-27.
CVII.	Peter's denial	— 69-75.	— 66-72	— 55-62.	
CVIII.	Christ before the sanhedrin, Pilate, and Herod	xxvii. 1-14.	xv 1-5.	{ — 66-71 xxiii 1-12	— 28-38
CIX.	——— condemned by Pilate	— 15-26.	— 6-15.	— 13-25.	{ — 39, 40. xix. 1-16
CX.	Judas hangs himself in guilty despair	— 3-10.			
CXI.	Christ crucified	— 31-56.	— 20-41.	— 25-49	— 16-37
CXII.	Christ's burial	— 57-61.	— 42-47.	— 50-56	— 38-42.
CXIII.	resurrection	xxviii 1-8.	xvi 1-8	xxiv. 1-12	xx. 1-10.
CXIV.	——— appearing to his disciples	— 9, 10.	— 9-14	— 13-48	— 11-20.
CXV.	——— appearance at the sea of Tiberias, and his discourse with Peter				xxi.
CXVI.	Christ commissions his disciples, and ascends to heaven	xxviii. 16-20.	xvi. 15-20.	xxiv. 49-53.	

R

CH. XXI.—CHRONOLOGICAL TABLE OF THE NEW TESTAMENT SCRIPTURES.

READERS of the Scriptures may profit greatly by knowing the times and occasions of writing the several books. The New Testament was originally written in the Greek language; perhaps the Gospel according to Matthew may, as some suppose, also have had an original in Hebrew. But concerning the exact year or season when each of the several books was written, some little differences of opinion have been entertained among commentators. The following table has been compiled from the best writers on the subject of the New Testament books.

BOOK.	AUTHOR.	WHERE WRITTEN.	FOR WHOSE USE.	DATE. A.D.
Matthew, Gospel of, in Hebrew	Matthew	Judea	Hebrew Christians	38
in Greek	Ditto	Ditto	Gentile Christians	60
1 Thessalonians	Paul	Corinth	Ditto	52
2 Thessalonians	Ditto	Ditto	Ditto	52
Galatians	Ditto	Ditto	Ditto	53
1 Corinthians	Ditto	Ephesus	Ditto	57
Romans	Ditto	Corinth	Ditto	58
2 Corinthians	Ditto	Macedonia	Ditto	58
James	James	Judea	Jewish nation	61
Mark, Gospel of	Mark	Rome	Gentile Christians	61
Ephesians	Paul	Ditto	Ditto	61
Philippians	Ditto	Ditto	Ditto	62
Colossians	Ditto	Ditto	Ditto	62
Philemon	Ditto	Ditto	Philemon	63
Hebrews	Ditto	Italy	Hebrew Christians	63
Luke, Gospel of	Luke	Greece	Theophilus and Gentile Christians	63
Acts	Ditto	Ditto	Ditto	64
1 Timothy	Paul	Macedonia	Timothy	64
Titus	Ditto	Ditto	Titus	64
1 Peter	Peter	Babylon	General	64
Jude	Jude	Unknown	Ditto	65
2 Peter	Peter	Babylon or Rome	Ditto	65
2 Timothy	Paul	Rome	Timothy	65
1 John, Epistle of	John	Ephesus	General	68
2 John, do.	Ditto	Ditto	The Elect Lady	69
3 John, do.	Ditto	Ditto	Gaius	69
Revelation	Ditto	Patmos	General	97
John, Gospel of	Ditto	Ephesus	Ditto	98

Ch. XXII.—The Miracles of Christ.

MIRACLES have never been wrought by any but the commissioned servants of God. Our Saviour's miracles illustriously prove the divinity of his mission: they were never wrought for his own advantage; but most benevolently to afford relief to those in distress, and to show his almighty power, being wrought as from himself: they were such as no enthusiast or impostor would attempt: he would never dare to say to the blind, Receive thy sight; to the deaf, Hear; to the dumb, Speak; to the dead, Arise; or to the raging waves of the sea, Be still, lest he should ruin his cause: but all these were done by our Lord. It is evident that only a small number of his mighty works are specified in the Gospels; but the following is a list of only the more particularly noted miracles of Christ.

MIRACLES.	PLACE.	RECORD.
Water turned into wine	Cana	John ii 1-11.
The Capernaum nobleman's son cured	Ditto	—— iv 46-54.
Surprising draught of fishes	S of Galilee	Luke v. 1-11.
Demoniac cured	Capernaum	Mark i. 22-28.
Peter's mother-in-law healed	Ditto	—— — 30, 31.
Many miracles	Thro' Galil	—— — 32-34.
Leper healed	Capernaum	—— — 40-45.
Centurion's servant healed	Ditto	Matt viii. 5-13.
Many healed	Thro' Galil.	Luke vi. 17-19.
Widow's son raised from the dead	Nain	—— vii. 11-17.
Tempest calmed	S. of Galilee	Matt viii. 23-27.
Demoniacs of Gadara cured	Gadara	—— — 28-34.
Man sick of the palsy cured	Capernaum	—— ix. 1-8.
Jairus's daughter raised to life	Ditto	—— — 18-26.
Sight restored to two blind men	Ditto	—— — 27-31.
Dumb demoniac cured	Ditto	—— — 32, 33.
Numbers cured	Thro' Galil	—— — 35
Woman diseased with issue of blood healed	Capernaum	Luke viii. 43-48.
Diseased cripple at Bethesda cured	Jerusalem	John v. 1-9
Man with a withered hand cured	Judea	Matt. xii. 10-13.
Demoniac cured	Capernaum	—— — 22, 23.
Five thousand fed	Decapolis	—— xiv. 15-21.
Many healed	Thro' Galil.	Mark vi. 55, 56.
Jesus walks on the sea	Ditto	Matt xiv. 22-32.
Canaanite woman's daughter cured	Near Tyre	—— xv. 23-28.
Man deaf and dumb cured	Decapolis	Mark vii 31-37.
Many healed	Thro' Galil	Matt xv. 29-31.
Four thousand fed	Decapolis	—— — 32-39.
Blind man restored to sight	Bethsaida	Mark viii. 22-26.
Boy possessed of a devil cured	Tabor	Matt. xvii.14-21.

MIRACLES.	PLACE.	RECORD.
Miracle to pay tribute	Sea of Galil.	Mat. xvii. 24-27.
Man born blind restored to sight	Jerusalem	John ix.
Woman of eighteen years' infirmity cured	Galilee	Luke xiii. 11-17.
Dropsical man cured	Ditto	—— xiv. 1-6.
Ten lepers cleansed	Samaria	—— xvii. 11-19.
Lazarus raised from the grave to life	Bethany	John xi.
Two blind men restored to sight	Jericho	Matt. xx. 30-34.
Many healed	Jerusalem	—— xxi. 14.
Fig tree blasted	Olivet	—— — 18-21.
The ear of Malchus healed	Gethsemane	Luke xxii. 50,51.
Wondrous draught of fishes	S. of Galilee	John xxi. 1-14.

Ch. XXIII.—Recorded Parables of Jesus Christ.

PARABLES are allegorical forms of instruction, founded on something real or apparent in nature or history. They were commonly employed by teachers in the East, in conveying offensive truths, that these might appear with greater force when fully explained. Our Saviour frequently used them, as best suited to the state of the minds of his hearers, and while impressing them as a means of guarding himself against the inveterate malice of the scribes and Pharisees.

Our Lord's character, as "a teacher sent from God," is proved by his parables; all of which exhibit perfect knowledge of human nature: they convey the sublimest sentiments, expressed in the purest language, containing the highest practical wisdom. Those deserving special regard are, the Good Samaritan; the Prodigal Son; the Rich Man and Lazarus; the Pharisee and Publican; and the Ten Virgins.

PARABLES.	PLACE.	RECORD.
Of the sower	Capernaum	Matt. xiii. 1-23.
— tares	Ditto	{ —— — 24-30. 36-43. }
— seed springing up imperceptibly	Ditto	Mark iv. 26-29.
— grain of mustard seed	Ditto	Matt. xiii. 31,32.
— leaven	Ditto	—— — 33.
— found treasure	Ditto	—— — 44.
— pearl of great price	Ditto	—— — 45, 46.
— net cast into the sea	Ditto	—— — 47-50.
— two debtors	Ditto	Luke vii. 36-50.
— unmerciful servant	Ditto	Mat. xviii. 23-35.
— good Samaritan	Jericho	Luke x. 25-37.

CH. XXIV.—REMARKABLE DISCOURSES OF CHRIST.

PARABLES.	PLACE.	RECORD
Of the rich fool	Galilee	Luke xii. 16-21.
— servants waiting for their lord	Ditto	—— 35-48
— barren fig tree	Ditto	—— xiii. 6-9.
— lost sheep	Ditto	—— xv. 3-7.
— lost piece of money	Ditto	—— — 8-10.
— prodigal son	Ditto	—— — 11-32.
— dishonest steward	Ditto	—— xvi 1-12.
— rich man and Lazarus	Ditto	—— — 19-31.
— unjust judge	Peræa	—— xviii. 1-8.
— Pharisee and publican	Ditto	—— — 9-14.
— labourers in the vineyard	Ditto	Matt. xx. 1-14.
— pounds delivered for trading	Jericho	Luke xix. 12-27.
— two sons	Jerusalem	Matt. xxi 28-32.
— vineyard	Ditto	—— — 33-46.
— marriage feast	Ditto	—— xxii. 1-14.
— ten virgins	Ditto	—— xxv. 1-13.
— talents	Ditto	—— — 14-30.
— sheep and goats	Ditto	—— — 31-46.
— true vine	Ditto	John xv 1-8.

CH. XXIV.—REMARKABLE DISCOURSES OF CHRIST.

OUR Saviour's consummate wisdom appears not only in his parables, but in his discourses. Many of these have been preserved; and they form a treasure to the church. Most of these arose out of incidents in the course of his ministry; but even his learned enemies never found him unprepared to silence their cavils; and those who heard him preaching the gospel of the kingdom, were astonished at his knowledge, holiness, and kindness; some of them declaring, "Never man spake like this man." Those discourses of Christ will perhaps appear most interesting, which he held with Nicodemus; with the woman of Samaria; with the people in his sermon on the Mount; with his apostles at their ordination; and again before he suffered in Gethsemane.

DISCOURSES.	PLACE.	RECORD.
Conversation with Nicodemus	Jerusalem	John iii. 1-21
———————— the Samaritan woman	Sychar	—— iv. 1-42.
Discourse in the synagogue	Nazareth	Luke iv. 16-31.
Sermon on the mount	Ditto	Matt. v vi vii.
Ordination charge to the apostles	Galilee	—— x.
Denunciations against Chorazin	Ditto	—— xi. 20-24.
Discourse concerning healing the infirm man at Bethesda	Jerusalem	John v

PARABLES.	PLACE.	RECORD.
Discourse concerning his disciples plucking ears of corn on the sabbath	Judea	Matt. xii. 1-8.
Refutation of the charge, of his working miracles by the agency of Beelzebub	Capernaum	—— 22-37.
Discourse on the bread of life	Ditto	John vi.
—— concerning internal purity	Ditto	Matt. xv. 1-20.
—— against giving or taking offence and the forgiving of injuries	Ditto	—— xviii.
—— at the feast of tabernacles	Jerusalem	John vii.
—— on occasion of the adulteress	Ditto	—— viii. 1-11.
—— concerning the sheep	Ditto	—— x.
—— with Martha and Mary	Bethany	—— xi. 21-44.
Denunciation against the scribes and Pharisees	Peræa	Luke xi. 37-45.
Discourse on humility and prudence	Galilee	—— xiv. 7-14.
Directions how to attain heaven	Peræa	Matt. xix. 16-30.
Discourse on the sufferings of Christ	Jerusalem	—— xx. 17-19.
Denunciations against the Pharisees	Ditto	—— xxiii.
Predictions concerning Jerusalem	Ditto	—— xxiv.
Discourse of consolation	Ditto	John xiv.—xvi.
—— on the way to Gethsemane	Ditto	Matt. xxvi. 31-36.
—— with Peter after his resurrection	Galilee	John xxi. 5-22.
—— with his disciples before his ascension	Mount Olivet	Matt. xxviii. 16-20; Luke xxiv. 50-53.

Ch. XXV.—Jewish Sects.

Ezra, having laboured among his people in the reformation of religion after the return of the Jews from Babylon, in connexion with Nehemiah, is thought to have established the " Great Synagogue," consisting of a hundred and twenty elders of Israel, for the perfection of the good work, Ezra vii. 1; x. 16; Neh. viii. 1—13. These, principally under his superintendence, completed the collection of the Old Testament books, nearly three hundred years before the coming of Christ. These elders were succeeded by others, who collected the opinions and interpretations of various passages of Scripture, as given by their predecessors, preserving them as valuable traditions. Two parties, therefore, arose among them, who manifested a regard for religion. One of them adhered to the Scriptures only, rejecting all human traditions. Professing to observe the whole law, they assumed the name Zadikim, the righteous. From these

proceeded the Samaritans and the Sadducees. The other party, besides the inspired Scriptures, superadded the traditions of the elders; and from a supposed superior degree of sanctity were called Chasidim, the pious. From these arose the Pharisees and Essenes.

1. The Samaritans were originally the idolatrous successors of the ten tribes, part of whom the king of Assyria sent to unite with the scattered few in repeopling Samaria and the land of Israel. At first, as a punishment for their idolatry, they were plagued with lions; but on this being reported to the king, a priest was sent from among the captives, to instruct them in the law of God. "So they feared the LORD, and made unto themselves of the lowest of them priests of the high places, which sacrificed for them in the houses of the high places, and served their own gods, after the manner of the nations whom they carried away from thence," 2 Kings xvii. 24—33.

Afterwards they became partially reformed, admitted the writings of Moses as divine, and the rest of the Old Testament, but as of inferior authority. They became, therefore, a sect of the Jewish professors of religion, built a temple on Mount Gerizim, and worshipped the God of Israel. In the time of our Saviour, as we learn from his conversation with the woman of Sychar, even the more corrupt class had some knowledge of the Messiah, and expected his appearance, John iv. 25.

2. The Sadducees were a kind of deists. They received their appellation from Sadoc their founder, who lived B. C. 280 years. At first they rejected only the oral or unwritten traditions of the elders, as being destitute of divine authority; but afterwards they adopted many impious notions like those of Epicurus, a heathen philosopher, who regarded pleasure as the chief good of man, and rejected the whole of the sacred writings except the five books of Moses. They denied the resurrection of the dead, the existence of angels, and the immortality of the soul. They admitted the being and providence of Almighty God; but they rejected the doctrine of rewards and punishments in a future state.

Josephus, the Jewish historian, observes, "Whenever they sat in judgment upon criminals, they always were for the severest sentence against them." He also says, "Their number was the fewest of all the sects of the Jews: but they were only those of the best quality, and of the greatest riches among them." Caiaphas, the high priest, and several of the chief priests also, at that time were Sadducees.

3. The Pharisees were the principal sect among the Jews, including almost all that professed any regard for religion; and though they were haughty despisers of the common people, the vulgar entertained such an opinion of the sanctity which they outwardly professed, that it became a common notion among them, that if only two persons were received into heaven one of them must be a Pharisee. The greater part of the doctors of the law and the scribes were of this party. They esteemed the traditions of the wise men, or rabbins, as of nearly equal authority with the word of God, and generally, for practical purposes, gave them the preference! They were intolerably proud of their religious attainments; supposing themselves to merit the Divine favour by their duties and observances. On these accounts they were justly characterized by our Lord as grossly hypocritical, and at a greater distance from the kingdom of God than even publicans and harlots, Matt. xxiii. 1—33.

4. The Essenes were a rigid sect of the Jews, a branch of the Pharisees; but they entered upon a more mortified way of living, and were probably more free from hypocrisy. Though our Saviour often censured the other sects, we have no account of his mentioning them; nor are they noticed specifically by the writers of the New Testament. This has been accounted for by their living in solitary places, somewhat in the manner of the Romish monks, and from their seldom coming to the temple or into public assemblies. Many suppose that John the Baptist lived among them. They believed in a future state of happiness, but doubted of the resurrection. They mostly disallowed marriage, adopting the children of the poor to train up in their principles.

Candidates for communion with them were in probation for three years, and when fully admitted, they were required to bind themselves to worship God, to practise justice, to conceal none of their mysteries from any of the society, and to communicate them to no other, even to save their lives. They despised riches, and held their property common; they were remarkably abstemious, ate at a common table, and were extremely plain in their apparel. In many things they resembled the Rechabites, Jer. xxxv. 1—10.

5. The Scribes among the Jews, principally Pharisees, were not a particular sect, but transcribers of the sacred books; also persons who addicted themselves to literary pursuits: they were interpreters of the law and instructors of the people, Matt. vii. 28.

6. The Herodians were not so much a religious sect as a political party. They complied with many heathen practices to ingratiate themselves with Herod and his patrons, the Romans, Matt. xxv. 16.

7. The Galileans, or Gaulonites, appear to have been a turbulent political party among the Jews, rather than a religious sect. Their first leader was Judas, the Galilean, Acts v. 37.

8. The Libertines, Acts vi. 9, were such Jews or proselytes as were free citizens of Rome, having a synagogue in Jerusalem peculiar to themselves.

CH. XXVI.—HERESIES AND SECTS MENTIONED IN THE NEW TESTAMENT.

It will be evident to every reader of the New Testament, that during the apostolic age many pernicious heresies infested the infant churches. Some of them were introduced by Judaizing teachers, who wished to incorporate the Levitical ceremonies with the simplicity of the gospel, Acts xv. 1; Gal. i. 6; v. 2; vi. 12. Others arose from a false philosophy which was borrowed from the heathen, and which the apostle denounces as vain

deceit, Col. ii. 8. To draw up a detailed account of these, specifying their Jewish or pagan principles, would be unsatisfactory in itself and unsuitable to this work; yet it seems indispensable to give some short notices concerning the chief of them.

1. The Nicolaitanes have, by some, been supposed to have had Nicolas, one of the seven deacons, for their leader in false doctrine and immorality: but this seems contrary to his character, as declared by the evangelists, Acts vi., and we have no evidence that Nicolas, the deacon, ever departed from the faith of the gospel. These corrupters of religion were a kind of practical Antinomians; they allowed themselves to participate in the sacrifices of the idolaters, and indulged in the vilest impurities, to the scandal of their Christian profession, and to the destruction of their souls, Rev. ii. 6.

2. The Antichrists mentioned by the apostle, 1 John ii. 18, were certain heretical teachers, whose principles contradicted the true doctrines of the gospel. They were called Ebionites, from one Ebion; Cerinthians, from one Cerinthus; and Gnostics, from gnosis, a Greek word signifying knowledge. Simon Magus, Acts viii. 9—24, is said to have been the parent of these heresies. It is difficult to ascertain precisely what doctrines these heretics taught; some making a distinction between Jesus and the Christ; some denying the Divine nature of our Lord, and others his humanity; some rejecting his vicarious atonement, and all disregarding his holy precepts. To refute and destroy their pernicious absurdities, the apostle John was inspired to write his Gospel and Epistles, testifying the proper Godhead, the real manhood, and the propitiatory sacrifice of our Lord and Saviour. John i. 1—3, 14; 1 John i. 1, 2; ii. 18—24; iii. 1, 3, 9, 10.

3. The Stoics, Acts xvii. 18, were pagan philosophers, the founder of whose sect was Zeno, who flourished about 350 years before the Christian era. They affected a perfect indifference to both pleasure and pain, professing to believe that all things are governed by an irresistible necessity called fate, which was regarded

by them as superior to the will of all their imaginary gods.

4. The Epicureans were another sect of philosophers, who were the disciples of Epicurus, an Athenian, who flourished about 300 years before the Christian era. They taught principles the very opposite to the Stoics; they ascribed all things to chance, and considered pleasure as the chief good. Some pretended intellectual pleasures; but the generality of Epicureans indulged in the corrupt gratifications of the flesh.

Ch. XXVII.—Fulfilled Prophecies of the Bible.

Prophecy, contained in the Bible, forms one of the most illustrious and convincng proofs of Divine Revelation. "Known unto God are all his works from the beginning of the world," Acts xv. 18. He alone can declare the nature and certainty of future events. Prophecy, therefore, can be given only by that infinite Being, the Almighty Jehovah, whose sole prerogative it is to "declare the end from the beginning," Isa. xlvi. 10. "Prophecy came not in old time by the will of man: but holy men of God spake as they were moved by the Holy Ghost," 2 Pet. i. 21. The evidence arising from the fulfilment of prophecy, therefore, that the "Holy Scriptures were given by the inspiration of God," while it is confounding to the infidel, is most edifying and consolatory to the believer on Jesus Christ.

"God in his goodness hath afforded to every age sufficient evidence of his truth. Miracles may be said to have been the greatest proofs of revelation to the first ages, that saw them performed. Prophecies may be said to be the greatest proofs of revelation to the last ages, that see them fulfilled."

Prophecy, in the Bible, regards numerous individuals, various nations, extensive regions, and remote ages: but the whole compass of it centres in one Person,—the Great Messiah,—the character, offices, ministry,

and everlasting kingdom of our Lord and Saviour Jesus Christ. Hence Jesus, after his resurrection, assured his apostles, "that all things must be fulfilled which were written in the Law of Moses, and in the Prophets, and in the Psalms, concerning himself," Luke xxiv. 27, 44. Hence the apostle Peter declares, "To Him give all the prophets witness," Acts x. 43: and hence also the declaration of the angel to the apostle John,—"The testimony of Jesus is the spirit of prophecy," Rev. xix. 10.

Section I.—PROPHECIES CONCERNING JESUS CHRIST.

Inspired prophecy foretold the advent of Messiah under the most significant names, revealing the dignity and importance of his mediatorial character with increasing clearness, throughout the former dispensations, to Malachi, the last of the prophets of the Old Testament. The following are a few of the names and titles of our Divine Redeemer taken from the Old Testament: many others might have been added, but these specimens will suffice for the present work.

1. SEED OF THE WOMAN. "I will put enmity between thy seed and her seed; He shall bruise thy head, and thou shalt bruise his heel," Gen. iii. 15.

Christian commentators generally, and many of the Jewish, regard this declaration of God, after the fall of Adam and Eve, as announcing a future Deliverer. It foretells that Messiah would be of human nature; in a peculiar sense, the offspring of a female; that he should, in a mysterious way, remedy the evil of man's transgression; and that, though a partial sufferer by that power which had brought sin and ruin into the world, yet he should overcome it by a glorious triumph.

Every reader of the New Testament perceives how all these things were fulfilled in Jesus Christ; and many passages refer to this paragraph. "God sent forth his Son, made of a woman," Gal. iv. 4. "The God of peace shall bruise Satan under your feet shortly," Rom. xvi. 20. "As the children are partakers of flesh and blood,

he also himself likewise took part of the same; that through death he might destroy him that had the power of death, that is, the devil," Heb. ii. 14. "For this purpose the Son of God was manifested, that he might destroy the works of the devil," 1 John iii. 8.

2. SEED OF ABRAHAM, CONFERRING BLESSINGS ON THE WORLD. God promised to Abraham, "And in thy SEED shall all the nations of the earth be blessed," Gen. xxii. 18. This gracious promise was several times repeated to Abraham, to Isaac, and to Jacob, who understood it as indicating the Messiah, expected by all the pious patriarchs from Adam. The ancient Jews understood this as predicting the Messiah; and our Lord declared to the Jews this faith of Abraham. "Your father Abraham rejoiced to see my day; and he saw it and was glad," John viii. 56. The inspired apostle applies this to Christ: "Now to Abraham and his seed were the promises made. He saith not, And to seeds, as of many; but as of one, And to thy seed, which is Christ," Gal. iii. 16. In Jesus, therefore, the greatest of Abraham's descendants, all true believers, of every nation, have received the knowledge of his gospel, the pardon of sin, peace of conscience, joy in God, and hope of immortal glory, by the teaching of God the Holy Spirit.

3. SHILOH; THE RIGHTFUL AND PACIFIC SOVEREIGN. Jacob declared, in blessing his sons, "The sceptre shall not depart from Judah, nor a lawgiver from between his feet, until Shiloh come; and unto him shall the gathering of the people be," Gen. xlix. 10. The general consent of both Jews and Christians, in all ages, has declared this to be a prophecy of the Messiah. Shiloh is interpreted as signifying *Peaceful*, the *Pacificator*, or *Giver of peace:* thus corresponding with other well-known descriptions of Messiah, in the Old Testament. Isaiah predicted his advent, as "The Prince of Peace," declaring that "of the increase of his government and peace there shall be no end," Isa. ix. 6, 7.

Agreeably to this prediction, Judah retained, not only its distinct tribal form, which the rest, except Levi

successively lost, but a governing power, through all its revolutions, until Christ appeared in the flesh. And no sooner was his work of mediation finished, than the Gentiles were gathered to Shiloh by the preaching of the apostles,—church privileges were transferred to the Christians, the Jewish government being destroyed. The remnant of the Jewish people, who, till that time continued to possess the land of promise, were scattered among the nations; and they have been permitted to exist as the living witnesses to the truth of prophecy and of Christianity.

4. A Prophet like Moses. A few days before the death of Moses, Jehovah declared unto him,—" I will raise them up a Prophet from among their brethren, like unto thee, and will put my words into his mouth; and he shall speak unto them all that I shall command him. And it shall come to pass, that whosoever will not hearken unto my words which he shall speak in my name, I will require it of him," Deut. xviii. 18, 19.

Moses, as the prophet of God, was the great deliverer of the people of Israel: but not one of the Jewish prophets or kings, not even David, the divinely anointed king and inspired psalmist, possessed the authority of lawgiver. Jesus is the only "Prophet like unto Moses," the founder of a new dispensation of religion; and the prediction intimates that the Messiah should be a man, an Israelite, a Prophet of the highest order, a Lawgiver, the Teacher, and Intercessor for the people, before the Divine Presence, procuring for the Jews the greatest blessings, and disobedience to whom would be marked with fearful manifestations of the Divine displeasure. These services were rendered to the Israelites, by Moses, under God's authority: but blessings of a higher order are to be expected from Messiah, "the Apostle and High Priest of our profession, Christ Jesus," Heb. iii. 1.

5. The Redeemer, the Living One. Job, in his deep affliction, foretold the manifestation of Messiah, declaring his lively faith:—" I know that my Redeemer liveth, and that he shall stand at the latter day upon the earth: and though, after my skin, worms destroy

this body, yet in my flesh shall I see God," Job xix. 25, 26.

Job possessed "the Spirit of Christ;" though he might not understand the full import of all that he was "moved by the Holy Spirit" to speak, 1 Pet. i. 11, on the occasion of his grievous calamity. But while he had little expectation of recovery to health and prosperity in this world, the patriarch protests his confidence, that the living God, the eternal and unchanging One, would be his Vindicator from unjust censures, and his Redeemer from all sorrows: that He would recover him from the state of death, to a future life of supreme happiness in the favour and enjoyment of God. This declaration of holy Job can apply only to the character and works of Him, "to whom all the prophets give witness." Jesus Christ, the Messiah, was manifested in the fulness of time, as the Redeemer from sin and death, the Living One, the "Resurrection and the Life;" who will come again the second time to judgment, whose voice the dead shall hear, "and they that hear shall live."

Regarding this language of Job, as "given by inspiration of God," a prophecy of the second coming of the only Redeemer and Judge of mankind, it must be received as designating our Lord and Saviour by the highest titles and attributes of Deity.

6. MESSIAH, SON OF GOD. Many predictions concerning Messiah are found in the Book of Psalms: in the second we read, "The kings of the earth set themselves, and the rulers take counsel together against the LORD, and against his Anointed [Messiah].—"Yet have I set my King upon my holy hill of Zion. I will declare the decree: the LORD hath said unto me, Thou art my Son; this day have I begotten thee.—Kiss the Son, lest he be angry, and ye perish from the way, when his wrath is kindled but a little. Blessed are all they that trust in Him," Psa. ii. 2, 6, 7, 12.

This sublime Psalm, written by David when assured by Nathan of the succession of Solomon to the throne of Israel, cannot fully apply to any temporal monarch.

Apostolical authority directs us to regard it as a prophecy of the opposed but invincible empire of Messiah, Acts iv. 25, 28; xiii. 33. The views that it gives of him are,—that He should be the Son of God, in a sense so peculiar and exalted, as to involve the right and power of universal dominion; that He should be openly declared to be the Son of God; that He should be entitled to the homage, love, confidence, and obedience of all mankind; that, by the appointment of the Almighty Father, He should support his own throne by the righteous exercise of his power; that safety and happiness would lie only in submission to him and reliance on his grace; and that those who will not yield to his mercy, shall be subdued by his invincible power. How all these declarations are fulfilled in Jesus Christ, the Son of God, is evident to every reader of the New Testament, and especially felt by every true Christian. The last clause merits particular attention, as demanding from all men that religious trust and confidence in the Messiah, which the Scriptures require to be reposed only in the Almighty and everlasting God: all this is demanded, in the New Testament, for our Saviour Jesus Christ. The ancient Jews considered this Psalm as referring to the Messiah.

7. SON OF MAN; LORD OF ALL THINGS. David, in adoring the Almighty Creator, was inspired to write, " What is man, that thou art mindful of him? and the Son of man, that thou visitest him? For thou hast made him a little lower than the angels, and thou hast crowned him with glory and honour. Thou madest him to have dominion over the works of thy hands," Psa. viii. 4—6.

This Psalm is applied to Christ by the inspired apostle, Heb. ii. 6—9. The honours which are here declared to have been conferred upon the human race by the Creator, had never, either generally, or in a single instance, been bestowed, till the man Christ Jesus was exalted " far above all principality, and power, and might, and dominion, and every name that is named, not only in this world, but also in that which is to come; and hath put all things under his feet," Eph. i. 21, 22.

Thus it appears a beautiful prophetical description and testimony of Christ,—who is the Head of the human race, the new Adam, the Restorer and Saviour of the world.

8. THE HOLY ONE OF GOD. David, in expressing his confidence in God, and his hope of eternal life, declared by the Spirit the resurrection of Messiah. Dr. Kennicott's translation is as follows:—

"I have set Jehovah before me continually: for He is on my right hand, I shall not be moved. Therefore my heart is glad, and my glory rejoiceth; my flesh also shall rest in hope. For thou wilt not abandon my life in the grave; thou wilt not give thy Holy One to see corruption," Psa. xvi. 8—10.

Dr. Kennicott calls this Psalm, "An hymn prophetically descriptive of the Messiah; as expressing his abhorrence of the general idolatry of mankind, and his own zeal for the honour of Jehovah; with the full assurance of his being raised from the dead, *before his body should be corrupted in the grave.*"

David himself might not perceive the full import of his own language in this Psalm: but he and the pious Jews probably understood it as prophetical; because the expressions in it could not correctly apply to the writer. And the apostles Peter and Paul positively affirm, by the same inspiring Spirit, that David spake only of the Messiah. Peter, in testifying of the resurrection and exaltation of Christ, declares, "David speaketh concerning him," in this paragraph; and adds, "The patriarch David is both dead and buried, and his sepulchre is with us unto this day. Therefore being a prophet, and knowing that God had sworn with an oath to him, that of the fruit of his loins, according to the flesh, he would raise up Christ to sit on his throne; he seeing this before, spake of the resurrection of Christ," Acts ii. 25—31.

This prophetical description of Messiah, therefore, declares his proper humanity, his perfect holiness, his acceptableness to God, his death, and his speedy resurrection to immortal felicity and glory. Messiah's proper designation in this Psalm became common among the

Jews; for even an impure spirit uttered it, though with terror and malice; "I know thee who thou art, the Holy One of God," Mark i. 24.

9. THE MESSENGER OF DIVINE BENEVOLENCE TO ATONE FOR SIN. David, in the middle of his reign, was inspired to write the fortieth Psalm: "Sacrifice and offering thou didst not desire; mine ears hast thou opened: burnt-offering and sin-offering hast thou not required. Then said I, Lo, I come: in the volume of the book it is written of me; I delight to do thy will, O my God: yea, thy law is within my heart," Psa. xl. 6—8.

That this was an inspired prediction of Messiah appears evident, from the language itself, which could not apply to the prophet. And this Psalm is expressly declared, in the Epistle to the Hebrews, to refer to Christ: the apostle showing the inefficiency of the Levitical sacrifices, by their constant repetition, until this prophecy was fulfilled by the infinitely precious offering of Christ. He says, "For it is not possible that the blood of bulls and goats should take away sins. Wherefore, when he cometh into the world, he saith, Sacrifice and offering thou wouldest not, but a body hast thou prepared me. In burnt-offerings and sacrifices for sin thou hast had no pleasure: then said I, Lo, I come (in the volume of the book it is written of me) to do thy will, O God. Above, when he said, Sacrifice and offering and burnt offerings and offering for sin thou wouldest not, neither hadst pleasure therein; which are offered by the law; then said he, Lo, I come to do thy will, O God. He taketh away the first, that he may establish the second. By the which will we are sanctified, through the offering of the body of Jesus Christ once for all," Heb. x. 4—10.

10. GOD TRIUMPHING AND REIGNING FOR EVER. David is believed to have composed the forty-fifth Psalm, on the occasion of Nathan's assuring him of the establishment of his son on the throne of Israel, 1 Chron. xvii. 11—15: but the inspiring Spirit led him to write,— "Thou art fairer than the children of men; grace is

poured into thy lips: therefore God hath blessed thee for ever. Gird thy sword upon thy thigh, O most Mighty, with thy glory and thy majesty. Thy throne, O God, is for ever and ever: the sceptre of thy kingdom is a right sceptre. Thou lovest righteousness, and hatest wickedness: therefore God, thy God, hath anointed thee with the oil of gladness above thy fellows," Psa. xlv. 2, 3, 6, 7.

Part of this address is quoted in the first chapter of the Hebrews, as declaring the Divinity and Messiahship of Jesus Christ; and comparing it with the other inspired predictions, it appears evidently a celebration, in the known imagery of prophecy, of the Divine Messiah, the dignity of his person, the power and grace of his kingly office, and the conversion of the Gentiles to the faith of him as their Redeemer. The seventh and eighth verses in particular contain the language of joyful homage to the LORD, the Messiah, from his redeemed church, congenial with the reason and feelings of every holy being on earth and in heaven. THY THRONE, O GOD, IS FOR EVER AND EVER:—in exact harmony with the universal assembly who shout, " Blessing, and honour, and glory, and power, be unto HIM that sitteth upon the throne, and unto the LAMB for ever and ever," Rev. v. 13.

11. THE LORD, THE IMMORTAL PRIEST AND CONQUEROR. David is believed to have composed the hundred and tenth Psalm on the same occasion as he wrote the forty-fifth. Inspired by the Spirit, therefore, he wrote, "The LORD said unto my Lord, Sit thou at my right hand, until I make thine enemies thy footstool. The LORD hath sworn, and will not repent, Thou art a priest for ever after the order of Melchizedek," Psa. cx. 1, 2, 4.

All admit these verses to be prophetical of the Messiah. They are so quoted in the New Testament, Acts ii. 34, 36; Heb. i. 13; v. 6; vii. 17, 21. Our blessed Lord referred to this Psalm in reply to the captious Pharisees and lawyers of the Jews, who had answered his questions, "What think ye of Christ? whose son is

he?" They readily declared, "The Son of David!" But he again proposed, "How then doth David in spirit call him Lord? saying, The LORD said unto my Lord, Sit thou on my right hand, till I make thine enemies thy footstool! If David then call him Lord, how is he his son?" Matt. xxii. 42—45.

Jesus here affirms, that the royal prophet, a thousand years before, and under the infallible teaching of the Holy Spirit, had a knowledge of the Messiah as the glory of Israel and the hope of salvation for the world: that he contemplated this exalted Being, as at that period a living person; and thus inspired, attributed to the Messiah the honours and dominion of Deity.

David mentions this dignified person, as his Lord and Sovereign, to whom his faith had been directed by the Divine inspiration. This Sovereign is here described as then receiving from Jehovah a dominion, the exercise of which is represented in characters far too exalted for any being who is a mere creature. He is made known to us as a King to reign, no less than a Priest to make propitiation for sin; as receiving the homage of innumerable willing subjects; and as employing invincible powers against all his enemies. He is called also, in the fifth verse, by the most sacred title "LORD," (Heb. *Adonai,)* which is peculiarly and exclusively appropriated to the only living and Almighty God. But all these most wonderful and glorious, though apparently contrary characters, are declared in the New Testament, as belonging most fully to our Lord Jesus Christ.

12. IMMANUEL, or GOD WITH US. Isaiah, the prophet, in an interview with Ahaz, king of Israel, when Jerusalem was besieged by the allied kings of Syria and Israel, proposed to him to ask a sign that God would deliver the city. This he declined, lest he should tempt God; when the prophet declared,—"Therefore the LORD himself shall give you a sign: Behold, a virgin shall conceive, and bear a son, and shall call his name Immanuel," Isa. vii. 14.

This most remarkable passage is attended with difficulty to us in some of the circumstances under which it

was originally given: but we have proof that it had a prophetical reference to the miraculous formation of the human nature of Christ; and was perfectly fulfilled only in the birth of our Saviour, and in his Divine character of Messiah, "God manifest in the flesh," 1 Tim. iii. 16. "Over all, God blessed for ever," Rom. ix. 5. Hence the evangelist Matthew records the event, adding, "Now all this was done, that it might be fulfilled which was spoken of the Lord by the prophet, saying, Behold, a virgin shall be with child, and bring forth a son, and they shall call his name Emmanuel; which being interpreted, is, God with us," Matt. i. 22, 23.

13. THE WONDERFUL, MIGHTY GOD, THE ETERNAL SOVEREIGN. Isaiah, by the inspiring Spirit, directed his distressed countrymen to look forward to the advent of Immanuel, their glorious Deliverer, and the Giver of all blessings. Hence he writes:—

"Unto us a child is born, unto us a son is given, and the government shall be upon his shoulder; and his name shall be called Wonderful, Counsellor, The Mighty God, The Everlasting Father, The Prince of Peace. Of the increase of his government and peace there shall be no end, upon the throne of David, and upon his kingdom, to order it, and to establish it with judgment and justice, from henceforth even for ever," Isa. ix. 6, 7.

Interpreters of every community, ancient and modern, have agreed in regarding this language as an illustrious prediction of Messiah. Inspired evangelists and apostles have delineated, in the New Testament, the character of Jesus Christ, in perfect accordance with this prediction by Isaiah; and in no other individual that ever existed can the same surprising qualities be found. The prophet of God has here represented Messiah in the opposite characters of humanity and Divinity; the nativity and infirmity of a mortal child, and the incommunicable attributes of the Almighty and eternal God! Most appropriately is his name, therefore, called WONDERFUL; for unsearchable are the mysteries of his person and offices. He alone is the COUNSELLOR, the Mediator of the gospel covenant, in whom are treasured

all the blessings of wisdom and grace for his people: He is the FATHER, PROTECTOR, and GUIDE of his family, the universal church, through the present world to life everlasting; and He is the celestial SOVEREIGN, reigning, by his Word and Spirit, in the hearts of his followers, as in a kingdom of joy, peace, and righteousness, extending to all nations.

14. THE OFFSPRING OF JESSE. Messiah was foretold to arise in the tribe of Judah, and from the royal house of David: his father, Jesse, is, therefore, mentioned in several sublime predictions. Hence Isaiah declared;—" And there shall come forth a rod out of the stem of Jesse, and a Branch shall grow out of his roots: and the Spirit of the LORD shall rest upon him, the spirit of wisdom and understanding, the spirit of counsel and might, the spirit of knowledge and the fear of the LORD; and shall make him of quick understanding in the fear of the LORD: and he shall not judge after the sight of his eyes, neither reprove after the hearing of his ears.—The earth shall be full of the knowledge of the LORD, as the waters cover the sea. And in that day there shall be a root of Jesse, which shall stand for an ensign of the people; to it shall the Gentiles seek; and his rest shall be glorious," Isa. xi. 1, 3, 9, 10.

Many Jewish commentators interpret this chapter as denoting their Messiah; and this judgment is proved to be correct by a quotation from it by the apostle Paul, Rom. xv. 12. The whole New Testament declares Jesus Christ to be of the house of David, born at the time of its deepest debasement, and represents him as endowed with the richest communications of the Holy Spirit, so as to possess extraordinary wisdom and holiness; as being a righteous Judge; a powerful Sovereign; and a benignant Saviour, receiving all nations to his merciful protection. His apostles being commissioned to preach the gospel to all nations, and their writings, with those of the Old Testament, being spread into all the world, "the earth" is now being made "full of the knowledge of the LORD," for all people to enjoy the blessings of Christianity.

15. JEHOVAH THE SAVIOUR AND SHEPHERD. Isaiah, in predicting the deliverance of Judah from captivity in Babylon, was inspired by the Spirit to declare a greater redemption by the King Messiah. Hence he prophesied: —" The voice of him that crieth in the wilderness, Prepare ye the way of the LORD, make straight in the desert a highway for our God. Every valley shall be exalted, and every mountain and hill shall be made low: and the crooked shall be made straight, and the rough places plain: and the glory of the LORD shall be revealed, and all flesh shall see it together: for the mouth of the LORD hath spoken it.—O Zion, that bringest good tidings, get thee up into the high mountain; O Jerusalem, that bringest good tidings, lift up thy voice with strength; lift it up, be not afraid; say unto the cities of Judah, Behold your God! Behold, the Lord GOD will come with strong hand, and his arm shall rule for him: behold, his reward is with him, and his work before him. He shall feed his flock like a shepherd: he shall gather the lambs with his arm, and carry them in his bosom, and shall gently lead those that are with young," Isa. xl. 3—5, 9—11.

Every Christian reader perceives that this prophecy indicates the forerunner and herald of the great Deliverer; and that the Redeemer himself is represented as the God of Israel, the Lord Jehovah. His character, as the careful and compassionate Shepherd, will remind the reader of the beautiful discourse delivered by Christ, assuming that relation to his universal flock.—" I am the GOOD SHEPHERD, and know my sheep, and am known of mine. As the Father knoweth me, even so know I the Father; and I lay down my life for my sheep. And other sheep I have, which are not of this fold: them also I must bring, and they shall hear my voice; and there shall be one fold, and one shepherd.—And I give unto them eternal life; and they shall never perish," John x. 14—16, 28. This description of our Saviour, by himself, so beautifully evident in his lively concern for his disciples, and his merciful engagements for all believers, exactly corresponds with the language of the

prophet, exhibiting him as "gathering the lambs," as the "chief Shepherd," and "Bishop of souls," the true and Divine Messiah. He also speaks in the same terms by another prophet;—"And ye, my flock, the flock of my pasture, are men, and I am your God, saith the Lord God," Ezek. xxxiv. 31.

16. BELOVED SERVANT OF GOD. Isaiah, in continuing his prophetical discourses for the comfort of the godly, is employed by Jehovah to call the nations to receive the Messiah:—

"Behold my Servant, whom I uphold; mine elect, in whom my soul delighteth: I have put my Spirit upon him; he shall bring forth judgment to the Gentiles. He shall not cry, nor lift up, nor cause his voice to be heard in the street. A bruised reed shall he not break, and the smoking flax shall he not quench: he shall bring forth judgment unto truth. He shall not fail nor be discouraged, till he have set judgment in the earth: and the isles shall wait for his law," Isa. xlii. 1—4.

Messiah is here commended to the nations, as distinguished above all the prophets of God: he is represented as, in human nature, the object of the Divine complacency; and endowed with the richest heavenly gifts, for imparting the knowledge of true religion to mankind: as being meek and compassionate; sympathizing with the afflicted and sorrowful; devoted to the evangelization of the world, and successful in his labours; overcoming all opposition by the sweetness of his doctrine and the power of the Spirit of God. Isaiah, as a divine and holy prophet, might be amiable in his character, in some degree answering this description, but it has its perfect fulfilment only in the ministry of Jesus Christ; to whom it is directly applied by the evangelist Matthew, Matt. xii. 18, 21.

17. JEHOVAH, THE SUPREME GOD, THE RIGHTEOUS, AND THE SAVIOUR. Isaiah was inspired to represent the Eternal God thus calling to mankind:—"I the LORD: and there is none else beside me; a just God and a Saviour: there is none beside me. Look unto me, and be ye saved, all the ends of the earth; for I am God,

and there is none else. I have sworn by myself, the word is gone out of my mouth in righteousness, and shall not return, That unto me every knee shall bow, every tongue shall swear. Surely, shall one say, in the LORD have I righteousness and strength: even to him shall men come; and all that are incensed against him shall be ashamed. In the LORD shall all the seed of Israel be justified, and shall glory," Isa. xlv. 21—25.

This sublime prediction is quoted and referred to in several places in the New Testament, as declaring our Lord Jesus Christ to be the only Judge and Saviour of mankind, in whom alone, as their Mediator and Redeemer, believers find righteousness and strength for their eternal salvation. This descriptive language perfectly corresponds with the uniform representations of Messiah in the Old Testament, and with the inspired testimonies of the apostles concerning Christ. The apostle Paul, in urging the consideration that "we must all stand before the judgment-seat of Christ," cites this passage in proof of his doctrine. "For it is written, As I live, saith the Lord, every knee shall bow to me, and every tongue shall confess to God. So then every one of us shall give account of himself to God," Rom. xiv. 10—12. That this application of the words to Jesus Christ is correct, appears from the argument of the apostle in another place, declaring his exaltation, as following his death for sinners: "God hath highly exalted him, and given him a name which is above every name. That at the name of Jesus every knee should bow, of things in heaven, and things in earth, and things under the earth. And that every tongue should confess that Jesus Christ is Lord, to the glory of God the Father," Phil. ii. 9—11.

18. JEHOVAH'S RIGHTEOUS SERVANT, SUFFERING AS OUR REDEEMER. Isaiah, in describing the mysterious sufferings and triumphs of Messiah, thus writes, by the inspiration of God:—

"Behold, my Servant shall deal prudently, he shall be exalted and extolled, and be very high. As many were astonied at thee; (his visage was so marred more

than any man, and his form more than the sons of men.) —He is despised and rejected of men, a man of sorrows, and acquainted with grief.—Surely he hath borne our griefs and carried our sorrows: yet we did esteem him stricken, smitten of God, and afflicted. But he was wounded for our transgressions, he was bruised for our iniquities; the chastisement of our peace was upon him; and with his stripes we are healed.—He shall see of the travail of his soul, and shall be satisfied: by his knowledge shall my Righteous Servant justify many; for he shall bear their iniquities," Isa. lii. 13, 14; liii. 3—5, 11.

This inspired picture of the diligent ministry, and exemplary holiness, the unequalled sufferings, and final exaltation of the "Righteous Servant" of Jehovah, compels all Christian commentators to regard it as the most remarkable prophecy of the vicarious humiliation of Jesus Christ. Many of the ancient Jews, who yet generally expected the Messiah, only as a glorious king and mighty conqueror, regarded this prophecy as applying to him, though in a state of suffering. As the prophet represents the "Righteous Servant" of Jehovah, rejected and wickedly cut off by his nation, as numbered with malefactors in his death, yet making his grave with the rich; we find all these things fully declared as realities in the history of the bitter persecutions of Jesus Christ by the Jews; and as it is variously repeated by the prophet, that he should suffer in the room of others, as a propitiatory sacrifice for the sins of us all; Jesus, as our High Priest and Redeemer, "bare our sins in his own body on the cross," and by laying down his life, pouring out his blood for sinners, so that all who believe his gospel have forgiveness and eternal salvation. The prophet directs the reader to consider Messiah as "seeing of the travail of his soul, and being satisfied;" and the inspired writers of the New Testament declare the glorious conquests of the gospel in their days; while our own eyes perceive the progress now making in the fulfilment of this prophecy by the advancement of Christianity.

19. JEHOVAH OUR RIGHTEOUSNESS. Jeremiah, in foretelling the restoration of the Jews from captivity in

Babylon, was inspired with a view of a more glorious deliverance, by the Messiah; and he wrote:—"Behold, the day is come, saith the LORD, that I will raise unto David a righteous Branch, and a King shall reign and prosper, and shall execute judgment and justice in the earth. In his days, Judah shall be saved, and Israel shall dwell safely; and this is the name whereby he shall be called, THE LORD OUR RIGHTEOUSNESS," Jer. xxiii. 5, 6. Nearly parallel is another passage, ch. xxxiii. 15, 16.

These two striking passages indicate the great Messiah; as is admitted by interpreters both Jewish and Christian. And it appears evident that the Messiah is here called by the incommunicable name of the self-existent JEHOVAH. This teaches us the essential Divinity of the Redeemer, which, as well as his humanity, is fully declared in the New Testament,—"God manifest in the flesh." Righteousness, the capital blessing of the gospel, the justification of a sinner before God, comes to us only by the perfect obedience and meritorious sufferings of Christ as our Mediator. The inspired apostle declares, "Christ is the end of the law for righteousness to every one that believeth," Rom. x. 4. "God was in Christ reconciling the world unto himself.—He hath made him to be sin for us, who knew no sin, that we might be made the righteousness of God in him," 2 Cor. v. 19, 21. This, with all other blessings, comes to guilty men by faith in Jesus, "who of God is made unto us wisdom, and righteousness, and sanctification, and redemption: that he that glorieth may glory in the Lord," 1 Cor. i. 30, 31. Hence Messiah's name in this prophecy; and the fact of the New Testament writers pouring forth the fulness of their souls in the most expressive language concerning the glory of their Lord and Saviour.

20. SON OF MAN UNITED WITH THE ETERNAL GOD, EXERCISING UNIVERSAL EMPIRE. Daniel thus describes what he beheld in a prophetical vision:—"I beheld till the thrones were cast down, and the ANCIENT OF DAYS did sit, whose garment was white as snow, and the hair

of his head like the pure wool: his throne was like the fiery flame, and his wheels as burning fire. A fiery stream issued and came forth from before him: thousand thousands ministered unto him, and ten thousand times ten thousand stood before him: the judgment was set, and the books were opened. I saw in the night visions, and behold, one like the SON OF MAN came with the clouds of heaven, and came to the ANCIENT OF DAYS, and they brought him near before him. And there was given him dominion, and glory, and a kingdom, that all people, nations, and languages should serve him: his dominion is an everlasting dominion, which shall not pass away, and his kingdom that which shall not be destroyed," Dan. vii. 9, 10, 13, 14.

Daniel's prophetic vision has engaged the attention of all biblical scholars, who have not supposed it to have been fulfilled in any other person than the Messiah; whom it is understood to represent as approaching the Eternal Father, in entering upon his mediatorial empire. While, therefore, it indicates the true humanity of Messiah, agreeably to the numerous predictions already noticed, as given before by the more ancient prophets, it intimates such powers, and these exercised in such a manner, as consist only with his possession of Divinity. Every reader of Daniel's description will be reminded of the vision of the exalted Saviour, as seen by the apostle John, and described in the Book of the Revelation.

21. MESSIAH THE PRINCE, CUT OFF TO MAKE RECONCILIATION FOR INIQUITY. Daniel was instructed by the angel Gabriel to foretell the precise period of the advent of Messiah.—" The man Gabriel talked with me, and said, O Daniel, I am now come forth to give thee skill and understanding.—Seventy weeks are determined upon thy people, and upon thy holy city, to finish the transgression, and to make an end of sins, and to make reconciliation for iniquity, and to bring in everlasting righteousness, and to seal up the vision and prophecy, and to anoint the Most Holy. Know, therefore, and understand, that from the going forth of the commandment to restore and to build Jerusalem, unto Messiah

the Prince, shall be seven weeks, and threescore and two weeks; and after threescore and two weeks shall Messiah be cut off, but not for himself," Dan. ix. 21, 22, 24—26.

"Seventy weeks" denote sabbatical weeks of years, Lev. xxv. 8, making *four hundred and ninety years;* and these form the period from a certain decree to the great sacrifice of Messiah. This was so far understood by the Jews, that one of their learned doctors, as stated by Dr. Gill, in his Commentary, Rabbi Nehemiah, " who lived about fifty years before the coming of Christ, declared the time of Messiah, as signified by Daniel, could not be deferred longer than those fifty years."

Daniel's prophecy was literally fulfilled in Jesus Christ, both as to the period and purposes of his death: for the "seventy weeks," or 490 years, reckoned from the seventh year of Artaxerxes, as remarked by Dr. Prideaux, coincide with the 4256th year of the Julian Period, and in the month Nisan, in which Ezra was commissioned to restore the Jewish state and polity, Ezra vii. 9—26, and bring us to the month Nisan of the 4746th year of the same period, or A. D. 33, the very month and year in which the work of our redemption was finished by the death of our Lord and Saviour!

22. SOVEREIGN, SHEPHERD, RESTORER. HE WHOSE ACTINGS HAVE BEEN FROM ETERNITY. Micah was contemporary with Isaiah; and, like him, while foretelling the recovery of the captive Jews from Assyria, predicts the great spiritual deliverance by Messiah.—" But thou, Bethlehem Ephratah, though thou be little among the thousands of Judah, yet out of thee shall He come forth unto me that is to be ruler in Israel; whose goings forth have been from of old, from everlasting.—And He shall stand and feed in the strength of the LORD, in the majesty of the name of the LORD his God; and they shall abide: for now shall he be great unto the ends of the earth," Micah v. 2, 4.

Micah's prophecy is not interpreted as being applicable to any one but the Messiah; and all its significant terms find their fulfilment in Jesus Christ, as testified

in the New Testament. This one, giving no intimation of suffering to Messiah, but indicating his local origin in connexion with a prior and eternal existence, was regarded with peculiar interest by the Jews: hence their "chief priests and scribes" immediately referred to this passage, in answer to the inquiry of king Herod, "where Christ should be born," Matt. ii. 1—6. One of their ancient commentaries thus paraphrases the prophecy:—" And thou, Bethlehem of Ephrata, little art thou, to be reckoned among the clans of the house of Judah; out of thee shall proceed in my presence, the Messiah, to exercise sovereignty over Israel; whose name has been called from eternity, from the days of the everlasting period."

Dr. Hales remarks, " This prophecy of Micah is perhaps the most important single prophecy in the Old Testament, and the most comprehensive, respecting the personal character of the Messiah and his successive manifestation to the world. It crowns the whole chain of prophecies descriptive of the several limitations of the Blessed Seed of the woman; to the line of Shem, to the family of Abraham, Isaac, and Jacob, to the tribe of Judah, and to the royal house of David, here terminating in his birth at Bethlehem, 'the city of David.' It carefully distinguishes his human nativity from his eternal generation; foretells the rejection of the Israelites and Jews for a season, their final restoration, and the universal peace destined to prevail throughout the earth in 'the regeneration.' It forms, therefore, the basis of the New Testament, which begins with his human birth at Bethlehem, the miraculous circumstances of which are recorded in the introduction of Matthew's and Luke's Gospels; his eternal generation, as the ORACLE, or WISDOM, in the sublime introduction of John's Gospel; his prophetic character and second coming, illustrated in the four Gospels and the Epistles; ending with a prediction of the speedy approach of the latter, in the Apocalypse," Rev. xxii. 20.

23. THE DESIRE OF ALL NATIONS. Haggai prophesied after the return of the Jews from Babylon, to en-

courage them in building the second temple at Jerusalem. He delivered this prediction:—" For thus saith the LORD of hosts, Yet once, it is a little while, and I will shake the heavens, and the earth, and the sea, and the dry land; and I will shake all nations, and the DESIRE of all nations shall come: and I will fill this house with glory, saith the LORD of hosts.—The glory of this latter house shall be greater than of the former, saith the LORD of hosts: and in this place will I give peace, saith the LORD of hosts," Hag. ii. 6—9.

Messiah is generally acknowledged to be here intended by the prophet, who represents Him as a bountiful Deliverer and giver of peace; as being the object of joyful expectation to other nations besides the Jews, and as appointed to appear in the second temple at Jerusalem. All this was fulfilled by Jesus Christ, for though Alexander the Great and the Romans took Jerusalem, they venerated its magnificent temple, and in their conquest spared that sacred building; so that Christ appeared, "a light to lighten the Gentiles, and the glory of his people Israel," filling the temple with the fame of his miracles, and the doctrine of reconciliation with God and of eternal salvation: and so, by his personal Divine presence, with greater glory than any which attended the splendours of king Solomon.

24. THE BRANCH, THE BUILDER AND SOVEREIGN OF THE CHURCH. Zechariah was contemporary with Haggai, and delivered several predictions concerning the Messiah: "Thus saith the LORD of hosts.—Hearken now, O Joshua, the high priest;—behold, I will bring forth my Servant, the BRANCH," Zech. iii. 7, 8. "Thus speaketh the LORD of hosts, saying, Behold the man whose name is The BRANCH; and he shall grow up out of his place, and he shall build the temple of the LORD: even he shall build the temple of the LORD; and he shall bear the glory, and shall sit and rule upon his throne; and he shall be a priest upon his throne: and the counsel of peace shall be between them both," ch. vi. 12, 13. "Rejoice greatly, O daughter of Zion; shout, O daughter of Jerusalem: behold, thy King cometh unto

thee: he is just, and having salvation; lowly, and riding upon an ass, and upon a colt the foal of an ass," ch. ix. 9.

Messiah is here foretold under characters represented by David, Isaiah, and Jeremiah; as a "Branch of the stem of Jesse," and a "Priest for ever after the order of Melchisedek;" far superior in dignity and ministry to Joshua, the high priest of the Jews, in the time of Zechariah: that he should erect a temple to Jehovah, different from the material building then in progress at Jerusalem; and as Shiloh, rule upon his sacred throne, being a priest as well as a king, "taking away the iniquity of the land in one day," ch. iii. 9. He is further described as the "King of Zion," meek and religious, and his triumphs not secured by force and violence, with the terrible war-horse, and marked with tears and blood: but his victories are those of truth, holiness, and beneficence, the conquests of reason and conscience, bringing the blessings of grace to all nations of men with the highest glory to God!

Jesus Christ answers the whole prediction; and he only of all the public persons that ever appeared among men: he entered Jerusalem in holy triumph literally as here described; and every other particular mentioned by the prophet, Zechariah, has been fully verified in his person and offices, as the great Mediator, "the Apostle and High Priest of our profession," who continues building up his church, a spiritual house, of living stones, and extending his conquests of knowledge and holiness by the gospel among all nations. The peaceful character of Messiah, as represented by the prophet, indicates the unsuitableness of war for promoting his religion; and intimates its final abolition by the prevalence of pure, vital Christianity.

25. SHEPHERD; ONE NEAREST TO JEHOVAH.—Zechariah thus represents the humiliation of Messiah: "Awake, O sword, against my Shepherd, and against the man that is my fellow, saith the LORD of hosts: smite the Shepherd, and the sheep shall be scattered; and I will turn mine hand upon the little ones," Zech. xiii. 7.

Messiah is many times represented by the prophets as a Shepherd; and here Zechariah foretells him in that office. But he predicts his being mysteriously smitten by the sword of Jehovah, to whom he is yet called a "Fellow," as an *Equal*, and in the nearest relationship to God! This appellation indicates his being the person whom God had appointed to be the Deliverer and Saviour of his people; yet he calls upon the fearful "sword" to smite him! These things have had no fulfilment in the history of any individual, except Jesus Christ: and when he was betrayed by Judas, he claimed the prophecy as referring to himself, Matt. xxvi. 31: but in his wonderful person, Immanuel, *God with us*, we see Jehovah's "Fellow:" and He only, with truth, could say, "I and the Father are One;—He that hath seen me hath seen the Father." This "good Shepherd" only was sold for "thirty pieces of silver," which were, by the guilty and tormented traitor, "cast down in the house of the LORD," and given "to the potter," as foretold by Zechariah, ch. xi. 12, 13. This "good Shepherd" voluntarily went to Jerusalem, to "lay down his life for his sheep," that they might obtain eternal glory. But the "Shepherd being smitten," his personal followers, "the sheep, were scattered," for a season, when they were again gathered to form the newly constituted church of God our Saviour.

26. SOVEREIGN, MESSENGER OF THE COVENANT. Malachi closed the long series of predictions contained in the Old Testament, foretelling the advent of Messiah, and of his forerunner, John the Baptist. He wrote, from the inspiring Spirit, "Behold, I will send my messenger, and he shall prepare the way before me: and the LORD, whom ye seek, shall suddenly come to his temple, even the Messenger of the covenant, whom ye delight in: behold, he shall come, saith the LORD of hosts," Mal. iii. 1. "Behold, I will send you Elijah the prophet before the coming of the great and dreadful day of the LORD," ch. iv. 5.

"Elijah the prophet," commentators generally understand of some minister resembling that great reformer

in spirit and zeal. Such was John the Baptist; who was intended by the Holy Spirit, as declared by Gabriel, the "angel of the LORD," to his father Zacharias, Luke i. 13—19. The same is also affirmed by our blessed Saviour, Matt. xi. 14.

Messiah, as the "Messenger of the covenant," and "LORD of his temple," is intended in the former verse: and his being described as Proprietor of the temple, indicates, in the constant style of the Old Testament, that he was Jehovah, the God of Israel. His being called "Messenger," or, Angel "of the covenant," refers to his mission; which he undertook for the purpose of fulfilling the designs of mercy in the salvation of men, as their Redeemer, this being promised to David, to Abraham, and even to Adam, the object of sacred hope to every pious Israelite. With this promise of the Divine mercy, the earliest intimation was made to our first parents concerning Messiah; and with its renewal, in the plainest and most solemn forms of speech, the prophet of God finished the wonderful series of evangelical declarations in the Old Testament. Those which are here noticed, and many more relating to the mighty Mediator between God and men, are commended to the intelligent faith of believers in the New Testament, as being perfectly fulfilled, to their peace and salvation, in the person, offices, and kingdom of our blessed Lord and Saviour, Jesus Christ!

Section II.—THE ARABS.

The Arabs claim their descent from Ishmael, the eldest son of Abraham. Concerning him, an angel of the Lord announced to his mother, before his birth: "I will multiply thy seed exceedingly, that it shall not be numbered for multitude. Behold, thou art with child, and shalt bear a son, and shalt call his name Ishmael; his hand shall be against every man, and every man's hand against him: and he shall dwell in the presence of his brethren," Gen. xvi. 10—12.

The Divine promise concerning Ishmael has been

wonderfully verified. Dismissed, with his mother, from the family of Abraham, by the direction of Heaven, on account of his impious tyranny over his younger brother Isaac, when weaned at the age of about three years, himself being seventeen years old,—and furnished by his father with a pastoral outfit of gifts with cattle for his support, Gen. xxi. 8—14; xxv. 6;—in a few years the family of Ishmael was so increased, that we read of Ishmaelites trading into Egypt. Ishmael's posterity was multiplied exceedingly in the Hagarenes, probably so called from his mother Hagar; in the Nabatheans, who had their names from his eldest son Nebaioth; in the Itureans, so called from his son Itur; and in the Arabs or Saracens, who overran a great part of the world, and who remain to this day a numerous people. Ishmael himself subsisted by rapine in the wilderness; and his posterity, in every succeeding age, infested Arabia and the neighbouring countries by predatory incursions. Every petty chief, in his own district, considers himself a sovereign prince; and though seemingly divided, they are all united in a sort of league. They live in a state of continual war with the rest of the world, generally robbers by land and pirates by sea. And, as they have been such enemies to the rest of mankind, it can excite no surprise, that, in return, mankind have always been enemies to them. In every age, travellers have been obliged to traverse their country in caravans or large companies, with arms for their protection, and, to defend themselves from the assaults of these freebooters, to march with their sentinels, to keep watch like an army—so literally has the prediction been fulfilled, " his hand shall be against every man."

As to that part of the prediction which declares, " He shall dwell (or tabernacle) in the presence of his brethren," it has been remarkably fulfilled. The country of Ishmael is situated in that part of the globe where society originated, and the first kingdoms were formed. The greatest empires of the world arose and fell around them. They have not been secluded from correspond-

ence with foreign nations, and thus through ignorance and prejudice remained attached to simple and primitive manners. In the early period of their history, they were united as allies to the most powerful monarchs of the east: under Mohammed they carried their arms over the most considerable kingdoms of the earth : through successive ages the caravans of the merchant, and the companies of Mohammedan pilgrims, passed regularly over their deserts; even their religion has undergone several total changes. Yet all these circumstances, which it might be supposed would have subdued the most stubborn prejudices, and have changed the most inveterate habits, produced no effect upon the Arabs; they still preserve, unimpaired, a most exact resemblance to the first descendants of Ishmael.

An eye-witness, after having lately visited an Arab camp, and examined their peculiarities, writes—" On the smallest computation, such must have been the manners of these people for more than three thousand years." Thus in all things verifying the predictions given of Ishmael at his birth, that he in his posterity should be a wild man, and continue to be so, though they shall dwell for ever in the presence of their brethren. And that an acute and active people, surrounded for ages by polished and luxurious nations, should, from their earliest to their latest times, be still found a wild people dwelling in the presence of their brethren, as we may call these nations, unsubdued and unchangeable, is indeed a standing miracle—one of those mysterious facts which establish the truth of prophecy.

Section III.—THE JEWS.

Moses, the appointed deliverer and venerable lawgiver of the Israelites, and many also of the prophets who succeeded him, foretold the future condition of the Jews. With a wonderful exactness they predicted their calamities and dispersion on account of their wickedness; and their preservation and ultimate recovery through sovereign mercy and divine goodness. Moses, foreseeing their apostacy and iniquities, wrote by the direction

of the Holy Spirit, the following among many other similar passages. "If ye will not hearken unto me, and will not do all these commandments; and if ye shall despise my statutes, or if your soul abhor my judgments so that ye will not do all my commandments, but that ye break my covenant; I will make your cities waste, and bring your sanctuaries into desolation; and I will scatter you among the heathen, and will draw out a sword after you; and your land shall be desolate. And thou shalt become an astonishment, a proverb, and a by-word, among all the nations whither the LORD shall lead thee," Lev. xxvi. 14, 15, 31, 33; Deut. xxviii. 37. The prophet Jeremiah predicted; "I will persecute them with the sword, with the famine, and with the pestilence, and will deliver them to be removed to all the kingdoms of the earth; to be a curse, and an astonishment, and a hissing, and a reproach among all the nations whither I have driven them: because they have not hearkened to my words, saith the LORD, which I sent unto them by my servants the prophets, rising up early and sending them," Jer. xxix. 18, 19. The prophet Hosea also declared; "For the children of Israel shall abide many days without a king, and without a prince, and without a sacrifice, and without an image, and without an ephod, and without teraphim," Hos. iii. 4. The prophets were also directed to write—"And yet for all that, when they be in the land of their enemies, I will not cast them away, neither will I abhor them, to destroy them utterly, and to break my covenant with them; for I am the LORD their God," Lev. xxvi. 44. "Afterward shall the children of Israel return, and seek the LORD their God, and David their king; and shall fear the LORD and his goodness in the latter days," Hos. iii. 5.

All these predictions are delivered with the confidence of truth, and the clearness of history. They represent the manner, the extent, the nature, and the continuance of their dispersion; their persecutions, their sufferings, their blindness, their hardened impenitence, and their grievous oppression; the universal mockery, the

unlimited diffusion, and the unextinguishable existence of that extraordinary people. Strong were the ties which bound the Jews to Canaan. It was not only a glorious land, but the land of their fathers, and the peculiar gift of Heaven, where only many of their religious customs could be observed. As nothing could separate them from their temple till multitudes perished in its flames, so nothing could tear them from their country but the overwhelming power of the Roman armies. They were rooted up as a nation and banished from their own land: and by an imperial edict it was death for a Jew to set his foot in Jerusalem, though every Gentile might tread upon its ruins.

But the extent of their dispersion is still more remarkable than the manner of its accomplishment. They have traversed the wide world; and there is not a kingdom upon the face of the earth in which they are not to be found. They are numerous in Poland, in Turkey, in Germany, and in Holland; in Russia, France, Spain, Italy, Britain, and America. In Persia, China, and India, on the east and the west of the river Ganges, they are found more thinly scattered. They have trodden the snows of Siberia, and the sands of the burning desert; and the European traveller hears of their existence in regions which he cannot reach, even in the very interior of Africa. From one end of the earth unto the other, the Jews, and the Jews only, have been dispersed among all nations.

As Christians we are looking forward to times more glorious than the present; when, as Hosea predicted, ch. iii. 5, " The children of Israel shall return and seek the LORD their God, and David (the Messiah) their king;" when they shall be brought into the church of Christ with the fulness of the Gentiles. That throughout all the changes which have happened in the kingdoms of the earth, from the days of Moses to the present time, a period of more than three thousand years, nothing should have transpired to prevent the accomplishment of these prophecies; but, on the contrary, that the state of the Jewish, and Christian, and Heathen nations at this day

should be such as renders them easily capable, even of a literal completion, in every particular, if the will of God be so, is a miracle, a standing miracle to us; and which hath nothing parallel to it in the phenomena of nature! The Jews were once the peculiar people of God: and Paul saith, "Hath God cast away his people? God forbid!" Rom. xi. 1. We see that after so many ages they are still preserved, by a miracle of Providence, a distinct people: and why is such a continual miracle exhibited, but for the greater illustration of divine truth and grace, and the accomplishment of the divine promises which are yet to be fulfilled, to the glory of the King Messiah, on whom Abraham and their fathers believed, and of whom the prophets spake?

Section IV.—JUDEA.

Judea, the country of the Jews, of which Jerusalem was the capital, was so exceedingly fertile, that it was ranked by the Greeks and Romans amongst the finest of their provinces. Celebrated ancient authors bear the most decided testimony to the great number of towns and villages with which it was overspread; to the eminence of several of its cities; the excellency of its climate, and the fertility of its soil; in which it outrivalled Italy as to the abundance and excellency of its fruits. Cultivation was carried to so high a degree, that the Greeks, who possessed a rich and beautiful country of their own, proverbially called Syria, including the land of Moab, Ammon, and Philistia, as well as Judea, a garden. Moses foretold the miserable condition of the country in the most affecting terms. "I will break the pride of your power; and I will make your heaven as iron, and your earth as brass. And your strength shall be spent in vain: for your land shall not yield her increase, neither shall the trees of the land yield their fruits. And I will bring the land into desolation; and your enemies who dwell therein shall be astonished at it," Lev. xxvi. 19, 20, 32. Isaiah, in similar language, said, "Your country is desolate, your cities are burned with fire; your land, strangers devour it in your presence, and it is desolate,

as overthrown by strangers. The land shall be utterly emptied, and utterly spoiled: for the LORD hath spoken this word. The earth also is defiled under the inhabitants thereof; because they have transgressed the laws, changed the ordinance, broken the everlasting covenant. Therefore hath the curse devoured the earth, and they that dwell therein are desolate; therefore the inhabitants of the earth are burned, and few men are left," Isa. i. 7; xxiv. 3, 5, 6. Jeremiah also wrote from the LORD; "I have forsaken mine house, I have left mine heritage; I have given the dearly beloved of my soul into the hand of her enemies. They have made it desolate, and being desolate it mourneth unto me; the whole land is made desolate, because no man layeth it to heart," Jer. xii. 7, 11. "And the cities that are inhabited shall be laid waste, and the land shall be desolate; and ye shall know that I am the LORD," Ezek. xii. 20.

The vision of the inspired prophets was as clear as the eyesight of any who now read the history of Judea, or look upon the face of the land; while the many vestiges of ancient cultivation; ruins abounding every where; the remains of Roman buildings and highways, and the natural richness of the soil, in many places yet unaltered, agree with the universal voice of history, in attesting the dismally altered state of the country. After a long and uninterrupted possession of Judea by the Israelites, the Chaldeans, Syrians, Egyptians, and Romans, were the strangers, who, in succession, brought destruction upon destruction, and prepared the way for more savage desolators. Early in the seventh century, the Arabian tribes, under the banners of Mohammed, seized, or rather laid it waste. Since that period, it has been torn by the civil wars of the Fatimites and the Ommiades; wrested from the caliphs by their rebellious governors; taken from them by the Turcoman soldiery; invaded by the European crusaders; retaken by the Mamelukes of Egypt, and ravaged by Tamerlane and his Tartars, till at length it has fallen into the hands of the Ottoman Turks.

The cities have been laid waste. By the concurring testimony of all travellers, Judea may now, with pro-

priety, be called a field of ruins. Heaps of ruins and rubbish are all that remain of Cesarea, Zabulon, Capernaum, Bethsaida, Gadara, and Chorazin, and many other places mentioned in the Bible. Columns covered with rubbish, and shapeless heaps of ruins, are scattered over the whole country.

The land is brought into desolation. The country is overrun by rebel tribes; the Arabs pasture their flocks at freedom. The most fertile plains lie untilled. The art of cultivation is in the most deplorable state, and the countryman sows with the musket in his hands.

The remains of highways no longer passable are still to be seen. In the interior parts of the country, there are neither great roads, nor canals, nor even bridges over the rivers and torrents, however necessary they may be in winter. The roads in the mountains are scarcely passable. There are no inns in any part of the country; neither ports, nor public conveyances; not a wagon nor a cart in all Syria. These statements are made by different and respectable travellers, who agree in testifying to the perfect fulfilment of the predictions, written by Moses three thousand three hundred years ago; and by Isaiah, at the distance of about two thousand five hundred years. It must be acknowledged, that in this is the hand of the righteous LORD, and here we behold the awful severity of God, and the truth of his word!

SECTION V.—IDUMEA.

Idumea, or Edom, was the country of Esau the son of Isaac, and brother of Jacob. This land formed the southern boundary of Judea; but though the people were descended from Isaac as were the Israelites, they were enemies to the Jews. They united with Nebuchadnezzar when he besieged Jerusalem, and urged him to raze it with its temple even to the ground. On account of their idolatry, wickedness, and enmity to the people and worship of God, Isaiah was directed to write, among others, the following awful predictions: "For my sword shall be bathed in heaven: behold, it shall come down upon Idumea, and upon the people of my curse, to judgment.

For the LORD hath a sacrifice in Bozrah, and a great slaughter in the land of Idumea. And thorns shall come up in her palaces, nettles and brambles in the fortresses thereof; and it shall be a habitation of dragons, and a court for owls," Isa. xxxiv. 5, 6, 13. "I have sworn by myself, saith the LORD, that Bozrah shall become a desolation, a reproach, a waste, and a curse, and all the cities thereof shall be perpetual wastes. Thy terribleness hath deceived thee, and the pride of thy heart, O thou that dwellest in the clefts of the rock, that holdest the height of the hill: though thou shouldest make thy nest as high as the eagle, I will bring thee down from thence, saith the LORD. As in the overthrow of Sodom and Gomorrah, and the neighbour cities thereof, saith the LORD, no man shall abide there, neither shall a son of man dwell in it," Jer. xlix. 13, 16, 18. "Thus saith the LORD God; Behold, O mount Seir, I am against thee, and I will stretch out my hand against thee, and I will make thee most desolate. Because thou hast had a perpetual hatred, and hast shed the blood of the children of Israel by the force of the sword in the time of their calamity, in the time that their iniquity had an end: therefore, as I live, saith the LORD God, I will prepare thee unto blood, and blood shall pursue thee. I will make thee perpetual desolations, and thy cities shall not return: and ye shall know that I am the LORD," Ezek. xxxv. 3, 5, 9. "Shall I not in that day, saith the LORD, even destroy the wise men out of Edom, and understanding out of Teman? And thy mighty men, O Teman, shall be dismayed, to the end that every one of the mount of Esau may be cut off by slaughter: and there shall not be any remaining of the house of Esau; for the LORD hath spoken it," Obad. 8, 9, 18.

An intelligent traveller remarks, "From the reports of the Arabs of Bakir, and from the inhabitants of Gaza, who frequently go to Maan (or Teman) and Karak, on the road of the pilgrims, there are, within three days' journey to the south-east of the Dead Sea, upwards of thirty ruined towns absolutely deserted. The Arabs, in general, avoid them, on account of the scor-

pions with which they swarm. We cannot be surprised at these traces of ancient population, when we recollect that this was the country of the Nabatheans, the most powerful of the Arabs, and of the Idumeans, who, at the time of the destruction of Jerusalem, were almost as numerous as the Jews." Yet the ruins of these cities are not the chief monuments of the ancient greatness of Edom. Its capital city, now without an inhabitant, except the wild animals foretold by the prophet a thousand years before it ceased to be tenanted by men, presents one of the most wonderful scenes that can possibly be conceived. In the vicinity of Mount Seir, the extensive ruins of a large city, heaps of hewn stones, foundations of buildings, fragments of columns, and vestiges of paved streets. are spread over a valley which is enclosed on each side by perpendicular cliffs, varying from four hundred to seven hundred feet in height, which are hollowed out into innumerable chambers of different dimensions, rising in the cliffs, tier above tier, till it seems impossible to approach the uppermost. Columns also rise above columns, and adorn the fronts of the dwellings; horizontal grooves for the conveyance of water, run along the face of the cliffs; flights of steps formed the means of ascent, and the summit of the heights, in various places, is covered with pyramids cut out of the rock. The identity of the scene, as described by the prophet, Jer. xlix. 16, in all the terribleness of the human power which pertained to it, and as depicted in the desolate aspect it now exhibits, is such as cannot be mistaken.

The mausoleums and sepulchres are very numerous and magnificent. They are of various periods and orders of architecture. One of them in particular is described as a work of immense labour and colossal dimensions, in perfect preservation, containing a chamber sixteen paces square, and about twenty-five feet high, crowned with a pediment highly ornamented, and all cut out of the rock. By these splendid monuments, dedicated to the memory of its rulers, the opulence of the city is demonstrated.

The enemies of the gospel might be admonished by the fate of the enemies of the ancient church, who have been cut off according to the word of the LORD; and whose very land, that especially of the Edomites, for their violence against their brethren of Israel, has been wasted with a curse which shall cleave to it for ever. The most high God will surely avenge the quarrel of his everlasting covenant, as certainly as he did that which was to be disannulled. And though the enemies of the Christian faith were to league together, as did the confederate tabernacles of Edom against Judah, all the terribleness of their strength would become like chaff before the whirlwind. Men of worldly wisdom should be instructed by the monuments of ruined Edom. If all their superior knowledge were unsanctified by religious principles and the fear of God, all their physical science would prove vain, as the skill of the wise men of Teman: all their mechanical discoveries and operations would end in destruction and eternal oblivion. "Seeing then that all these things" are perishable; that even "the heavens shall pass away with a great noise, and the elements shall melt with fervent heat; the earth also, and the works that are therein shall be burned up, what manner of persons ought we to be in all holy conversation and godliness!" According to the promise of God, we are "looking for new heavens and a new earth wherein dwelleth righteousness," 2 Pet. iii. 10, 13.

Section VI.—EGYPT.

Egypt was one of the most ancient, and one of the mightiest of kingdoms. If it were not the birth-place, it was early the protector of the sciences; and it cherished every species of knowledge, which distinguished the most enlightened men of remote times. Egypt was, therefore, famous for its wisdom: but it was no less superstitious; and at a very early period of its history excessively addicted to idolatry. This profanity and folly they carried to a greater height than any other people, worshipping the sun, moon, stars, men, animals,

plants, reptiles, and even the most despicable insects. What history records of its population, cities, and public buildings, would surpass credibility, were it not attested by their monuments which remain to this day. Egypt is a scene of antiquities: walking among ruins, the traveller forgets the present to contemplate the past, and amid the traces of a degenerate race, he marks the remains of a mighty nation. The pyramids of Egypt have always ranked among the wonders of the world. Three of them still remain, at the distance of a few leagues from Grand Cairo, where the ancient Memphis stood. It has been calculated by a French engineer, that the stones in the largest of the three, called the great pyramid, are six millions of tons; and would be sufficient to build a wall round the whole of France, (about eighteen hundred miles,) ten feet high and one foot broad! It forms a square, each side of whose base is seven hundred and forty-six feet, and covers nearly fourteen acres of land. It is said to be as large as the area of Lincoln's-inn Fields, London. The perpendicular height is about five hundred and sixty feet; being one hundred and seventeen feet higher than St. Paul's cathedral in London. The summit, which viewed from below appears a point, is found to be a platform, each side of which is eighteen feet. Some of the stones of which this enormous edifice is built, are thirty feet long. These stupendous works of man were originally designed as tombs of their kings; from which we may infer the grandeur and resources of the nation.

Concerning Egypt it was prophesied:

"Thus saith the LORD God: Behold, I am against thee, Pharaoh king of Egypt, the great dragon that lieth in the midst of his rivers, which hath said, My river is mine own, and I have made it for myself! Behold, therefore I am against thee, and against thy rivers, and I will make the land of Egypt utterly waste and desolate, from the tower of Syene even unto the border of Ethiopia. It shall be the basest of the kingdoms; neither shall it exalt itself any more above the nations. Thus saith the LORD God; I will also destroy the idols,

and I will cause their images to cease out of Noph; and there shall be no more a prince of the land of Egypt: and I will put a fear in the land of Egypt," Ezek. xxix. 3, 10, 15; xxx. 13.

These predictions have been fulfilled with awful minuteness. Egypt is still full of wonders, as its ancient cities and temples are heaps of ruins. Those stupendous temples, abounding with massy and lofty columns, are profusely covered with hieroglyphics; and, though they were erected by mortals, who had " changed the glory of the incorruptible God into an image made like to corruptible man, and to birds, and four-footed beasts, and creeping things," they seem destined to pay homage to the only living and true God, by illustrating both the historical and the prophetical truth of his inspired word.

Deprived twenty-three centuries ago of her natural proprietors, Egypt has seen her fertile fields successively a prey to the Persians, the Macedonians, the Romans, the Greeks, the Arabs, the Georgians; and, at length, the race of Tartars, distinguished by the name of Ottoman Turks. The Mamelukes, purchased as slaves, and introduced as soldiers, soon usurped the power and elected a leader. They have been replaced by slaves brought from their original country. The system of oppression in Egypt is methodical. Every thing which the traveller sees or hears, reminds him that he is in the country of slavery and tyranny. In Egypt there is no middle class: neither nobility, clergy, merchants, nor landholders. Ignorance prevailing over the whole population, extends its effects to every species of moral and physical knowledge.

There has not been a prince in the land of Egypt. It has been laid waste, and all by the hand of strangers. It is a base kingdom, and "the basest of kingdoms;" governed by strangers and slaves. The pashas have been oppressors and strangers, and the price paid for his authority and power, and the whole property of the country, being at the will of every succeeding pasha, show how it has been literally sold into the hands of the wicked.

The fate of Egypt, as of Idumea and of Judea, demonstrates the Bible to be no cunningly devised fable; but gives the most overpowering evidence, that the prophets who foretold these things, spake and wrote as they were moved by the Holy Ghost.

Section VII.—NINEVEH.

Nineveh was the capital city of Assyria, founded by Ashur, or by Nimrod, both grandsons of Noah. It was situated on the eastern bank of the river Tigris, about 280 miles north-west of Babylon. Nineveh rose to its highest glory many ages after, under its second founder, Ninus II., about the year B. C. 1230; it then became the greatest city in the world. Its walls are described by heathen historians, as having been one hundred feet in height, and sixty miles in circuit, fortified by fifteen hundred towers, each two hundred feet high. The expression used by Jonah, the prophet, that "Nineveh was a great city of three days' journey," justifies the description of profane historians. The population is supposed to have been, at least, six hundred thousand. A succession of warlike princes had established the greatness of Nineveh on the ruins of the neighbouring states; and the greater part of Asia submitted to the Assyrian power. By this growing prosperity, the rulers and people became dreadfully corrupted: rapacity, cruelty, and oppression marked the progress of their conquests: under their king Shalmaneser they exterminated the kingdom of Israel, 2 Kings xvii.; and king Sennacherib purposed the same concerning Judah, besieging Jerusalem, ch. xviii. xix.; Isa. xxxvi. xxxvii.; before whose walls the angel of the LORD blasted in death, during one night, the Assyrian army of one hundred and eighty thousand men. Jonah had preached repentance to the Ninevites; and they had humbled themselves before God; by which means their threatened overthrow was suspended about 200 years: but returning to their wickedness, the prophet Nahum was raised up to declare the righteous judgments of God upon their proud and guilty metropolis. "The burden of Nineveh. God is jealous, and the LORD revengeth;

the LORD will take vengeance on his adversaries, and he reserveth wrath for his enemies. With an overrunning flood he will make an utter end of the place thereof, and darkness shall pursue his enemies. For while they be folden together as thorns, and while they are drunken as drunkards, they shall be devoured as stubble fully dry. The gates of the rivers shall be opened, and the palace shall be dissolved. Take ye the spoil of silver, take the spoil of gold: for there is none end of the store and glory out of all the pleasant furniture. Behold, thy people in the midst of thee are women; the gates of thy land shall be set wide open unto thine enemies: the fire shall devour thy bars. There is no healing of thy bruise; thy wound is grievous: all that hear the bruit of thee shall clap the hands over thee; for upon whom hath not thy wickedness passed continually?" Nahum i. 1, 2, 8, 10; ii. 6, 9; iii. 13, 19. "He will stretch out his hand against the north, and destroy Assyria; and will make Nineveh a desolation, and dry like a wilderness. And flocks shall lie down in the midst of her, all the beasts of the nations: both the cormorant and the bittern shall lodge in the upper lintels of it; their voice shall sing in the windows; desolation shall be in the thresholds: for he shall uncover the cedar work. This is the rejoicing city, that said in her heart, 'I am, and there is none beside me:' how is she become a desolation, a place for beasts to lie down in! Every one that passeth by her shall hiss, and wag his hand," Zeph. ii. 13—15.

These predictions have been remarkably accomplished upon Nineveh. A Greek historian, in describing the manner of its destruction, relates that the proud city was besieged by the allied armies of the Medes and Babylonians for three years; that the king Sardanapalus, being encouraged to hold out, by an ancient oracle, that *Nineveh should never be taken by assault until the river became its enemy;* when a mighty inundation of the river, swollen by long-continued rains, threw down about twenty furlongs of the city wall, through which the besiegers entered, and the king, in his desperation, conceiving that the oracle was near its accomplishment,

heaped an immense funeral pile in his palace, set fire to it; and thus destroyed himself, his concubines, eunuchs, and treasure, in the year B. C. 606. It is also related, that after the allied army took the city, they sacked and razed it, carrying away many talents of gold and silver to the city of Ecbatana.

The very site of Nineveh was long unknown to the moderns; so completely have the predictions been fulfilled: but it is believed to have been opposite to the city of Mosul, now flourishing on the western side of the Tigris. Travellers find on the eastern side heaps of ruins, overgrown with grass, resembling the remains of the intrenchments and fortifications of ancient Roman camps. The appearance of other mounds and ruins less marked, extend for ten miles, and seem to be the wreck of former buildings. There is not one monument of royalty, nor one token of splendour: the places are not known where they were. There are not even bricks, stones, or other materials of buildings, discernible, in the larger mounds. The place is a desolation—an utter ruin—empty, void, and waste. The very ruins have perished; and it is reduced to even less than the wreck of its former grandeur. It shows not the least signs of the greatness of its kings, nobles, or merchants: but even the want of these proclaims, most powerfully, the truth of the word of God!

Section VIII.—BABYLON.

Babylon was the capital of Babylonia, an ancient kingdom founded by the first descendants of Noah, soon after the deluge; and enlarged by Nimrod, his great-grandson, about two thousand years before the birth of Christ. Many additions were made to it by queen Semiramis, and it was greatly strengthened and beautified by various succeeding sovereigns: but it was Nebuchadnezzar and his queen, called Nitocris, by Herodotus, and who was regent during his distraction of seven years, that brought the city to such a degree of splendour, as rendered it one of the wonders of the world. Babylon stood in the midst of an extended plain, of

inexhaustible fertility, exciting the astonishment of the Greeks, though theirs was a plentiful country. The city was divided into two parts by the river Euphrates, which flowed through it from north to south. Both these divisions were enclosed by one wall; and the whole formed a complete square, four hundred and eighty furlongs, or sixty miles in compass. The walls were of extraordinary strength, being eighty-seven feet broad, capable of admitting six chariots abreast to run upon them, and three hundred feet high. On each side of the river was built a quay, and high walls of the same thickness with the walls around the city. The entrances to the city were by one hundred gates, made of solid brass, and of prodigious size, from which fifty streets, twenty-five from each side, and fifteen miles long, traversed the whole area from gate to gate; and intersecting each other, the whole was divided into six hundred and twenty-five squares. The two parts of the city were connected by a remarkable bridge across the river, a furlong in length, and sixty feet wide; and to prevent inconvenience from the swellings of the river, two canals were cut, above the city, by which the superabundant waters were carried off into the Tigris. Besides, prodigious embankments were made, effectually to confine the stream within its channel, and as a security against inundation. The materials for these stupendous works were taken, principally, from the western side of the city, where an extraordinary lake was dug, the depth of which was thirty-five feet, and its circumference forty-five miles.

At the two ends of the bridge were two magnificent palaces, which some describe as having had a subterraneous communication with each other, by means of a vault or tunnel under the bed of the river. The old palace, on the east side, was about thirty furlongs in compass, surrounded by three separate walls, one within another. The new palace, on the opposite side, was about four times as large as the other, and is said to have been eight miles in circumference. Within this were "hanging gardens," forming an area of four hundred feet

square, containing about three and a half acres: they consisted of terraces raised one above another, till they equalled the city wall, supported by twenty walls very thick and eleven feet asunder, covered with large flat stones. On the highest level was a reservoir with a machine, by which water was drawn from the river for the supply of the whole gardens, in which trees were planted in soil of sufficient depth for them to grow fifty feet high. This magnificent work was prepared for the gratification of the queen Amyitis, daughter of king Astyages; that she might behold something resembling the hills and woodlands of her native country Media. Near to the old palace stood the temple of Belus, or Jupiter, forming a square nearly three miles in compass. In the middle of the temple was an immense tower, six hundred feet in height. This large pile of building consisted of eight towers, each seventy-five feet high, and which were ascended by stairs winding round the outside. On this temple of Belus, or, as some say, on its summit, was a golden image forty feet in height, and equal in value to three and a half millions sterling. There was, besides, such a multitude of other statues and sacred utensils, that the whole of the treasure contained in this single edifice, has been estimated at forty-two millions of pounds sterling! These things displayed the prodigious wealth and power of the Babylonian empire, and were, certainly, among the mightiest works of mortals. Babylon was called, "the glory of kingdoms," "the golden city," "the lady of kingdoms," and "the praise of the whole earth:" but its pride, idolatry, and wickedness, have been visited in its utter desolation, agreeably to the inspired predictions of the holy prophets of the Most High.

"Babylon, the glory of kingdoms, the beauty of the Chaldees' excellency, shall be as when God overthrew Sodom and Gomorrah. It shall never be inhabited, neither shall the Arabian pitch his tent there; neither shall the shepherds make their fold there. But wild beasts of the desert shall lie there; and their houses shall be full of doleful creatures; and owls shall dwell there,

and satyrs shall dance there. And the wild beasts of the islands shall cry in their desolate houses, and dragons in their pleasant palaces: and her time is near to come, and her days shall not be prolonged. For I will rise up against them, saith the LORD of hosts, and cut off from Babylon the name, and remnant, and son, and nephew, saith the LORD. I will also make it a possession for the bittern, and pools of water: and I will sweep it with the besom of destruction, saith the LORD of hosts. Thus saith the LORD to his anointed, to Cyrus, whose right hand I have holden, to subdue nations before him; and I will loose the loins of kings, to open before him the two-leaved gates; and the gates shall not be shut; I will go before thee, and make the crooked places straight: I will break in pieces the gates of brass, and cut in sunder the bars of iron; and I will give thee the treasures of darkness, and hidden riches of secret places, that thou mayest know that I, the LORD, who call thee by thy name, am the God of Israel. Publish, and conceal not: say, Babylon is taken, Bel is confounded, Merodach is broken in pieces; her idols are confounded, her images are broken in pieces. Because of the wrath of the LORD, it shall not be inhabited, but it shall be wholly desolate: every one that goeth by Babylon shall be astonished, and hiss at all her plagues. Come against her from the utmost border, open her storehouses: cast her up as heaps, and destroy her utterly: let nothing of her be left. One post shall run to meet another, and one messenger to meet another, to show the king of Babylon that his city is taken at one end. And Babylon shall become heaps, a dwelling-place for dragons, an astonishment, and a hissing, without an inhabitant," Isa. xiii. 19—22; xiv. 22, 23; xlv. 1—3; Jer. l. 2, 13, 26; li. 31, 37.

The particulars of the siege of Babylon are detailed by Herodotus and Xenophon, two eminent heathen historians. In exact accordance with the inspired predictions of Isaiah and Jeremiah, they say, that Cyrus, with a large army of the Medes and Persians, invaded Babylon; that the Babylonians, after having been defeated

in a pitched battle in the plain, were driven within the city, which was then closely besieged; and that they, having laid up provisions for several years, were under no apprehensions; and conceiving their walls impregnable, could not be provoked to an engagement; that Cyrus contrived a snare for the Babylonians, by turning the course of the river Euphrates through the great lake in a canal made by his soldiers; that the waters being thus dried up, the soldiers marched to the bridge in the channel of the river; that, from the negligence of the guards, some of the gates, leading to the city, were left open; that the troops of Cyrus, entering by this means, took Babylon during the night of an idolatrous festival; that its princes, nobles, and captains, being drunk with their feasting, were suddenly slaughtered, and that the glorious city, never before conquered, was thus taken without the knowledge of the king, till messengers ran with the information, which he had scarcely time to receive before he was also numbered among the multitudes of the slain, in the year 536 before the advent of Christ, as described by the prophet Daniel, chapter v. Babylon soon began to decline. Darius Hystaspes broke down its lofty walls, and took away the gates, which Cyrus had spared; and from an imperial, it was reduced to a tributary city. Xerxes, a successor of Cyrus on the Persian throne, after his ignominious retreat from Greece, seized the sacred treasures, plundered the temples, and destroyed the images of precious metal. Alexander the Great, having conquered Persia, attempted to restore Babylon, designing to make it the metropolis of a universal empire. Ten thousand men were employed by him for two months, in removing the rubbish for the repairing of the embankments of the Euphrates, and the rebuilding of the temple of Belus: but the work was abandoned on the premature death of Alexander.

Seleucus Nicator, successor of Alexander in the kingdom of Syria, dismantled and spoiled the city, to build New Babylon; which, to immortalize his name, was called Seleucia. With the same design several other

cities were built in those regions by succeeding sovereigns, by which the population was drained from the old city; and the fairest parts of Babylon were destroyed by a Parthian conqueror, about a hundred and thirty years before the birth of Christ.

Babylon, at the commencement of the Christian era, was but very thinly peopled; and Strabo describes the greater part of the site as a desert, at that period. It continued to decline, and its desolations to increase, till, in the fourth century, its walls formed an enclosure for the breeding of wild beasts; and it was reserved as a hunting park for the Persian monarchs. For a long series of ages no record was made concerning Babylon; while it was approaching its desolation, a dwelling-place for dragons, as testified by the inspired prophets.

The site on which Babylon stood has been completely ascertained; and the ruins have been visited and described by several intelligent English travellers. From being the "glory of kingdoms," Babylon is now the greatest of ruins; and after the lapse of two thousand four hundred years, it exhibits to the view of every traveller the precise scene defined by the prophets of God.

The name and remnant are cut off from Babylon. There the Arabian pitches not his tent: there the shepherds make not their folds; but wild beasts of the desert lie there, and their houses are full of doleful creatures. It is a place for the bittern, and a dwelling-place for dragons: it is a dry land and a desert—a burnt mountain—empty—wholly desolate—pools of water—heaps—and utterly destroyed—a land where no man dwelleth—every one that passes by it is astonished.

The superstitious dread of evil spirits, and the natural terror at the wild beasts which dwell among the ruins of Babylon, restrain the Arab from pitching his tent, or shepherds from making their folds there. The princely palaces and habitations of the wondrous city, utterly destroyed, are now nothing but unshapely heaps of bricks and rubbish: instead of their stately chambers, there are now caverns, where porcupines creep, and owls and bats nestle; where lions find dens, and jackals, hyænas,

and other noxious animals, their unmolested retreats, from which issue loathsome smells; and the entrances to which are strewed with the bones of sheep and goats. On one side of the Euphrates, the canals are dry, and the crumbled bricks on an elevated surface exposed to the scorching sun, cover an arid plain, and Babylon is a wilderness, a dry land, a desert. On the other, the embankments of the river, and with them the vestiges of ruins over a large space, have been swept away: the plain is in general marshy, and in many places inaccessible, especially after the annual overflowing of the Euphrates: no son of man doth pass thereby; the sea or river is come upon Babylon, she is covered with the multitude of the waves thereof.

Birs Nimrod, or the temple of Belus, which was standing after the beginning of the Christian era, is still to be distinguished. It has been visited and described by several modern English travellers, who have given sketches of it, from one of which the following is taken.

It is still worthy, from its immensity, of being a relic of Babylon the great: for though a mass of ruins, it is no less than two hundred and thirty-five feet high. On these ruins there are vast fragments of brickwork that have been completely molten; they ring, on striking them, like glass, and must have been subjected to a heat equal to that of the strongest furnace. From the summit of this

mass there is a distinct view of the frightful heaps which constitute all that now remains of ancient and glorious Babylon; and a more complete picture of desolation could scarcely be imagined by the human mind!

Thus we behold the proudest works of the greatest of mortals brought to nothing, and the loftiest monuments of their power, genius, and riches, levelled with the dust, and preserved in ruins, for the purpose of illustrating and confirming the faithful testimony of the eternal God, as recorded in his most holy word. How wonderful are the predictions of his commissioned servants, when compared with the events to which they direct our minds; and what a convincing demonstrative proof do we see of the truth and divinity of the Holy Scriptures! With what admirable propriety does Jehovah allege this memorable instance of his foreknowledge, in relation to Babylon, and challenge all the false divinities and their votaries to produce any thing of similar import! "Who hath declared this from ancient time? Who hath told it from that time? have not I the LORD? And there is no God else beside me, a just God and a Saviour, there is none else beside me. Declaring the end from the beginning, and from ancient times the things that are not yet done, saying, My counsel shall stand, and I will do all my pleasure," Isa. xlv. 21; xlvi. 10.

Babylon, in its pride, wickedness, and doom, is, as we find, regarded by the inspired writers of the New Testament, as typical of antichrist, the "mystery of iniquity," the "man of sin," the great ecclesiastical imposture, and called, "BABYLON THE GREAT!" 2 Thess. ii. 3—10; Rev. xvii. xviii. Dr. Hales, therefore, remarks, "These awful prophecies against Babylon acquire an additional interest from the numerous references thereto in the New Testament. Rome, the corrupt and idolatrous mistress of the western world, is compared to her prototype in the east, by the apostle Peter, in his Epistles, and by John, in the Apocalypse."

Ch. XXVIII.—Unfulfilled Prophecy.

The Bible scheme of prophecy is manifestly divine. Upon this subject the foregoing chapter, on several prophecies remarkably fulfilled, will serve as a demonstration to every reflecting reader. Considered in its first dawning; its gradual advancement; its partial completion, in the overthrow of the great monarchies; the advent of the Messiah; the perfection of his mediation; the dispersion of the Jews, his enemies; the establishment of his kingdom among the Gentiles; and the prevailing influence of its saving knowledge and the fear of the Lord covering the earth, preparatory to the great day of God; prophecy is an object the most sublime that imagination can conceive, and the most important that a devout mind can contemplate.

In the Bible we behold the spirit of prophecy pervading all time; commencing so early as the first man, and extending to the final consummation of all things: we see it uniformly characterizing one person; first, by dark and obscure intimations, then gradually unfolding itself with brighter lustre as it advances, till the appearance of Him who was its ultimate end and object. In Him, and in his apostles, especially in his beloved disciple, we behold it renewed, predicting, with peculiar exactness, every important event which should befall his church, even from its earliest establishment, down to that period of awful expectation, when the great plan of the Divine mercy shall be brought to a glorious conclusion, and the mysterious counsels of the Almighty, respecting the Christian dispensation, shall be closed in judgment and consummated in glory.

In the mean time, many great and blessed things are to be effected among the nations of mankind, as declared in the "sure word of prophecy" contained in the Bible. We will notice several particulars.

1. Concerning the Lord our Redeemer, it is said, " Of the increase of his government and peace there shall be no end," Isa. ix. 7. " He shall come down like rain upon the mown grass: as showers that water the earth.

In his days shall the righteous flourish; and abundance of peace so long as the moon endureth. He shall have dominion also from sea to sea, and from the river unto the ends of the earth. His name shall endure for ever: His name shall be continued as long as the sun: and men shall be blessed in him; all nations shall call him blessed," Psa. lxxii. 6—8, 17.

To this end,

2. The gospel is to be preached among all the nations and people upon the earth. " And he said unto them, Go ye into all the world, and preach the gospel to every creature," Mark xvi. 15. " Many shall run to and fro, and knowledge shall be increased," Dan. xii. 4. " And I saw another angel fly in the midst of heaven, having the everlasting gospel to preach unto them that dwell on the earth, and to every nation, and kindred, and tongue, and people," Rev. xiv. 6. " The earth shall be filled with the knowledge of the glory of the LORD, as the waters cover the sea," Hab. ii. 14.

3. The saving influences of the Holy Spirit are to accompany the ministry of the gospel, to give it the necessary efficacy. " And it shall come to pass afterwards, that I will pour out my Spirit upon all flesh," Joel ii. 28. " And when he (the Comforter) is come he will reprove the world of sin, and of righteousness, and of judgment," John xvi. 8. " I will pour water upon him that is thirsty, and floods upon the dry ground: I will pour my Spirit upon thy seed, and my blessing upon thine offspring: and they shall spring up as among the grass, as willows by the water courses. One shall say, I am the LORD's; and another shall call himself by the name of Jacob; and another shall subscribe with his hand unto the LORD, and surname himself by the name of Israel," Isa. xliv. 3—5.

4. As the consequence of the effusion of the Spirit, the church of Christ is to include all nations, in an extraordinary state of knowledge, holiness, and happiness. " All the ends of the world shall remember and turn unto the LORD: and all the kindreds of the nations shall worship before thee," Psa. xxii. 27. " But in

the last days it shall come to pass, that the mountain of the house of the LORD shall be established in the top of the mountains, and it shall be exalted above the hills; and people shall flow into it. And many nations shall come, and say, Come, and let us go up to the mountain of the LORD, and to the house of the God of Jacob; and he will teach us of his ways, and we will walk in his paths; for the law shall go forth of Zion, and the word of the LORD from Jerusalem. And he shall judge among many people, and rebuke strong nations afar off; and they shall beat their swords into ploughshares, and their spears into pruning-hooks: nation shall not lift up sword against nation, neither shall they learn war any more," Micah iv. 1, 3. "They shall not hurt nor destroy in all my holy mountain, for the earth shall be full of the knowledge of the LORD, as the waters cover the sea," Isa. xi. 9.

" And the Gentiles shall come to thy light, and kings to the brightness of thy rising; I will make thy officers peace, and thine exactors righteousness. Violence shall no more be heard in thy land, wasting nor destruction within thy borders; but thou shalt call thy walls Salvation, and thy gates Praise," Isa. lx. 3, 17, 18. "In that day shall there be upon the bells of the horses, HOLINESS UNTO THE LORD," Zech. xiv. 20.

5. Of the Jews it is predicted that their infidelity shall be removed; and, by conversion they shall be brought into the church of Christ, with the fulness of the Gentiles. "For the children of Israel shall abide many days without a king, and without a prince, and without a sacrifice, and without an image, and without an ephod, and without teraphim. Afterward shall the children return, and seek the LORD their God, and David their king; and shall fear the LORD and his goodness in the latter day," Hos. iii. 4, 5. "I will pour upon the house of David, and upon the inhabitants of Jerusalem, the spirit of grace and of supplication: and they shall look upon me whom they have pierced," Zech. xii. 16. "Thus saith the LORD GOD; Behold, I will take the children of Israel from among the heathens, whither they be

gone, and will gather them on every side, and bring them into their own land: and I will make them one nation in the land upon the mountains of Israel; and one king shall be king to them all. I will save them out of all their dwelling-places, wherein they have sinned, and will cleanse them: so shall they be my people, and I will be their God. And David my servant shall be king over them: and they all shall have one shepherd over them; they shall also walk in my judgments, and observe my statutes, and do them. My tabernacle also shall be with them: yea, I will be their God, and they shall be my people. And the heathen shall know that I the LORD do sanctify Israel, when my sanctuary shall be in the midst of them for evermore," Ezek. xxxvii. 21—24, 27, 28. Neither will I hide my face any more from them: for I have poured out my Spirit upon the house of Israel, saith the LORD GOD," Ezek. xxxix. 29. "Blindness in part is happened to Israel, until the fulness of the Gentiles be come in. And so all Israel shall be saved: as it is written, There shall come out of Sion the Deliverer, and shall turn away ungodliness from Jacob; for this is my covenant unto them, when I shall take away their sins," Rom. xi. 25—27.

These are a few of the predictions which abound in the word of God: and that all these prophecies shall be perfectly fulfilled, we have the most confident assurance, arising from the faithful word of the LORD OF HOSTS. He has said, "For as the snow and the rain cometh down from heaven, and returneth not thither, but watereth the earth, and maketh it bring forth and bud, that it may give seed to the sower and bread to the eater: so shall the word be that goeth forth out of my mouth: it shall not return unto me void, but it shall accomplish that which I please, and it shall prosper in the thing whereto I sent it," Isa. lv. 9, 10.

Besides the infallible word of God, the signs of the times, and the various means which Providence has brought into operation within the last fifty years especially, indicate the approaching accomplishment of all

the merciful purposes of God towards mankind; though, in accordance with the prophetical declarations, there are also increasing indications of dark and trying times to be passed through previously. Scriptural truth appears to be better understood by the church of God. Christians of different denominations manifest a greater disposition to seek to extend the kingdom of their Saviour, in blessing the whole family of man. For this purpose missionary societies have been established; they are supported by the voluntary contributions of the several bodies of Christians, whose agents have been eminently honoured of God in diffusing the saving knowledge of Jesus Christ. By their means many nations have abandoned idolatry with its degrading brutalities, and many have received the truth as it is in Jesus. It is computed that a thousand protestant missionaries are disseminating the doctrines of their Saviour among the heathen, assisted by at least a thousand preachers and teachers from among the native converts. To further their object, the Scriptures have been translated by the missionaries and others into about sixty different languages, which before had never been sanctified by the inspired word of God; and the Bible Society has published the Scriptures, in whole or in part, in about one hundred and fifty languages. Innumerable religious tracts have been published in various languages. Schools have been established at the various missionary stations; and it is calculated, that not less than 100,000 pagan children and adults are receiving Christian instruction in day and Sunday schools. The fruits of evangelical instruction are appearing in multitudes of devoted converts to Christ among the heathen, and the blessed morning has, we trust, evidently dawned upon the world, which, though it may be for a time clouded, shall be succeeded by the rising of the Sun of righteousness, and by the meridian glory of truth and holiness, when "all shall know the LORD from the least even to the greatest," and "the kingdoms of this world shall become the kingdoms of our Lord and of his Christ," Rev. xii. 10.

Ch. XXIX.—Figurative Language of the Bible.

"I have multiplied visions, and used similitudes by the ministry of the prophets," Hos. xii. 10. This declaration of the Lord God Almighty must be practically regarded, fully to profit by studying the Holy Scriptures. To adopt this mode of instruction was a merciful condescension to human weakness on the part of God; especially in the early ages of the world, when symbolical language originated from the necessary scarcity of words. Figures of speech, as all allow, were occasioned by the very poverty of language. The advancement of society in arts, sciences, and refinement, has produced the addition of a multitude of words. Still, in the highest state of improvement, all languages continue to be more or less figurative both in speech and writing.

Probably there are no writings in existence whose style is not, in some degree, metaphorical; which, indeed, imparts to them much essential beauty.

The language of the Bible is highly figurative, particularly the Old Testament; for which, besides its remote antiquity, two particular reasons have been assigned. First, the eastern nations, possessing warm imaginations, and living in climates rich and fertile, surrounded by objects equally grand and beautiful, naturally delighted in a figurative mode of expression, far beyond that of the colder taste of Europeans in less luxuriant regions. The other is, that many of the books of the Old Testament consist of Hebrew poetry; in the style of which the author illustrates his productions by images and similitudes, drawn from every striking subject which may be present to his imagination. Moses, David, Solomon, Isaiah, and other sacred poets, abound with figurative expressions, on every occasion their compositions are adorned with the richest flowers and the most instructive metaphors, to impress the minds and affect the hearts of their readers. But their propriety, design, and beauty, can be appreciated fully only by possessing a tolerable idea of the country in which the

inspired poets flourished, the peculiarities of its inhabitants, and the idioms of its language.

The style of the New Testament also, especially the discourses of our Saviour, are remarkably metaphorical; by mistaking which the most extravagant notions have been published as divine doctrine; some professors of Christianity adopting a literal application of those expressions which were figuratively intended. A few examples will show the incorrectness of a literal interpretation of some of the words of our Lord. Speaking of Herod the king, Christ says, "Go ye, and tell that fox," Luke xiii. 32. Here, as every reader perceives, the word fox is transferred from its literal signification, that of a beast of prey, proverbial for its profound cunning, to denote a cruel tyrant, and that use of the term conveys, as was designed, the idea of consummate hypocrisy.

Our Lord said to the Jews, "I am the living bread which came down from heaven: if any man eat of this bread he shall live for ever: and the bread that I will give is my flesh, which I will give for the life of the world," John vi. 51. The sensual Jews understood his words literally; and said, "How can this man give us his flesh to eat?" ver. 52, not considering that he intended the sacrifice of his life, which he gave as an atonement for the sins of the world.

In the institution of the Lord's supper, our Saviour said of the bread, "This is my body;" and of the wine, "This is my blood," Matt. xxvi. 26—28. Upon these words the Roman Catholics, since the twelfth century, have put a forced construction; and in opposition to other passages of the Scriptures, as well as every principle of nature and sound reason, they have attempted to establish their monstrous doctrine of transubstantiation; or, the conversion of the bread and wine in the Lord's supper into the real body and blood of Christ, when the priest pronounces the words of pretended consecration, though to all the senses it remains just the same bread and wine unchanged. The evident meaning of our Lord was, that the bread represented his body, and the wine signified his blood. This mode of expression

may be seen used in the Old Testament, Gen. xli. 26 27; Exod. xii. 11; Dan. vii. 24; and by our Saviour himself in his parables, Matt. xiii. 38, 39; John x. 7—9. Also, Christ calls himself the door, John x. 9; a vine, John xv. 1; a shepherd, John x. 11.

The most common and remarkable figures of speech in the Bible are the following:

I. A Metaphor is a figurative expression, founded on some similitude which one object bears to another, as, To bridle the tongue, James i. 26. For the sword to devour flesh, Deut. xxxii. 42. To be born again, John iii. 3.

II. A Proverb is a concise, sententious saying, founded on a penetrating observation of men and manners. Brevity and elegance are essential to a proverb, Prov. x. 15; Luke iv. 23.

III. A Parable is the representation of some moral or spiritual doctrine under an ingenious similitude, as that of the Sower, Matt. xiii. 2—23; the Prodigal Son, Luke xvi. 11—32; and the Ten Virgins, Matt. xxv. 1—13.

IV. An Allegory is a continued metaphor, as the discourse of our Saviour concerning eating his flesh, John vi. 35—65.

V. Metonymy is a figure of speech in which one word is put for another; as, "They have Moses and the prophets," Luke xvi. 29; meaning not their persons, but their writings.

VI. Prosopopœia, or Personification, attributes the actions of persons to things, as in Psa. lxxxv. 10, it is said, "Mercy and truth are met together; righteousness and peace have kissed each other."

VII. Synecdoche puts a part for the whole of any thing, or the whole for a part, as Luke ii. 1, "All the world;" and Acts xxiv. 5, "Throughout the world;" by which is meant the Roman empire, or parts of it. In Acts xxvii. 37, the word "souls" is put for the whole persons.

VIII. Irony is a figure in which a different thing is intended from that which is spoken. Examples of this kind are not very frequent in the Bible; yet there are

a few. Such is the address of Elijah to the priests of Baal, 1 Kings xviii. 27; and the remark of Job to his friends, Job xii. 2.

IX. Hyperbole is a representation of any thing as being much greater or smaller than it is in reality. For examples of this figure, see Numb. xiii. 33; Deut. i. 28; ix. 1.

Ch. XXX.—Index to the Symbolical Language of the Bible.

Abaddon, in Hebrew, } A name derived from the title
Apollyon, in Greek— } of the Arabian kings, and applied to the Mohammedan powers, by which the Christian church in the east was oppressed, Rev. ix. 11.

Abomination—1. Sin, in general, Isa. lxvi. 3; Ezek. xvi. 50, 51.
    2. An idol, 2 Kings xxiii. 13; Isa. xliv. 19.
    3. Idolatrous rites and ceremonies of popery, Rev. xvii. 4.

Abomination of desolation—The idolatrous ensigns of the Roman army, Matt. xxiv. 15.

Adulteress, or Harlot—An apostate city or church, Isa. i. 21; Rev. xvii. 5.

Adultery—Idolatry and apostacy, Jer. iii. 8, 9; Rev. ii. 22.

Angels—1. Intelligent beings employed by God as ministers of his providence, Ezek. x. 8, etc.; Heb. i. 4—7, 14; Rev. iv. 6; v. 11.
    2. Apostate spirits, Matt. xxv. 41; Jude 6.
    3. The pastors or bishops of churches, Rev. i. 20; ii. 1, 8, 12, 18.
    4. Angel of the Lord, Jesus Christ, Zech. i. 11.

Arm—1. The omnipotence of God, Jer. xxvii. 5; xxxii. 17.
    2. The power and miracles of Christ, Isa. liii. 1; John xii. 38.

Arm—3. Gracious influences of God on mankind, Isa. li. 9; lii. 10.
Armour—Spiritual graces, Rom. xiii. 2; Eph. vi. 11.
Arrows—1. Judgments of God, Job vi. 4.
    2. Slanderous words, Psa. lxiv. 3.
Babes—1. Unskilful and foolish princes, Isa. iii. 4.
    2. Young or feeble Christians, 1 Cor. iii. 1; Heb. v. 13.
Babylon—Papal Rome, Rev. xiv. 8; xvii. xviii.
Balaam—The errors and impurities of that apostate, 2 Pet. ii. 15; Jude 11; Rev. ii. 14.
Beast—1. A heathen power, Dan. vii. 17.
    2. The papal antichrist, Rev. xiii. 2, 12; xvii. 3, 7, 8, etc.
Beasts — The four living creatures, improperly called beasts, Rev. iv. They denote the cherubim described Ezek. i. x.
Black, Blackness—Afflictions, Jer. xiv. 2; Joel ii. 6.
Blasphemy — Idolatry, especially that of popery, Rev. xiii. 1, 5, 6; xvii. 3.
Blindness—Ignorance of divine doctrine, Isa. xxix. 18; Rom. xi. 25; Eph. iv. 18.
Blood—1. Slaughter and mortality, Isa. xxxiv. 3; Ezek. xxxii. 6; Rev. xiv. 20.
    2. Symbol of the atonement by Christ, Matt. xxvi. 28; Heb. xiii. 20.
Body—The sanctified church of Christ, 1 Cor. xii. 13, 27.
Book—Symbol of the Divine decrees, Psa. xl. 7; Heb. x. 7.
Book of Life—The heavenly register of the people of God, Rev. iii. 5; xx. 12, 15; xxii. 19; Mal. iii. 16.
Bow—1. Vigorous health, Job xxix. 20.
    2. Symbol of evangelical conquest, Rev. vi. 2.
Bowels—Tender sympathy, Phil. ii. 1; Luke i. 78. Gr. bowels of mercy.
Branch—Christ, Isa. xi. 1; Jer. xxiii. 5; xxxiii. 15; Zech. iii. 8.
Bread, food—1. Divine doctrine, Deut. viii. 3; Isa. lv. 2; Matt. iv. 4.

2. Christian fellowship, 1 Cor. x. 17.
Bride—The church of Christ, Rev. xxi. 9.
Bridegroom—Christ, the husband of the church, John iii. 29; Rev. xxi. 9.
Briers—Persons of pernicious principles, Isa. lv. 13.
Brimstone—1. Perpetual desolations, Job xviii. 15; Isa. xxxiv. 9.
   2. Emblem of torment, Rev. xiv. 10.
   3. Pernicious doctrines, Rev. ix. 17.
Bulls—Violent men, Psa. xxii. 12.
Candlestick—See Lamp.
Cedars—Eminent men, Zech. xi. 2.
Cedars of Lebanon—Kings, princes of Judah, Isa. ii. 13.
Cedars, twigs of—Nobility, military chiefs, Ezek. xvii. 4.
Chaff—Worthless, irreligious persons, Psa. i. 4; Matt. iii. 12.
Chain—Calamity or affliction, Lam. iii. 7.
Clouds—Armies, multitudes, Jer. iv. 13; Isa. lx. 8; Heb. xii. 1.
Crown of life—of glory—Immortality, felicity, and glory of heaven, James i. 12; Rev. ii. 10.
Cup—1. Blessings of Divine providence and grace, Psa. xxiii. 5.
   2. Divine judgments, Isa. li. 17.
Cup of salvation—Thankful acknowledgment of Divine mercies, Psa. cxvi. 13.
Cup of blessing—Cup at the Lord's supper, in allusion to the paschal cup, 1 Cor. x. 16.
Darkness—1. Calamity and misery, Jer. xxiii. 1.
   2. Irreligion and ignorance, Rom. xiii. 12.
Darkness of the sun, stars, etc.—Disorders in the government, Isa. xiii. 10.
Day—1. A year, Ezek. iv. 6; Rev. ii. 10; xi. 9; xii. 6.
   2. An appointed season, Isa. xxxiv. 8.
   3. A state of evangelical knowledge, 1 Thess. v. 5.
Death, Natural—Separation of the spirit from the body, Gen. xxv. 1.
Death, Moral—Insensibility to the evil of sin, and to the duties and pleasures of the Divine friendship Eph. ii. 2; Rev. iii. 1.

Death, Second—Eternal banishment from God, Rev. ii. 11; xx. 14.

Death, Evangelical—Mortification of sinful affection, Rom. vi. 8; 1 Pet. ii. 24.

Dew—Power of Christ in the resurrection, Isa. xxvi. 19.

Dogs—1. Gentiles, as sunk in impurity, Matt. xv. 26.
    2. Idle, luxurious ministers of religion, Isa. lvi. 10.
    3. Cavilling, unprincipled teachers, Phil. iii. 2; Rev. xxii. 15.

Door—1. The commencement of a new government, Rev. iv. 1.
    2. The entrance, or enlarged exercise of the gospel ministry, 1 Cor. xvi. 9.

Dragon—1. Symbol of a royal enemy, Ezek. xxix. 23—the king of Egypt.
    2. Satan actuating his agents, Rev. xii. 9.
    3. Dangers or difficulties, Psa. xci. 13.

Drunkenness—1. Emblem of folly, Isa. xxviii. 1—3; Jer. xiii. 13.
    2. Senselessness, the effect of the Divine judgments, Isa. xxix. 9; li. 21.

Dust and ashes—Human nature, Gen. iii. 19; xviii. 27.

Eagle—1. A king or kingdom, Ezek. xvii.
    2. The Roman army, whose standards were eagles, Matt. xxiv. 28.
    3. Emblem of renewed strength, Psa. ciii. 3; Isa. xl. 31.

Earthen vessels—The human body, 2 Cor. iv. 7.

Earthquakes—Political revolutions, Rev. vi. 12; Hag. ii. 6, 7; Heb. xii. 26.

Egypt—Symbolical name for wickedness, Rev. xi. 3.

Elders, The twenty-four—Eminent saints, perhaps patriarchal believers, Rev. iv. 10; Heb. xi. 2.

Eyes—I. Applied to the Almighty, denote,
    1. His infinite knowledge, Prov. xv. 3; Psa. xi. 4.
    2. His watchful providence, Psa. xxxii. 8; xxxiv. 15.
  II. Applied to Jesus Christ, they denote his omnipresence, Rev. ii. 23; v. 6; Heb. iv. 13.
  III. Applied to man, they denote,

1. The understanding, the eyes of the mind, Psa. cxix. 18; Eph. i. 18.
2. A friendly counsellor, Job xxix. 15.
3. The whole man, Rev. i. 7.
4. Human designs, Deut. xxviii. 54—56.

Face—1. The favour of God, Psa. xxxvi. 16; Dan. ix. 17.
2. The infidel profaneness of impenitent man, Jer. v. 3.

Family—The church of God, Eph. iii. 15.

Fat—1. The most excellent of every thing, Psa. lxxxi. 16.
2. Riches, Psa. xxii. 29; Jer. v. 28.

Father—God, whose we are by creation and gracious adoption, Mal. i. 6; ii. 10; Jer. xxxi. 9; Rom. viii. 15, 16; Eph. i. 5.

Field—The world, Matt. xiii. 38.

Fire—Destructive calamity, Isa. xlii. 25; lxvi. 15; Ezek. xxii. 31.

Flesh—1. Riches, Isa. xvii. 4.
2. Mortal man, Isa. xl. 6.
3. Human virtues or religious privileges, Phil. iii. 3, 4.

Forehead—Public profession of religion, Rev. vii. 3; xiii. 16.

Fox—Consummate hypocrisy and deceit, Ezek. xiii. 4; Luke xiii. 32.

Fruit—Religious virtues and enjoyments, Psa. i. 3; xcii. 14.

Furnace—Trying affliction, or the place of affliction, Deut. iv. 20; Jer. ix. 7; xi. 4.

Garments—Souls of men, Rev. iii. 4.

Garments, White—Emblems of purity and joy, Isa. lii. 1; lxi. 10; Rev. iii. 4, 5; xix. 8.

Gates—Symbol of security, Psa. cxlvii. 13.

Gates of the daughter of Sion—The ordinances of divine worship, Psa. ix. 14.

Gates of death—Imminent danger, Psa. ix. 13; Job xxxviii. 17.

Gog with Magog—1. Great Scythian powers in former ages, Ezek. xxxviii. 2.
2. Infidel nations in the last days, Rev. xx. 8.

Gold—Graces of the Holy Spirit, Rev. iii. 18.
Grapes—Virtues of religion, Isa. v. 2.
Grapes, Wild—Sinful tempers and manners, Isa. v. 2.
Hail—The incursions of violent enemies, Isa. xxviii. 2; xxxii. 19; Rev. viii. 7.
Hand, Right—Protection and favour, Psa. xviii. 35; lxxiii. 23.
Hand, Laying on of the—Communication of blessings or authority, Gen. xlviii. 14—20. Appointment to office, Numb. xxvii. 18; 1 Tim. v. 22.
Hand of the Lord on a prophet—Influence of the Holy Spirit, Ezek. viii. 1.
Harvest—Extreme judgment, Joel iii. 13, or end of the world, Matt. xiii. 39.
Head—1. The understanding or governing principle in man, Isa. i. 6; Dan. ii. 28.
  2. Chief of a people, Micah iii. 1, 9, 11.
  3. The metropolis of a country, Isa. vii. 8, 9.
Heavens—1. The powerful providence of God, Dan. iv. 26.
  2. God, Matt. xxi. 25; Luke xv. 18.
  3. Political or ecclesiastical governments, Isa. xiii. 13; Hag. ii. 2, 21.
  4. The visible church, Rev. xii. 7, 9.
Hell—1. The general receptacle of departed souls, Isa. xiv. 7; Rev. i. 18.
  2. The place of eternal torment for the impenitent, Psa. ix. 17; Matt. x. 28; xxiii. 33.
Horn—1. Strength, Rev. v. 6.
  2. Divine protection, Psa. xviii. 2; Amos iii. 14; Luke i. 69.
  3. Royal power, Jer. xlviii. 25; Zech. i. 18, 21; Dan. vii. 20, 22.
Horse—Emblem of conquest, the work of its rider, Joel ii. 4: Hab. i. 8; Jer. iv. 13.
Horse, White—Emblem of happy conquest, Rev. vi. 2—Red, of bloody war—Black, of disease and pestilence—Pale, of famine and misery, Rev. vi. 2, 8; Zech. vi. 2.
House—1. Church of God, Isa. ii. 2; 1 Tim. iii. 15; Heb. iii. 6.

2. Human body, 2 Cor. v. 1.

Hunger and Thirst—1. Natural desires after happiness, Prov. xix. 15; Isa. lv. 1; Rev. xxii. 17.

    2. Spiritual desires, Amos viii. 11; Matt. v. 6; Luke i. 53.

Idolatry—Covetousness, Col. iii. 5. An object excessively beloved, 1 John v. 21.

Image of gold, silver, brass, and iron—The four universal monarchies, Assyrian, Persian, Macedonian, Roman, Dan. ii. 31, 45.

Incense—Devotional exercises, Psa. cxli. 2; Rev. v. 8.

Infirmities—1. Bodily weaknesses, Matt. viii. 17; Isa. liii. 4.

    2. Spiritual weakness, Rom. viii. 26.

Jerusalem—1. Church of God, Psa. cxx. 6; Isa. lxv. 18; lxvi. 13.

    2. Heavenly glory, Heb. xii. 22; Rev. iii. 12; xxi. xxii.; Gal. iv. 24, 26.

Keys—1. Power and authority, Rev. i. 18; Isa. xxii.

    2. Commission of the gospel ministry, Matt. xvi. 19.

    3. Means of scriptural knowledge, Luke xi. 52.

Labourers—Gospel ministers, Matt. ix. 37, 38; 1 Cor. iii. 9.

Lamb—The Messiah, typified by the paschal lamb, and the daily Israelitish sacrifice, Exod. xii. 11; xxix. 38, 41.

Lamp—1. A successor, 1 Kings xv. 4; Psa. cxxxii. 17.

    2. Profession of religion, Matt. xxv. 3, 4.

    3. Divine illumination and comfort, 2 Sam. xxii. 29.

    4. A Christian church, not candlestick, Gr. lamps, Rev. i. 12, 20.

Leaven—Corrupt principles and practices, Matt. xvi. 6; 1 Cor. v. 6, 8.

Leopard—1. A subtle, rapacious enemy, Dan. vii. 6.

    2. A person of similar disposition, Isa. xi. 6.

    3. Antichristian power, Rev. xiii. 2.

Life—1. Immortal felicity, Psa. xvi. 11.

    2. Evangelical doctrine, John vi. 33.

    3. A state of justification, John v. 24; Col. iii. 3.

4. Christ the source of life, natural, spiritual, and eternal, John i. 4; xi. 25; xiv. 6; Col. iii. 4.

Light—1. Joy, peace, and prosperity, Esth. viii. 16.
   2. Evangelical knowledge and holiness, Isa. viii. 20; Eph. v. 8; 1 John i. 7.

Lion—1. An emblem of fortitude, the ensign of the tribe of Judah, Gen. xlix. 9.
   2. A title of Christ, Rev. v. 5.

Locusts—Teachers who corrupt the gospel, Rev. ix. 3.

Manna—The felicities of immortality, Rev. ii. 17.

Moon—The Jewish ecclesiastical state, Joel ii. 31; Rev. xii. 1.

Mountain—1. A kingdom, state, republic, or city, Isa. ii. 12, 14; Zech. iv. 7.
   2. The kingdom of Christ's church, Isa. ii. 2; xi. 9; Dan. ii. 35.

Mystery—A thing or doctrine unknown until revealed, Rom. xvi. 25; 1 Cor. ii. 7; Col. i. 26; Rev. i. 20.

Naked—Destitute of the garment of holiness, Rev. iii. 17.

Names—Persons, Acts i. 15; Rev. iii. 4.

Night—Ignorance, error, adversity, Rev. xxi. 25.

Number two—A few, 1 Kings xvii. 12; Isa. vii. 21.

Number three, or third—Excellency, Isa. xix. 24; Zech. xiii. 9.

Number four—Universality, Isa. xi. 12; Ezek. vii. 2.

Number seven—Perfection, Rev. i. 4, and throughout the book.

Number ten—Many, Dan. i. 20; Amos vi. 9; Zech. viii. 23.

Oaks—Princes, Isa. ii. 13.

Olive, Wild—Sensual man, Rom. xi. 17.

Olive, Cultivated—The church of Christ, Rom. xi. 24.

Palm—An emblem of joy and victory, Rev. vii. 7.

Paradise—Heaven, the residence of the redeemed, Luke xxiii. 43; Rev. ii. 7.

Passover—Jesus Christ, 1 Cor. v. 7.

Physician—Jesus Christ, Matt. ix. 12.

Pillar—1. The chief support of a family, city, or state, Gal. ii. 9.

Pillar—2. A monument of grace in the temple of glory, Rev. iii. 12.

Poison—Lies, evil principles, Psa. cxl. 3; Rom. iii. 13.

Rain—1. Emblem of saving doctrine, Deut. xxxii. 2.
    2. Spiritual influences, Isa. xliv. 3.

River—1. The irruption of an invading army, Isa. lix. 19; Jer. xlvi. 7, 8.
    2. An emblem of exuberant blessings, Job xxix. 6; Psa. xxxvi. 8.
    3. Overflowings of Divine love and grace, Rev. xxii. 1; Ezek. xlvii.

Rock—1. A secure refuge, Psa. xviii. 2; Isa. xvii. 10.
    2. The founder of a nation, Isa. li. 1.

Rod—1. Powerful authority, Psa. ii. 9.
    2. Divine faithfulness, Psa. xxiii. 4.

Salt—1. The principles and virtues of Christians, Matt. v. 13.
    2. The wisdom of Christian prudence, Col. iv. 6.

Sea—1. The remote islands and countries of the Gentiles, Isa. lx. 5.
    2. The river Euphrates, or Nile, Isa. xxi. 1; Jer. li. 36.

Seal, Sealed—1. Symbol of security, Sol. Song iv. 12.
    2. Symbol of secrecy, Isa. xxix. 11.
    3. Restraint, Job ix. 7; xxxvii. 7.
    4. Token of special commission, John vi. 27.
    5. Emblem of peculiar interest, Eph. i. 13; iv. 30; Rev. vii. 2—4.

Seed—Evangelical doctrine, Luke viii. 5, 11; 1 Pet. i. 23; 1 John iii. 9.

Serpent - Satan, the devil, Gen. iii. 1; 2 Cor. xi. 3; Rev. xii. 9.

Sheep—The disciples of Christ, Zech. xiii. 7; John x. 11, 16; 1 Pet. ii. 25.

Shield—Faith in the Divine promises, Eph. vi. 16.

Sleep—1. Death, Dan. xii. 2; John xi. 11; 1 Thess. iv. 14.
    2. Carnal security, Rom. xiii. 11.

Sodom and Gomorrah—An apostate, wicked city, Isa. i. 10; Rev. xi. 8.

Sores—Spiritual maladies, Isa. i. 6; liii. 5.
Sower—A gospel preacher, Matt. xiii. 3, 37.
Star—1. A prince or ruler, Numb. xxiv. 17; Rev. xxii. 16.
    2. Eminent pastors of churches, Rev. i. 20.
    3. Apostate teachers, Jude 13.
Stone—1. Jesus Christ, Psa. cxviii. 22; Isa. xxviii. 16; Matt. xxi. 42.
    2. A true believer, 2 Pet. ii. 5.
Stone, White—Seal or token of full absolution, Rev. ii. 17.
Sun—1. The Lord God, Psa. lxxxiv. 11.
    2. Jesus Christ, Mal. iv. 2.
Sun and Moon—States, civil and ecclesiastical, Joel ii. 31; Acts ii. 20.
Swine—Unclean, infidel persons, Matt. vii. 6.
Sword—1. The symbol of destruction, Deut. xxxii. 41, 42.
    2. The word of God—the weapon of a Christian, Eph. vi. 17.
Tabernacle—The human body, 2 Cor. v. 1; 2 Pet. i. 13, 14.
Talents—The gifts of God bestowed on man, Matt. xxv. 15.
Tares—Wicked infidels, Matt. xiii. 38.
Teeth—Symbols of cruelty, Prov. xxx. 14.
Thorns—1. Worldly cares, riches, and pleasures, Luke viii. 14.
    2. Perverse unbelievers, Ezek. ii. 6.
Throne—1. Government or kingdom, Gen. xli. 4; 2 Sam. vii. 12, 16.
    2. An order of angels, Col. i. 16.
Thunders—Prophecies, Rev. x. 4.
Towers—Protectors, Isa. ii. 12, 15.
Travail—1. Anguish and misery, Jer. iv. 31; xiii. 21; Mark xiii. 8.
    2. Solicitude of Christian ministers, Gal. iv. 19.
Tree of life—The pleasures of immortality, Rev. ii. 7; xxii. 2.
Trees—Good or bad men, Psa. i. 3; Matt. iii. 10.
Vine—1. The Hebrew church, Psa. lxxx. 8; Jer. ii. 21

Vine—2. Christ the Head of the church, John xv. 1.
Vineyard—The church of Israel, Isa. v. 1, 6; Jer. xii. 10.
Vipers—Wicked children of wicked parents, Matt. iii. 7; xii. 34.
Voice of the bridegroom—Nuptial festivities, invitations of the Saviour, Jer. xvi. 9; John iii. 29.
Walk—The habit of life.
To walk after the flesh—To be guided by sensual appetites, Rom. viii. 1.
To walk after the Spirit—To follow the motions of the Holy Spirit, and the counsels of the word of God, Rom. viii. 1.
To walk with God—To live in secret communion with God, acting as in his sight to please and glorify him, Gen. v. 24; vi. 9.
Wash, Washed, Washing, } Purification, { 1. Moral, Psa. xxvi. 6; lxxiii. 13. 2. Spiritual, Psa. li. 2; Ezek. xvi. 9.
  Pardon and sanctification, 1 Cor. vi. 11; Rev. i. 5; vii. 14.
Water—The grace of the Holy Spirit, Isa. xliv. 3; John iii. 5; iv. 10.
Waters—1. Afflictions and troubles, Psa. lxix. 1.
  2. Multitudes of people, Isa. viii. 7; Rev. xvii. 15.
  3. Evangelical ordinances, Isa. lv. 1.
  4. The blessings of the Holy Spirit, Isa. xliv. 3; John vii. 37.
Week—Seven years, Dan. ix. 24; Lev. xxv. 8. Seventy weeks of years, are four hundred and ninety years.
Wilderness—1. General desolation, Isa. xxvii. 10; Jer. xxii. 6.
  2. This world of trial, 1 Cor. x. 5, 6; Isa. xli. 18.
Wind—1. The operations of the Holy Spirit, John iii. 8.
  2. Divine judgments, Isa. xxvii. 8.
  3. Desolation, Jer. li. 1; iv. 11, 12.
Winds, Four—General destructions, Jer. xlix. 36; Dan. vii. 2; Rev. vii. 2.
Wine—1. Temporal blessings, Hos. ii. 8; Psa. iv. 7.
  2. Gospel provision, Isa. xxv. 6; lv. 1.
  3. Divine indignation, Psa. lxxv. 8; Rev. xvi. 19.

Wings—1. Protection, Psa. xvii. 8; xxxvi. 7; xci. 4.
    2. Evangelical blessings, Mal. iv. 4.
Witnesses—Persecuted churches or their pastors, Rev. xi. 3—6.
Wolf, Wolves—1. Fierce, irreligious men, Isa. xi. 6; lxv. 25.
    2. Bitter persecutors, Luke x. 3.
    3. Avaricious men, professedly Christian ministers, John x. 12; Acts xx. 29.
Women—1. A state or city, Ezek. xxiii. 2, 3.
    2. The church of Christ, Rev. xii. 1.
    3. The antichristian church, Rev. xvii. 3.
Yoke—1. Oppressive servitude, Deut. xxviii. 48.
    2. Painful religious rites, Acts xv. 10; Gal. v. 1.
    3. The delightful service of Christ, Matt. xi. 29, 30.
    4. Moral restraints, Lam. iii. 27.

Ch. XXXI.—Character and Influence of Christianity, and its Claims upon all Mankind.

The Holy Scriptures, as we have seen, are the living oracles of God. They are addressed to perishing sinners, and designed to make men wise unto salvation, through faith in Jesus Christ.

In every point of view Christianity exhibits to us the perfection of heavenly wisdom, and is incomparably superior to all the systems which have ever been presented to mankind, under the sacred name of religion.

Its institutes have been written by holy men of God, prophets, apostles, and evangelists: they have been confirmed by an innumerable multitude of intelligent, learned, and pious believers, in the character of confessors and martyrs for their truth, divinity, and saving efficacy; and their transforming influence on those who receive the love of the truth, still corresponds with their primitive claims, and demonstrates that they came from God.

The Bible alone has clearly revealed the self-existence,

the universal providence, and the infinite perfections of the one only living and eternal God. It has both published and illustrated his holy law, as the immutable rule of moral duty for all his intelligent creation. It announces a future judgment, in which all men shall be righteously rewarded or punished according to their character and their works. It contemplates man in that condition, which all history portrays—a fallen, miserable mortal, a guilty transgressor against God. It exhibits to his terrified mind, and brings to his awakened conscience, the rich provisions of mercy, full forgiveness and free justification, through the substitution of an almighty Surety. The understanding of man being darkened, and his heart corrupted, it sends him an omnipotent Sanctifier, whose influence illuminates and purifies the soul by regeneration and sanctification. Christianity thus destroys the deeply rooted enmity of the heart, and brings the alienated rebel to God, as his heavenly Father, to receive the unspeakable blessings of adoption into the family of God, and to enjoy the sweet assurances of immortality in the life everlasting.

This system of sovereign mercy implants the principles and enforces the practice of every virtue which can exalt, adorn, and improve the human character. Even its partial reception has annihilated the cruel barbarities and degrading customs inseparable from former ages. It alone has elevated woman to her just equality with man: it alone has sanctified the conjugal relation: it alone has inculcated the duty, and exemplified the expression of domestic harmony, and of parental and filial affection: it alone enforces mutual forgiveness, confidence, and brotherly love, irrespective of clime, and age, and nation. Christianity binds all classes together in universal sympathy, under a sense of our common necessities, as equally children of the same almighty Parent; and, being Christians, as members of the body of Christ, and fellow heirs of the grace of life.

Christianity is the angel of celestial mercy to the sons of wretchedness, affliction, and woe; and that even where superstition has been mingled with it. "To the influence

of Christianity are to be attributed those asylums for the relief of the miserable, which humanity has consecrated as monuments of beneficence. Constantine was the first who built hospitals for the reception of the sick and wounded in the different provinces of the Roman empire. These establishments were multiplied in the sixth, seventh, and eighth centuries, in Italy, France, and Spain. They were afterwards so generally adopted, that, according to Matthew Paris, not less than 19,000 charitable houses for leprosy alone existed in the Christian states in the tenth century. Rome contained forty hospitals for various charitable purposes. The number of similar establishments in Petersburg is almost incredible to those who recollect the sudden growth of that capital. In Paris, besides private establishments, there were before the revolution, forty-eight public foundations for the relief of disease and indigence."

London, the metropolis of our favoured country, is eminently distinguished by such noble monuments of Christian charity above every city in the world. In every part of it are to be seen hospitals, infirmaries, dispensaries, and asylums, built and endowed by the benevolence of Christians; and provided to relieve the sick and the poor, the blind and the dumb, the aged and the orphan. The detail would show a list of some hundreds in our British capital, besides the incalculable numbers of the same refuges of mercy, which are found in every city and large town in the kingdom.

Christianity has given to us our inestimable sabbaths; thus sanctifying a seventh portion of our days, for the benign purposes of rest, instruction, and devotion. It prescribes our social meetings on the day of the Lord, for cherishing fraternal affection, for increasing rational piety, and mutually to encourage our sublimest anticipations of a glorious immortality at the termination of our earthly sorrows.

The sacred exercises of the Christian sabbath promote the purest, the most enlarged philanthropy; and they have been the means of constraining the disciples of Christ to care for the souls of others. The immortal

welfare of their neighbours, of their fellow countrymen, and of the whole earth's population, has engaged their benevolent solicitude. It is computed that more than fifty thousand children of the indigent, are, in Great Britain, supported and educated in the principles of the Bible, by means of the bounty of deceased Christians! Scarcely fewer than two millions of the children, chiefly of the labouring and mechanical classes, are collected every sabbath; and by nearly two hundred thousand disciples of Christ, they are gratuitously taught to read and understand the words of everlasting life. Thus they are directed in the paths of virtue by the gospel of salvation, and instructed how they may glorify God and enjoy him for ever.

For the divine purpose of advancing knowledge and religion among all the families of mankind, British Christians annually contribute largely. Among the degraded heathen they support some hundreds of apostolical missionaries,—to learn their languages—to translate for them the sacred Scriptures—to preach among them the unsearchable riches of Christ—to instruct their children in heavenly wisdom—to show forth to guilty nations the unspeakable blessings of redeeming grace—and by the only Mediator between God and sinners, to lead them to the possession of life everlasting!

Such is the noble spirit, and such the imperishable fruits of Christianity, as contained in the Holy Bible. Its language still addresses equally every child of man; the monarch and the peasant—the rich and the poor—the learned and the illiterate—the master and the servant—the parent and the child, are alike invited and commanded to return to the Lord our God, by repentance and faith, in humble sincerity. To believe with the heart the record which God has given of his Son Jesus Christ, is to possess an interest in eternal life; to reject or disbelieve the gospel, is to make God a liar; and how shall we escape if we neglect so great salvation?

Ch. XXXII.—Plan for the Annual Reading through of the Bible.

"Search the Scriptures," is the authoritative injunction of our Lord and Saviour, in obedience to which every believer finds both profit and delight. While some appear contented to limit their attention to a few select chapters, the consistent Christian feels his obligation to regard every part of the Divine word. To imitate the worthy example of eminent devout men of former days, many are commendably solicitous to read through the Bible at least once a year, but they have no plan for their direction. For the assistance of such, the following Tables have been compiled.

It will be readily perceived that the reading of each day is divided into three parts, containing generally a chapter each of the *historical*, the *prophetical*, and the *devotional* Scriptures. While it is readily admitted, that some parts of the oracles of God are far more important for devotional and family reading than others, it must not be forgotten that the apostle Paul has declared, " All Scripture is given by inspiration of God, and is profitable for doctrine, for reproof, for correction, for instruction in righteousness: that the man of God may be perfect, throughly furnished unto all good works," 2 Tim. iii. 16, 17. To distinguish all the chapters and sections which are less necessary to be read in a daily course, would be difficult on a small scale; a few, however, have been marked, and the rest must be left to the enlightened reader.

JANUARY.				FEBRUARY.				MARCH.			
Jan.	Genesis	1 Chron.	Matt.	Feb.	Genesis	2 Chron.	Mark	Mar.	Exodus	2 Chron.	Luke
1	1	1	1 f. v. 17	1	32	4	4	1	11	32	17
2	2	2	2	2	33	5	5	2	12	33	18
3	3	3	3	3	34	6	6	3	13	34	19
4	4	4	4	4	35	7	7	4	14	35	20
5	*5	5	5	5	*36	8	8	5	15	36	21
6	6	6	6	6	37	9	9	6	16	Ezra 1	22
7	7	7	7	7	*38	10	10	7	17	*2	23
8	8	8	8	8	39	11	11	8	18	3	24
9	9	9	9	9	40	12	12	9	19	4	John 1
10	10 f. v. 9.	10	10	10	41	13	13	10	20	5	2
11	11	11	11	11	42	14	14	11	21	6	3
12	12	12	12	12	43	15	15	12	22	7	4
13	13	13	13	13	44	16	16	13	23	8	5
14	14	14	14	14	45	17	Luke 1	14	24	9	6
15	15	15	15	15	*46	18	2	15	25	10 to v. 18	7
16	16	16	16	16	47	19	3 to v. 22	16	*26	Neh. 1	8
17	17	17	17	17	48	20	4	17	*27	2	9
18	18	18	18	18	49	21	5	18	28	3	10
19	19	19, 20	19	19	50	22	6	19	29	4	11
20	20	21	20	20	Exod. 1	23	7	20	30	5	12
21	21	22	21	21	2	24	8	21	31	6	13
22	22 to v. 19	23 f. v. 24	22	22	3	25	9	22	32	7 f. v. 66	14
23	23	*24	23	23	4	26 v. 1–10	10	23	33	8	15
24	24	*25	24	24	5	26 v. 11–23	11	24	34	9	16
25	25	*26	25	25	6 to v. 13	27	12	25	35	10 f. v. 28	17
26	26	*27	26	26	7	28	13	26	*36	11	18
27	27	28	27	27	8	29	14	27	37	12 f. v. 22	19
28	28	29	28	28	9	30	15	28	*38	13	20
29	29	2 Chron. 1	Mark 1	29	10	31	16	29	39	Esther 1	21
30	30	2	2					30	40	2	Acts 1
31	31	3	3					31	Lev. 1	3	2

APRIL.

Apr.	Lev.	Esther	Acts
1	2	4	3
2	3	5	4
3	4	6	5
4	5	7	6
5	6	8	7
6	7	9	8
7	8	10	9
8	9	Job 1	10
9	10	2	11
10	11	3	12
11	12	4	13
12	13	5	14
13	14	6	15
14	15	7	16
15	16	8	17
16	17	9	18
17	*18	10	19
18	19	11	20
19	20	12	21
20	21	13	22
21	22	14	23
22	23	15	24
23	24	16	25
24	25	17	26
25	26	18	27
26	27	19	28
27	Numb. 1	20	Psalm 1, 2
28	2	21	3—5
29	3	22	6—8
30	4	23	9, 10

MAY.

May	Numb.	Job	Psalm
1	5	24	11—13
2	6	25	14—16
3	7	26	17
4	8	27	18
5	9	28	19—21
6	10	29	22
7	11	30	23—25
8	12	31	26—28
9	13	32	29, 30
10	14	33	31
11	15	34	32
12	16	35	33
13	17	36	34
14	18	37	35
15	19	38	36
16	20	39	37
17	21	40	38
18	22	41	39, 40
19	23	42	41—43
20	24	Prov. 1	44
21	25	2	45
22	*26	3	46—48
23	27	4	49
24	28	5	50
25	29	6	51, 52
26	30	7	53—55
27	31	8	56, 57
28	32	9	58, 59
29	*33	10	60, 61
30	34	11	62, 63
31	35	12, 13	64, 65

JUNE.

June	Numb.	Prov.	Psalm
1	36	14	66, 67
2	Deut. 1	15	68
3	2	16	69
4	3	17, 18	70, 71
5	4	19	72
6	5	20	73
7	6	21	74
8	7	22	75, 76
9	8	23	77
10	9	24	78
11	10	25	79, 80
12	11	26	81, 82
13	12	27	83, 84
14	13	28	85, 86
15	14	29	87, 88
16	15	30	89
17	16	31	90, 91
18	17	Eccles. 1	92, 93
19	18	2	94, 95
20	19	3	96, 97
21	20	4	98, 99
22	21	5, 6	100, 101
23	22	7	102
24	23	8	103
25	24	9	104
26	25	10	105
27	26	11, 12	106
28	27	Song 1, 2	107
29	28	3, 4	108, 109
30	29	5, 6.	110—112

JULY.

July	Deut.	Song	Psalm
1	30	7	113, 114
2	31	8	115, 116
3	32	Isaiah 1	117, 118
4	33	2	119 to v. 40
5	34	3	41—80
6	Josh. 1	4	81—128
7	2	5	129—176
8	3	6	120—124
9	4	7	125—127
10	5	8	128—130
11	6	9	131—134
12	7	10	135, 136
13	8	11	137—139
14	9	12	140—142
15	10	13	143, 144
16	11	14	145—147
17	*12	15	148—150
18	*13	16	Rom. 1
19	14	17	2
20	15 to v. 19	18	3
21	16	19	4
22	17	20	5
23	18	21	6
24	*19	22	7
25	20	23	8
26	*21	24	9
27	22	25	10
28	23	26	11
29	24	27	12
30	Judges 1	28	13
31	2	29	14

AUGUST.

Aug.	Judges	Isaiah	Romans
1	3	30	15
2	4	31	16
3	5	32	1 Cor. 1
4	6	33	2
5	7	34	3
6	8	35	4
7	9	36	5
8	10	37	6
9	11	38	7
10	12	39	8
11	13	40	9
12	14	41	10
13	15	42	11
14	16	43	12
15	17	44	13
16	18	45	14
17	19	46	15
18	20	47	16
19	21	48	2 Cor. 1
20	Ruth 1	49	2
21	2	50	3
22	3	51	4
23	4	52	5
24	1 Sam. 1	53	6
25	2	54	7
26	3	55	8
27	4	56	9
28	5	57	10
29	6	58	11
30	7	59	12
31	8	60	13

SEPTEMBER.

Sep.	1 Sam.	Isaiah	Galatians
1	9	61	1
2	10	62	2
3	11	63	3
4	12	64	4
5	13	65	5
6	14	66	6
7	15	Jer. 1	Eph. 1
8	16	2	2
9	17	3	3
10	18	4	4
11	19	5	5
12	20	6	6
13	21	7	Phil. 1
14	22	8	2
15	23	9	3
16	24	10	4
17	25	11	Col. 1
18	26	12	2
19	27	13	3
20	28	14	4
21	29	15	1 Thess. 1
22	30	16	2
23	31	17	3
24	2 Sam. 1	18	4
25	2	19	5
26	3	20	2 Thess. 1
27	4	21	2
28	5	22	3
29	6	23	1 Tim. 1
30	7	24	2

OCTOBER.

Oct.	2 Sam.	Jer.	1 Tim.
1	8	25	3
2	9	26	4
3	10	27	5
4	11	28	6
5	12	29	2 Tim. 1
6	13	30	2
7	14	31	3
8	15	32	4
9	16	33	Titus 1
10	17	34	2
11	18	35	3
12	19	36	Philemon
13	20	37	Heb. 1
14	21	38	2
15	22	39	3
16	23	40	4
17	24	41	5
18	1 Kings 1	42	6
19	2	43	7
20	3	44	8
21	4	45	9
22	5	46	10
23	6	47	11
24	7	48	12
25	8	49	13
26	9	50	James 1
27	10	51	2
28	11	52	3
29	12	Lam. 1	4
30	13	2	5
31	14	3	1 Peter 1

NOVEMBER.

Nov.	1 Kings	Lam.	1 Peter
1	15	4	2
2	16	5	3
3	17	Ezek. 1	4
4	18	2	5
5	19	3	2 Peter 1
6	20	4	2
7	21	5	3
8	22	6	1 John 1
9	2 Kings 1	7	2
10	2	8	3
11	3	9	4
12	4	10	5
13	5	11	2 John
14	6	12	3 John
15	7	13	Jude
16	8	14	Micah 1, 2
17	9	15	3, 4
18	10	16	5, 6
19	11	17	7
20	12	18	Nah. 1, 2
21	13	19	3
22	14	20	Hab. 1
23	15	21	2
24	16	22	3
25	17	23	Zeph. 1, 2
26	18	24	3
27	19	25	Hag. 1, 2
28	20	26	Zech. 1
29	21	27	2, 3
30	22	28	4, 5

DECEMBER.

Dec.	2 Kings	Ezek.	Zech.
1	23	29	6, 7
2	24	30	8
3	25	31	9
4	Hosea 1	32	10, 11
5	2	33	12, 13
6	3, 4	34	14
7	5	35	Mal. 1
8	6	36	2
9	7	37	3, 4
10	8	38	Rev. 1
11	9	39	2
12	10	*40	3
13	11	*41	4
14	12	*42	5
15	13	43	6
16	14	44	7
17	Joel 1	*45	8
18	2	*46	9
19	3	47	10
20	Amos 1	*48	11
21	2	Dan. 1	12
22	3	2	13
23	4	3	14
24	5	4	15
25	6	5	16
26	7	6	17
27	8	7, 8	18
28	9	9	19
29	Obadiah	10	20
30	Jonah 1, 2	11	21
31	3, 4	12	22

Ch. XXXIII.—Geography of the New Testament.

The geography of the New Testament extends little beyond the countries bordering on the Mediterranean Sea, or *Great Sea*. The only seas which are spoken of in the New Testament are, *the Sea of Galilee*, called *the Sea of Tiberias*, which is the Lake of Gennesaret; *the Red Sea*, and parts of the Mediterranean. At the period of our Saviour's ministry, almost all the countries mentioned in the New Testament were included in the Roman empire, or were subject to the Romans. The journeyings of our Lord were limited to the land of Israel. This country, on the western side of Jordan, was divided into three provinces; *Judea* in the south, *Samaria* in the middle, and *Galilee* in the north. *Beyond Jordan*, on the eastern side, the country was called Perea; in which were situated Decapolis, including ten cities, John i. 28; Mark vii. 31. The missionary labours of Paul were chiefly confined to Palestine, Syria, Asia Minor, Greece, and Italy; though it is believed by many that he visited Spain, Gaul or France, and even Britain. The countries of *Asia Minor*, mentioned in the New Testament, were Mysia, Lydia, Caria, Troas, Bithynia, Pontus, Asia, Galatia, Phrygia, Lycaonia, Cappadocia, Lycia, Pamphylia, and Cilicia. The *Roman, Proconsular* Asia, embraced the western part, comprehending Mysia, Lydia, and Caria, in whose cities, of which Ephesus was the chief, the seven churches were planted, Rev. i.

ABBREVIATIONS.

A. M.	Asia Minor.	mt	mountain.
Gr.	Greece.	Pal.	Palestine.
J.	Jerusalem.	pr.	province.
Jud.	Judea.	s. p.	seaport.
Lake of G.	Lake of Genesareth.	t.	town.
Mac.	Macedonia.	v.	village.
Med.	Mediterranean Sea.		

Abile'ne, pr. between the mt. of Libanus and Antilibanus in Syria, Luke iii. 1.
Acel'dama, field near J. Matt. xxvii. 8.

Acha'ia, the southern part of Gr., of which Corinth was the capital.
A'dria, a name of the Gulf of Venice, Acts xxviii. 27.
Alexan'dria, s. p. of Egypt; for a long time the most commercial city in the world, and distinguished as a place of learning. Its library of 700,000 volumes was destroyed, A. D. 638, by the Saracens.
Amphipo'lis, now Emboli, a city of Mac.
An'tioch, now Antachia, once the chief city of Syria, in which the Christians were first so called.
An'tioch of Pisidia, now Akshehr, t. of A. M.
Antipa'tris, t. of Samaria.
Apollon'ia, t. of Mac.
Appii Fo'rum, t. of Italy, 40 miles from Rome.
Ara'bia, a country of Asia, east of the Red Sea. It was divided into *Arabia Felix* or *Happy*, *Arabia Petræa* or *Stony*, and *Arabia Deserta* or *Desert*.
Areop'agus, or the *Hill of Mars*, where the supreme court at Athens was held.
Arimathe'a, t. of Jud.
Armaged'don, mt. of Megiddo in Samaria.
A'sia, in the New Testament, means A. M., sometimes only the western province of it, but never the continent now so called.
As'sos, s. p. of A. M.
Ath'ens, the capital of Attica, and the most famous city of Gr., 25 miles from Corinth.
Attali'a, a city of Pamphylia.
Azo'tus or Ash'dod, now Ezdoud, t. of Pal.
Bab'ylon, capital of Babylonia or Chaldea, situated on the Euphrates.
Bere'a, now Veria, t. of Mac., the birth-place of Alexander the Great.
Bethaba'ra, t. of Jud., east of Jordan.
Beth'any, t. of Jud., 2 miles from J.
Beth'lehem, t. of Jud., the birth-place of our Saviour.
Beth'phage, v. of Jud., 2 miles from J.
Bethsa'ida, t. of Galilee, on the Lake of G.
Bithyn'ia, a country of A. M.
Cal'vary, a hill or place on the north side of J.
Ca'na, t. in Galilee.
Caper'naum, t. in Gal., on the Lake of G.
Cappado'cia, country of A. M.
Ce'dron, or Kid'ron, rivulet near J.
Cen'chrea, s. p. of Gr., near Corinth.
Cesare'a, city and s. p. of Pal.
Cesare'a-Philip'pi, now Paneas, t. of Pal
Char'ran or Ha'ran, t. of Mesopotamia.

Chi'os, now Scio. Gr. island in the Ægean Sea.
Chora'zin, t. in Galilee.
Cili'cia, country of A. M.
Clau'da, a small Gr. island.
Cni'dus, now Crio, t. of A. M.
Colos'se, t. of A. M. in Phrygia.
Coos or Cos, now Stanchio, an island in the Med.
Cor'inth, a celebrated city in Gr.
Crete, now Candia, the largest island of Gr.
Cy'prus, an island in the Med.
Cyre'ne, now Curen, a city in Africa, and s. p. on the Med., west of Egypt.
Dalmanu'tha, t. on the Lake of G.
Dalma'tia, pr. of Illyricum on the Gulf of Venice.
Damas'cus, a famous city of Syria, 50 miles from the Med.
Dead Sea, Sea of Sodom, or Lake Asphaltites, salt lake in Pal., 70 miles long and 10 or 15 broad, occupying the spot on which Sodom, Gomorrah, Adma, and Zeboim stood.
Decap'olis, a district of ten cities of Pal.
Der'be, t. of A. M. in Lycaonia.
E'gypt, a celebrated country in the north-east of Africa.
E'lam, an ancient name of Persia.
Emma'us, t. seven miles from J.
E'non, t. of Jud., near to Jordan.
Eph'esus, city of A. M., celebrated for its temple dedicated to Diana.
E'phraim, t. of Pal. of the tribe of Ephraim.
Epi'rus, country of Gr.
Ethio'pia, country of Africa, south of Egypt.
Fair-Ha'vens, s. p. of Crete.
Gada'ra, t. of Pal. on the Lake of G.
Gala'tia, a country of A. M.
Gal'ilee, the northern division of Pal.
Ga'za, t. of Pal. of the Philistines.
Genne'saret, Lake of, or Sea of Galilee, or Sea of Tiberias, a lake of Pal., 17 miles long and 6 miles broad.
Gergesenes', people of Gergesa, t. on the Lake of G.
Gol'gotha, a part of Calvary.
Gomor'rha, one of the four cities on the plain of Sodom destroyed by fire.
Greece, a country on the south-east part of Europe, celebrated for learning, etc.
Hierap'olis, t. of A. M. in Phrygia.
Ico'nium, city of A. M., capital of Lycaonia.
Idume'a, country north of Arabia, south of Jud.
Illyr'icum, country on the east of Adria.
It'aly, country of Europe, whose capital is Rome.
Jer'icho, city of Jud.

Jeru'salem, capital of Jud. It was built on four hills, Zion, Moriah, Acra, and Bezeta. The modern city is built on Moriah.
Jew'ry, another name for Judea.
Jude'a, the south of Pal., a name often applied to the whole country.
Laodice'a, now Eski-hissar, t. of A. M.
Li'bya, a country of Africa, west of Egypt.
Lycao'nia, a country of A. M.
Ly'cia, a country of A. M. on the Med.
Lyd'da or Lod, t. of Jud.
Lys'tra, t. of A. M.
Macedo'nia, a country in the north of Gr.
Mag'dala, t. of Pal., on the Lake of G.
Me'dia, a country near Persia.
Mel'ita, now Malta, an island in the Med.
Mesopota'mia, a country between the rivers Euphrates and the Tigris, in Asia.
Mile'tus, a city and s. p. of A. M.
Mile'tum, a t. in Crete.
My'ra, a city of A. M., capital of Lycia.
My'sia, a country of A. M.
Nain, a t. of Galilee.
Na'zareth, a t. of Galilee.
Neap'olis, now Cavala, a t. of Mac.
Ne'pthali or Nepthalin, Land of, a district in the north of Galilee.
Nicop'olis, now Prevesa, a city of Epirus in Gr.
Nin'eveh, an ancient city and capital of Assyria.
O'lives, Mount of, or Olivet, mt. of Jud.
Pamphy'lia, a country of A. M.
Paphlago'nia, a country of A. M.
Pa'phos, a t. of Cyprus.
Par'thia, a country near to Persia.
Pat'ara, s. p. of A. M. in Lycia.
Pat'mos, now Patno or Palmosa, a small rocky island near Miletus.
Per'ga, a city of A. M., capital of Pamphylia.
Per'gamus, now Pergamo, a city of A. M.
Per'sia, a great empire in Asia.
Pheni'ce or Phenicia, country of the Philistines, in Pal.
Philadel'phia, now Allah Shehr, a city of A. M., in Lydia.
Philip'pi, now Datos, a city of Mac.
Phry'gia, a country of A. M.
Pisid'ia, a country of A. M.
Pon'tus, a country of A. M.
Ptolemai's, now Acre, s. p. of Pal.
Pute'oli, now Pozzuolo, a t. of Italy.

Ra'ma, a t. of Jud.
Red Sea, or Arabian Gulf, about 1400 miles long, dividing Arabia from Africa.
Rhe'gium, now Reggio, a s. p. of Italy.
Rhodes, an island near A. M.
Rome, a city of Italy; it was built on seven hills, and was the capital of the Roman empire.
Sal'amis, a city of Cyprus.
Sa'lim, a t. of Samaria.
Sama'ria, the middle division of Pal.
Sama'ria, now Sebaste, the capital city of Samaria.
Sa'mos, an island in the Med.
Samothra'cia, now Samotraki, a small island of Gr.
Sar'dis, now Sart, a city of A. M.
Sarep'ta, or Sarephath, a city of Phenicia.
Sa'ron, or Sha'ron, a t of Samaria.
Seleu'cia, a s p. of Syria
She'ba, a country of Arabia.
Si'don, or Zi'don, now Saida, a s. p. of Phenicia.
Sil'oam, a fountain and tower near J.
Si'nai, a mt. in Arabia, near Mount Horeb.
Si'on, or Zi'on; see Jerusalem.
Smyr'na, a city and s. p. of A. M.
Sod'om, one of the three cities destroyed by fire; see Dead Sea.
Spain, a large country of Europe.
Syr'acuse, a city on the island of Sicily.
Sy'char, or Shechem, a city of Samaria
Syr'ia, a large country of Asia
Syro-Phenicia, Phenicia, bordering on Syria.
Ta'bor, a mt. of Pal., the scene of the transfiguration.
Tar'sus, the capital of Cilicia, in A. M.
Thessalon'ica, now Salonica, a city and s. p. of Mac.
Three Taverns, a place 30 miles from Rome.
Thyati'ra, now Akhiser, a t. of A. M.
Tibe'rias, now Tabaria, the capital of Galilee.
Trachoni'tis, a district of Pal.
Tro'as, a district of A. M.
Trogyl'lium, a t. of A. M.
Tyre, now Sur, a s. p. of Phenicia.
Zab'ulon, tribe of, a district of Pal.

Ch. XXXIV.—Monies, Weights, and Measures of the Scriptures.

The several monies, weights, and measures mentioned by the sacred writers, were not all of Hebrew origin. Some of them were Greek, and others Roman, as these people in succession conquered the East; for with their government they introduced their coins and methods of policy. There is therefore considerable difficulty in making accurate calculations respecting both coins and measures; and learned men differ in several particulars relating to them. The following tables have been prepared from the most judicious writers on the subject, reckoning silver at 5s. per oz. and gold at £3 10s. per oz.

I. MONEY.

Copper Coin.

	£	s.	d.	qr
1. Mite, Mark xii. 42, it weighed half a barleycorn, and was in value about $\frac{3}{8}$ of a farthing English	0	0	0	$0\frac{3}{8}$
2. Farthing, or quadrans, two mites, or about $\frac{3}{4}$ of our farthing	0	0	0	$0\frac{3}{4}$
3. Assarium, or ass, Matt. x. 29, the tenth part of a Roman penny, or about three farthings English	0	0	0	3

Silver Money.

	£	s.	d.	qr
1. Gerah, Exod. xxx. 13, about	0	0	1	2
2. Penny, denarius, ten Roman asses, or Gr. drachma, Matt. xx. 2, the fourth of a shekel	0	0	7	2
3. Bekah, Exod. xxxviii 26, half a shekel	0	1	3	0
4. Shekel, Exod. xxx. 13, or silverling, Isa. vii. 23, or stater, Matt. xvii. 27, was stamped on one side with Aaron's rod, and on the other with the pot of manna	0	2	6	0
5. Maneh, mina, or pound, Luke xix. 13, fifty shekels	6	5	0	0
6. Talent, sixty manehs or pounds	375	0	0	0

Gold Money.

	£	s.	d.	qr
1. A solidus aureus, or sextula, was worth about	0	12	2	0

CH. XXXIV.—MONIES, WEIGHTS, ETC.

	£	s.	d.	qr.
2. Shekel of gold, about fourteen times the value of silver	1	15	0	0
3. Talent of gold, 3000 shekels	5250	0	0	0

II. WEIGHTS.

	lbs.	oz.	dwts	grs.
1. Gerah, about	0	0	0	12
2. Bekah, ten gerahs, or half a shekel	0	0	5	0
3. Shekel, two bekahs	0	0	10	0
4. Mina, sixty shekels	2	6	0	0
5. Talent, fifty minas	125	0	0	0

III. MEASURES.

Measures of Length.

	yds	ft	in.
1. Finger, Jer. lii 21, the breadth of a man's finger, about	0	0	$0\frac{3}{4}$
2. Hand breadth, Exod. xxv. 25, four fingers	0	0	$3\frac{1}{2}$
3. Span, Exod. xxviii. 16, three handbreadths	0	0	$10\frac{1}{2}$
4. Cubit, Gen. vi. 15, two spans	0	1	9
5. Fathom, Acts xxvii. 28, four cubits	2	1	0
6. Reed, Ezek. xl. 3—5, nearly eleven feet, or	3	2	0
7. Line, Ezek. xl. 3, eight cubits, or	46	2	0
8. Furlong, or stadium, Luke xxiv. 13, a Greek measure	233	0	0
9. Mile, Matt. v. 41, eight furlongs	1864	0	0
10. Sabbath day's journey, Acts i. 12, a mile: some say two miles.			

Liquid Measures.

	gals.	qts.	pts.
1. Log, Lev. xiv. 10, equal to six egg-shells full	0	0	$0\frac{3}{4}$
2. Hin, Exod. xxix. 4.	1	1	0
3. Bath, 1 Kings vii. 26, or firkin, John ii. 6, six hins	7	2	0
4. Cor, or homer, Ezek. xlv. 14; Isa. v. 10, the largest measure	75	0	0

Dry Measures.

	gals.	qts.	pts.
1. Pot, or sextarius, Mark vii. 4.	0	0	$1\frac{1}{2}$
2. Cab, 2 Kings vi. 25, or chenix, Rev. vi. 6, the measure of corn allowed to a slave for a day's food	0	1	1
3. Omer, Exod. xvi. 36, or tenth-deal, ch. xxix. 4.	0	3	0
4. Seah, Matt. xiii. 33, about	2	2	0
5. Ephah, or bath, Ezek. xlv. 11, about	7	2	0
6. Homer, Ezek. xlv. 11—14; Numb. xi. 32.	75	0	0

CH. XXXV.—CHRONOLOGICAL INDEX TO THE BIBLE.

Referring to the principal Events recorded in the Holy Scriptures, and including a Period of 4100 years, according to Usher; and 5511 years, according to Hales.

CHRONOLOGY affords great light to the sacred history; and it is, therefore, of high importance to the profitable reading of the Scriptures. For this reason dates are placed in the margins of our larger Bibles; and the system employed is that formed by Archbishop Usher, from the Jewish notes on the Hebrew Bible. It reckons 4000 years from the creation of the world to the birth of Christ: but the Jews generally computed 5344 years: the Septuagint, or Greek translation, exhibits 5872 years; but Dr. Hales, in his corrected system, reckons 5411 years. This great difference arises principally by the Septuagint declaring many of the patriarchs, at the birth of their sons, a hundred years older than is stated by the Hebrew, as will be seen in the following table of the ages preceding Noah. It may also be remarked, that Dionysius, a Roman abbot, about A. D. 527, was the first that formed the system of chronology called *Anno Domini;* and his system has been completed by more modern writers: though the true date of the birth of Christ is believed to be *four* years earlier than the common era of Anno Domini.

Ages at the Birth of their Sons.	Heb.	Sept.	Lived after. Heb.	Sept.	Length of Lives. Heb.	Sept.
Adam	130	230	800	700	930	930
Seth	105	205	807	707	912	912
Enos	90	190	815	715	905	905
Cainan	70	170	840	740	910	910
Mahalaleel	65	165	830	730	895	895
Jared	162	162	800	800	962	962
Enoch	65	165	300	200	365	365
Methuselah	187	187	782	782	969	969
Lamech	182	188	595	565	777	752
Noah, at the Deluge	600	600				
To the Deluge	1656	2262				

PERIOD or AGE I.

From the Creation to the Deluge, containing 1656 years, according to Usher; 2256 years, according to Hales.

Hales.		Usher.			
A.M.	B.C.	A.M.	B.C.		
	5411		4000	The creation of the world	Gen. i. ii.
		1	3999	Fall of our first parents, Adam and Eve, from holiness and happiness, by disobeying God.—Promise of a Saviour	— iii.
130	5281	2	3998	Cain born	— iv. 1.
131	5280	3	3997	Abel born	— — 2.
229	5182	129	3871	Abel murdered by his brother Cain	— — 8.
230	5181	130	3870	Seth born, his father, Adam, being 130 years old	— v. 3.
1122	4289	622	3378	Enoch born	— — 18, 19.
1287	4124	687	3313	Methuselah born	— — 21.
930	4481	930	3070	Adam dies, aged 930 years	— — 5.
1487	3914	987	3013	Enoch translated, aged 365 years	— — 24.
1042	4269	1042	2958	Seth dies, aged 912 years	— — 8.
1656	3755	1056	2944	Noah born	— — 28, 29.
2136	3275	1536	2464	The Deluge threatened, and Noah commissioned to preach repentance during 120 years	— vi. 3—22. 1 Pet. iii. 20. 2 Pet. ii. 5.
2256	3155	1656	2344	Methuselah dies, aged 969 years. In the same year Noah enters into the ark, being 600 years old	Gen. v. 27. — vii. 6, 7.

PERIOD or AGE II.

From the Deluge to the Call of Abraham, containing 427 years, according to Usher; 1077 years, according to Hales.

Hales.		Usher.			
A.M.	B.C.	A.M.	B.C.		
2257	3154	1657	2343	Noah, with his family, leaves the ark after the Deluge, and offering sacrifice, he receives the covenant of safety, of which the rainbow was the token	Gen. viii. 18, 20; ix. 8-17.
2797	2614	1770	2230	Babel built	— xi.
2857	2554	1770	2230	The confusion of language, and dispersion of mankind	— —
2857	2554	1771	2229	Nimrod lays the first foundation of the Babylonian or Assyrian monarchy	— x. 8—11.
2857	2554	1816	2184	Mizraim lays the foundation of the Egyptian monarchy	— — 13.
3074	2337			Trial of Job, according to Hales	Job i. ii.
2506	2905	2006	1994	Noah dies, aged 950 years	Gen. ix. 29.
3258	2153	2008	1992	Abraham born	— xi. 26.

PERIOD or AGE III.

From the Call of Abraham to the Exodus of Israel from Egypt, 430 years, according to Usher; 445 years, according to Hales.

Hales.		Usher.			
A.M.	B.C.	A.M.	B.C.		
3318	2093	—	—	Abraham called from Chaldean idolatry, at 60 years of age . .	Gen. xi. 31.
3333	2078	2083	1917	Abraham's second call, to Canaan	— xii. 1—4.
3341	2070	2091	1909	Abraham's victory over the kings, and rescue of Lot	— xiv. 1-24.
3344	2067	2094	1906	Ishmael born, Abraham being 86 years old	— xvi.
3356	2055	2107	1893	God's covenant with Abram, changing his name to *Abraham*,—circumcision instituted,—Lot delivered, and Sodom, Gomorrah, Admah, and Zeboim destroyed by fire on account of their abominations. . . .	— xvii.-xix.
3357	2054	2108	1892	Isaac born, Abraham being 100 years old	— xxi. — xxii.
3383	2028	2133	1867	Abraham offers Isaac as a burnt sacrifice to God	Heb. xi. 17-19; Jam. ii. 21.
3395	2016	2145	1855	Sarah, Abraham's wife, dies, aged 127 years	Gen. xxiii. 1.
3398	2013	2148	1852	Isaac marries Rebecca	— xxiv.
3418	1993	2168	1832	Jacob and Esau born, Isaac being 60 years old	— xxv. 26.
3433	1978	2183	1817	Abraham dies, aged 175 years .	— — 7, 8.
3495	1916	2245	1755	Jacob goes to his uncle Laban in Syria, and marries his daughters, Leah and Rachel . . .	— xxviii.
3508	1903	2258	1742	Joseph born, Jacob being 90 years old	— xxx. 23, 24.
3515	1896	2265	1735	Jacob returns to Canaan . .	— xxxi. xxxii.
3525	1886	2275	1725	Joseph sold as a slave by his brethren	— xxxvii.
3538	1873	2288	1712	He explains Pharaoh's dreams, and is made governor of Egypt	— xli.
3548	1863	2298	1702	Joseph's brethren settle in Egypt	— xliii.—xlvi.
3565	1846	2315	1685	Jacob foretells the advent of Messiah, and dies in Egypt, aged 147 years	— xlix.
3618	1793	2368	1632	Joseph dies, aged 110 years . .	— l. 26.
3680	1731	2430	1570	Aaron born	Ex. vi. 20; vii. 7.
3683	1728	2433	1567	Moses born	— ii. 1—10.
3723	1688	2473	1527	Moses flees into Midian . . .	— — 11-13.
3763	1648	2513	1487	Moses commissioned by God to deliver Israel	— iii. 2.

PERIOD or AGE IV.

From the Exodus of Israel from Egypt to the Building of Solomon's Temple, 487 years, according to Usher; 628 years, according to Hales.

Hales.		Usher.			
A.M.	B.C.	A.M.	B.C.		
3763	1648	2513	1487	Miraculous passage of the Red Sea by the Israelites	Ex. xiv. xv.
3764	1647	2514	1486	The law delivered on Sinai	— xix.—xl.
3802	1609	2552	1448	Miriam, sister of Moses, dies, aged 130 years	Num. xx. 1.
				Aaron dies, aged 123 years	— — 28, 29.
3803	1608	2553	1447	Moses dies, aged 120 years, Joshua being ordained his successor	Deu. xxxiv.
				The Israelites pass the river Jordan, the manna ceases, and Jericho taken	Josh. i.—vi.
3829	1582	2561	1439	Joshua dies, aged 110 years	— xxiv.
4259	1152	2849	1151	Samuel born	1 Sam. i. 19.
4301	1110	2888	1112	Eli, the high priest, dies. Ark of God taken by the Philistines	— iv. 1.
4301	1110	2909	1091	Saul anointed king of Israel	— x. xi. 12.
4311	1100	2919	1081	David born.	
4331	1080	2941	1059	David anointed to be king, and slays Goliath	— xvi. 13. — xvii. 49.
4341	1070	2949	1051	Saul is defeated in battle, and in despair kills himself. David acknowledged king by Judah	— xxxi.
4348	1063	2956	1044	Ishbosheth, king of Israel, assassinated, and the whole kingdom united under David	2 Sam. i.
4348	1063	2957	1043	Jerusalem taken from the Jebusites by David, and made the royal city	— v.
4359	1052	2969	1031	David commits adultery with Bathsheba, and contrives the death of her husband Uriah	— xi.
4360	1051	2970	1030	David brought to repentance for his sin by Nathan the prophet, sent to him by the LORD	— xii.
4361	1050	2971	1029	Solomon is born	— — 24.
4375	1036	2981	1019	Absalom rebels against his father and is slain by Joab	— xv.-xviii.
4381	1030	2989	1011	David causes Solomon to be proclaimed king, defeating the rebellion of Adonijah	1 Kings i.
4381	1030	2990	1010	David dies, aged 70 years	— ii.
4391	1020	3000	1000	Solomon's temple finished, after seven years building	— vi. vii.

PERIOD OR AGE V.

From the Building of Solomon's Temple to the Destruction of Jerusalem and Captivity of the Jews in Babylon, 412 years, according to Usher; 434 years, according to Hales.

Hales.		Usher.			
A.M.	B.C.	A.M.	B.C.		
4392	1019	3001	999	Solomon's temple dedicated	1 Kings viii.
4421	990	3029	971	Solomon dies. The Ten Tribes revolt to Jeroboam. He sets up a golden calf at each end of his kingdom, establishing idolatry instead of the worship of God. Great numbers of the priests and Israelites, on account of his idolatry, withdraw from his government and unite with Judah	— xii. 2 Chron. xi. 13—16.
4426	985	3033	967	Rehoboam abandons himself to impiety, so that the Lord permits Shishak, king of Egypt, to take Jerusalem, and pillage the palace and temple.	1 Kings xiv. 25. 2 Chron. xii. 1—9.
		3108	892	Elijah the prophet, being translated to heaven, is succeeded by Elisha	2 Kings ii.
		3165	835	Elisha the prophet dies	— xiii.
4602	809	3190	810	Uzziah, called also Azariah, begins to reign in Judah for 52 years; in whose time Isaiah and Amos prophesy in Judah, and Jonah and Hosea in Israel	— xv. 1—5. 2 Ch. xxvi.
4685	726	3274	726	Hezekiah endeavours to effect a complete reformation in religion in Judah, and establishes a society of scribes for copying the Scriptures	— xxix.— xxxi. 2 Kin. xviii. Prov. xxv. 1.
4692	719	3279	721	The kingdom of Israel totally destroyed by the Assyrians, after it had subsisted apart from Judah 254 years under nineteen wicked kings	2 Kin. xvii.
		3288	712	Micah and Nahum prophesy	Micah i. Nahum i.
		3304	696	Isaiah, as is believed, is sawn asunder, as a martyr for God, under Manasseh, the wicked king of Judah	Heb. xi. 37.
		3359	641	Zephaniah prophesies	Zeph. i.
		3377	623	Joel prophesies	Joel i.

Hales.		Usher.			
A.M.	B.C.	A.M.	B.C.		
		3391	609	Habakkuk prophesies	Hab. i.
4807	604	3394	606	Nebuchadnezzar takes Jerusalem, makes the king tributary, and carries many captives to Babylon, among whom were Daniel and his three companions	2 Kin. xxiv. 1. Dan. i. 1.
				Judah's seventy years' captivity begins, as foretold by Jeremiah	Jer. xxv. 11, 12. — xxix. 10.
		3406	594	Ezekiel carried captive to Chaldea	Ezek. i. 1, 2.
4825	586	3412	588	Jerusalem with its temple, after a long siege by Nebuchadnezzar, destroyed by fire; and the Jews, except the poorest, carried captives to Babylon	2 Kin. xxv. 1—21. 2 Chr. xxxvi. 14—21.

PERIOD or AGE VI.

From the Destruction of Jerusalem by Nebuchadnezzar to the Birth of Christ, 588 *years, according to Usher;* 586 *years, according to Hales.*

Hales.		Usher.			
A.M.	B.C.	A.M.	B.C.		
4825	586	3412	588	The first destruction of Jerusalem	2 Kin. xxv.
		3413	587	Jeremiah carried into Egypt . .	Jer. xliii. 6.
		3420	580	Nebuchadnezzar sets up a golden idol: the three Hebrews preserved in the fiery furnace . .	Dan. iii.
		3462	538	Belshazzar's impious feast; Babylon taken by Cyrus the Persian, and the kingdom transferred to his uncle Darius the Mede. Thus the Assyrian, or *first universal empire* ended	— v. — ii. 36—38. — vii. 5.
4875	536	3464	536	Cyrus succeeds Darius, and issues an edict to release the Jews, and for the rebuilding of the temple at Jerusalem, delivering up all the sacred vessels to the prince of Judah	Ezra i. Isa. xlv. 1.
		3480	520	Haggai and Zechariah prophesy	Ezra v. 1.
		3484	516	Esther, a Jewish captive, married by Ahasuerus	Esth. i. ii.
		3485	515	The second temple of Jerusalem finished and dedicated . . .	Ezra vi.
		3546	454	Nehemiah obtains leave to rebuild Jerusalem, as governor . . .	Neh. i. ii.
		3559	441	Nehemiah returns to the king Artaxerxes	— v. 14.

CH. XXXV.—CHRONOLOGICAL INDEX

Hales.		Usher.			
A.M.	B.C.	A.M.	B.C.		
		3561	439	Nehemiah goes again to Jerusalem, and completes the reformation of religion. Ezra revises those books of the Old Testament which had been written, and compiles the Books of Chronicles . .	Neh. v. 14. — viii. — xiii. 6.
4991	420	3602	398	Malachi prophesies, the last of the writers of the Old Testament	Mal. i. 1.
5011	400	3600	400	The Old Testament history closes about this time.	
		3668	332	Alexander the Great, having entered Asia, visits Jerusalem, reverences Jaddua the high priest, and favours the Jews.	
		3670	330	Alexander overthrows the Medo-Persian, or *second universal empire*, slays Darius, and sets up the Macedonian or Grecian empire	Dan. ii. 39 — vii. 6. — xi. 1—3.
		3716	284	The Old Testament translated into Greek about this time: the version now called the *Septuagint*.	
		3833	167	Seven Jewish brethren and their mother martyred by order of Antiochus king of Syria	2 Maccab. vii.
		3855	165	Judas Maccabeus recovers Jerusalem from the Syrians, and restores the worship of God.	
		3935	65	The Romans conquer Syria, terminate the *third* or Grecian *empire*, and establish their own or *fourth universal empire*	Dan. ii. 40—43.
5348	63	3937	63	Judea made a Roman province. John Baptist born six months before Jesus Christ	Luke i.

PERIOD or AGE VII.

From the Birth of Jesus Christ to the end of the First Century.

Usher. A. M.	Year of J. C.	Before A. D.		
4001	1	5	Nativity of Jesus Christ	Luke ii. 1—16.
		A. D.		
4008	12	8	Jesus visits Jerusalem	— ii. 41—52.
4026	30	26	Pilate sent from Rome as governor of Judea	— iii. 1.
4029	33	29	John Baptist begins his ministry	Matt. iii. 1.
4030	34	30	Jesus baptized by John	— —
4033	37	33	Jesus Christ crucified, and rose from the dead	— xxvii. xxviii.
4035	39	35	Saul converted—Paul his Roman name	Acts ix. xiii. 9.
4044	48	44	James beheaded by Herod: Peter liberated by an angel	— xii. 1—19.
4060	64	60	Paul sent a prisoner to Rome	— xxvi.— xxviii.
4063	67	63	Paul suffers martyrdom at Rome by order of Nero	2 Tim. iv. 6, 7.
4065	69	65	The Jewish war begins.	
4067	71	67	The Roman general raises the siege of Jerusalem, by which an opportunity is afforded for the Christians to retire to Pella, beyond Jordan, as admonished by Christ	Matt xxiv. 16—20.
4070	74	70	Jerusalem besieged and taken, by Titus Vespasian, according to the predictions of Christ; when 1,100,000 Jews perished, by famine, sword, fire, and crucifixion; besides 97,000 who were made captives and sold as slaves, and vast multitudes who perished in other parts of Judea	Luke xix. 41-44.
4071	75	71	Jerusalem and its temple razed to their foundations	Matt. xxiv. 2.
4095	99	95	John banished to the isle of Patmos, by the emperor Domitian	Rev. i. 9.
—	—	—	John writes the Revelation at Patmos.	
4097	101	97	John liberated from exile, and writes his Gospel.	
4100	104	100	John, the last surviving apostle, dies, being about 100 years old.	

Ch. XXXVI.—Scripture Names.

The scripture names of both persons and things are generally remarkable for their significations. A knowledge of these materially assists the reader in understanding many passages in the Bible. In several instances names were given immediately by God; in others they were imposed by a spirit of prophecy; and many, both persons and things, received their denominations from some particular circumstances in their history.

Thus God called our first parents Adam, which signifies earth, or red earth, because from the earth man was created, Gen. ii. 7; v. 2. He changed the name of Abram, which signifies high father, to Abraham, the father of a great multitude, or of nations, Gen. xvii. 5; and that of his wife, Sarai, my lady, to Sarah, lady or princess of a multitude, ver. 15, 16; and Jacob, a supplanter, to Israel, a prince with God, ch. xxxii. 28.

By a prophetic spirit some names were imposed, as Noah, signifying comfort, and Jesus, a saviour. Many names were given on account of some peculiar circumstances in their history: as Isaac, laughter or gladness, Gen. xvii. 17; xviii. 12; xxi. 3—6; Bethel, the house of God, Gen. xxxviii. 17—19; Moses, taken from the water, Exod. ii. 10.

It should be observed, that those names which begin or terminate with EL, or begin with JE, or end with IAH, were generally designed to express some relation to God: as Bethel, the house of God; Israel, a prince with God; Jeremiah, the exaltation of the Lord.

Some persons and things had two or more names, and they are sometimes called by one and sometimes by the other. For example, Jacob was called Israel; Jethro, the father-in-law of Moses, was called Reuel, Exod. ii. 18; iii. 1; Uzziah was called Azariah, 2 Kings xv. 1; 2 Chron. xxvi. 1; Isa. i. 1; Paul was the Roman name of the apostle, while his Jewish name was Saul, Acts xiii. 9.

Many names also of persons are spelled differently in the New Testament, as they were taken from the Greek translation of the Old Testament: as Noe for Noah,

Elias for Elijah, Osee for Hosea, and Jeremy for Jeremiah. In some of the names also in the New Testament, it will be observed that their Latin form has been retained in several places, by an oversight in the translators, as Timotheus for Timothy, Silvanus for Silas, and Marcus for Mark. Joshua is also called Jesus, Acts vii. 45; Heb. iv. 8.

AARON, signifies, a mountain of strength, or a teacher.
Abaddon, the destroyer.
Abednego, servant of light.
Abel, Adam's son, vanity, a city, mourning
Abel-Mizraim, the mourning of the Egyptians.
Abiathar, excellent father.
Abib, green fruits.
Abiel, God my father.
Abigail, father of joy.
Abijah, the LORD is my father.
Abimelech, father of the king.
Abner, father of light.
Abram, a high father.
Abraham, father of a great multitude.
Absalom, father of peace.
Achan, he that troubles.
Adam, earthy, or red earth.
Adonibezek, lord of lightning.
Adonijah, the Lord is my master.
Adonizedek, lord of justice.
Ahab, brother of the father.
Ahimelech, brother of the king.
Ahithophel, brother of ruin.
Ahitub, brother of goodness.
Alleluia, praise the Lord.
Amalek, a people licking or ill-using.
Amaziah, strength of the Lord.
Amnon, faithful, or foster-father.
Ananias, the cloud of the Lord.
Anna, or Hannah, gracious.
Arabia, a desert
Areopagus, the hill of Mars.
Asa, physician.
Asher, blessedness or happiness.
Azotus, or Ashdod, pillage.
Baal, master, or lord, an idol.
Baal-berith, lord of the covenant.

Baalim, idols, masters, false gods
Baalzebub, or Beelzebub, lord of flies.
Babel, or Babylon, confusion.
Baca, mulberry tree.
Balaam, destruction of the people.
Balak, a waster
Barnabas, son of consolation.
Beer, a well
Beersheba, the well of the oath.
Bel, ancient, nothing.
Belial, wicked, devil.
Belshazzar, master of the treasure.
Bethany, the house of humility, or of song.
Bethel, the house of God
Bethesda, the house of affliction.
Bethlehem, the house of bread
Bethshemesh, the house of the sun.
Beulah, married
Boanerges, sons of thunder
Bochim, weepers.
Cain, possession
Caleb, dog, basket, hearty
Calvary, the place of skulls.
Capernaum, the field of repentance or pleasure.
Carmel, vineyard of God.
Cush, black
Cushan, Ethiopia.
Dagon, corn, fish.
Dan, judgment.
Daniel, judgment of God.
David, beloved, dear.
Deborah, oracle, or bee.
Diotrephes, nourished by Jupiter.
Easter, the name of a Saxon goddess,—the word in Acts xii. 4, is, properly, passover.
Ebenezer, the stone of help.

Eden, pleasure, delight.
Edom, red.
Egypt, in Hebrew Mizraim, tribulation.
El-bethel, the God of Bethel.
Eliab, God my father.
Eliezer, help of my God.
Elihu, my God himself.
Elijah, God the Lord.
Eliphaz, endeavour of God.
Elizabeth, oath of God.
Elisha, salvation of God.
Enoch, dedicated.
Enos, fallen man.
Ephraim, very fruitful.
Ephratah, abundance.
Esau, perfectly formed.
Eshcol, a bunch of grapes.
Ethiopia, burnt face.
Eve, living.
Ezekiel, strength of God.
Ezra, a helper.
Felix, happy.
Festus, joyful.
Gabriel, God my excellency.
Gad, a troop.
Gedaliah, God my greatness.
Gilead, heap of witness.
Gomorrah, a rebellious people.
Goshen, approaching.
Habakkuk, a wrestler.
Hagar, a stranger, fearing.
Haggai, a solemn feast.
Halleluiah, praise the Lord.
Haman, noise, preparation.
Hannah, Anna, gracious.
Heber, a passer over, as Abraham over the river Euphrates, to dwell in Canaan, from which he was called the Hebrew.
Hephzibah, my delight is in her.
Herod, glory of the skin.
Hezekiah, strong in the Lord.
Hiram, exaltation of life.
Hobab, beloved.
Horeb, dryness, desert.
Hosea, Hoshea, a saviour or salvation.
Jabez, sorrow or trouble.
Jacob, a supplanter.
JAH, self-existent, everlasting.
Jazer, helper.
Ichabod, where is the glory?
Jebus, contempt.
Jedidiah, well beloved.
Jehoiada, knowledge of the Lord.
Jehoshaphat, judgment of the Lord.
Jehovah, the incommunicable name of God, self-existing.
Jehovah-jireh, the Lord will see or provide.
Jehovah-nissi, the Lord my banner.
Jehovah-shalom, the Lord send peace.
Jehovah-shammah, the Lord is there.
Jehovah-tsidkenu, the Lord our righteousness.
Jemima, handsome as the day.
Jeremiah, exaltation of the Lord.
Jeroboam, fighting against the people.
Jerubbaal, let Baal defend his cause.
Jerusalem, vision of peace.
Jeshurun, upright or righteous.
Jesse, my present.
Jesus, saviour.
Jews, the people of Judah.
Immanuel, God with us.
India, praise.
Joanna, grace or gift of the Lord.
Job, a weeper.
Jochebed, glory of the Lord.
Joel, willing, swearing.
Johanan, John, grace of the Lord.
Jonah, Jonas, a dove.
Joseph, increase.
Joshua, saviour.
Isaac, laughter.
Isaiah, salvation of the Lord.
Iscariot, a man of the bag or of murder.
Ishmael, God will hear.
Israel, a prince with God.
Issachar, recompence.
Ithiel, God with me.
Jubilee, sounding of the trumpet.
Judah, praise the Lord.
Jupiter, a helping father, a heathen idol god.
Kadesh, holiness.
Kedar, blackness.
Kenaz, this possession.
Kidron, obscurity.
Korah, bald, frozen.
Laban, shining.
Lamech, poor, debased.
Laodicea, just people.
Lazarus, help of God.
Lemuel, God with them.
Levi, joined, associated.
Lo-ammi, not my people.

CH. XXXVI.—SCRIPTURE NAMES.

Lois, better.
Lo-ruhamah, not having obtained mercy.
Lot, wrapt up, or myrrh.
Lucas, Lucius, Luke, luminous.
Manasseh, forgetfulness.
Manoah, rest.
Mark, Marcus, polite.
Mars-hill, the court hall at Athens.
Martha, becoming better.
Mary, bitterness, or myrrh of the sea.
Massah, temptation.
Matthias, gift of the Lord.
Matthew, given of the Lord.
Melchizedek, king of righteousness.
Mercurius, Mercury, the name of an idol god.
Messiah, anointed.
Methuselah, he has sent his death.
Micah, humble.
Michael, Micaiah, Michaiah, who is like God?
Miriam, Mary, myrrh of the sea.
Misraim, tribulation.
Moab, of the father.
Molech, Melek, king.
Mordecai, contrition.
Moriah, bitterness of the Lord.
Moses, taken out of the water.
Naaman, agreeable
Nabal, a fool, senseless.
Nahum, comforter.
Naomi, beautiful.
Naphtali, my wrestling.
Nazareth, separated
Nebuchadnezzar, Nebo's conqueror of treasures, or groans of judgment.
Nebuchadrezzar, Nebo's roller of treasures.
Nebuzadan, Nebo's winnower of lords.
Nehemiah, comfort of the Lord.
Nethinims, given or devoted.
Nimrod, rebellious.
Nineveh, handsome.
Noah, rest or consolation.
Nod, vagabond.
Obadiah, servant of the Lord.
Obed, servant.
Obed-edom, servant of Edom.
Onesimus, profitable
Onesiphorus, bringing profit.
Othniel, the time of God.

Padan-aram, the field or palace of Aram or Syria.
Paul, a worker.
Peniel, face or vision of God
Peninnah, pearl, or precious stone.
Peter, a rock or stone.
Pharaoh, the revenger, the crocodile.
Philadelphia, love of brethren.
Philemon, affectionate.
Philip, a lover of horses.
Pihahiroth, the pass of Hiroth.
Pisgah, a fortress.
Potiphar, a fat bull.
Quartus, the fourth.
Rabbi, my master.
Rachel, a sheep.
Rahab, proud.
Ramah, lofty.
Rameses, thunder.
Rebekah, pacified.
Rehoboam, enlarger of the people.
Reuben, a vision of the sun.
Rhoda, a rose.
Rome, strength.
Rufus, red.
Ruth, satisfied.
Salem, Salmon, Salome, peace.
Samaria, guard, prison.
Samson, his son.
Samuel, asked of the Lord
Sarah, lady or princess. Sarai, my lady or princess.
Satan, adversary.
Saul, demanded, or sepulchre.
Seth, placed
Sharon, a princely plain
Shem, name or renown.
Shiloh, peace, salvation.
Simeon, Simon, hearing, obedient.
Sin, Sinai, a bush.
Sion, noise, tumult.
Sodom, their secret.
Solomon, peaceable.
Stephanas, Stephen, a crown.
Susanna, a lily, rose, or joy.
Tabitha, clear-sighted.
Tammuz, concealed, the name of a Hebrew month, and of an idol god.
Tekel, weight.
Teraphim, images.
Tertullus, an impostor.
Theophilus, a lover of God.
Timeus, honourable, admirable.
Timotheus, Timothy, honoured of God.

Titus, honourable.
Tophet, a drum; the name of a place near Jerusalem, where children were burned as offerings to Molech, and drums beaten to drown their cries.
Trophimus, well educated.
Tryphena, delicious.
Tryphosa, very shining.
Tubal, the world.
Tubal-Cain, worldly possession.
Ur, fire, or light.
Uriah, Urijah, light of the Lord.
Uriel, the light of God.
Urim and Thummim, lights and perfections.
Uz, counsel.
Uzziah, the strength of the Lord.
Uzziel, the strength of God.
Vashti, a drinker.
Zaccheus, just, justified.
Zachariah, memory of the Lord.
Zadok, justified.
Zebedee, abundant portion.
Zedekiah, righteousness of the Lord.
Zelotes, jealous.
Zephaniah, secret of the Lord.
Zerubbabel, stranger of Babylon.
Zeruiah, chains of the Lord.
Zidon, fishing, hunting.
Zion, heap of stones.
Zipporah, beauty, trumpet.
Zoar, little, small.
Zurishaddai, the Almighty is my rock.

FINIS.

THE RELIGIOUS TRACT SOCIETY:
INSTITUTED 1799.